SHANGHAIED AND SHACKLED

BY LAUCHLAN CAMPBELL

British Library Cataloguing in Publication Data:
A catalogue record for this book is available from
the British Library

ISBN-13:
978-1-9163867-1-6

Cover design
David Stanyer

Printed & bound by PrintGuy
Published Up North

Part One: Shanghaied and Shackled
Part Two: A Civilised Prison in China

Lauchlan aged 19, best man at his friend Brian Cochrane's wedding.

Introduction

Here is a true-life story of a father who has taken his two sons out into the world to teach them to look beyond their own backyard. It had been all very innocent to begin with but his sons were street wise Glasgow boys and no wool was being pulled over their eyes. Scott was 18 and Lochy 16 both had travelled with their father in the past. This story of selfish errors in life and the results of a father behaving irresponsibly, Shanghai and Shackled tells a tale of life behind bars in communist China, an education not advisable to be experienced. A story of squandered opportunity and the desperate consequences of lessons learned the hard way.

My Family

Lauchlan Campbell. Born 23/5/1950 in a city called Glasgow Scotland the sixth child of a family of eight survivors having four elder sisters Helen, Sarah, Agnes and Patricia also one elder brother George. Then there is Robert just one year younger, followed by Tommy, the child who, surprisingly to us all, would grow to become the tallest and most notorious as the infamous TC Campbell headlined in the Ice Cream Wars killings, which resulted in setting up Free the Glasgow Two Campaign. TC Campbell tells his own story written in two books regarding his ordea,l Trial by Fire his 'INDICTMENT' of the British legal establishment tells of his harrowing battles to overturn police corruption. Book two, The Wilderness Year is an account of his past.

My Dad was called Bobbie Campbell he boxed for the army and loved that sport thus supplying his three sons with daily lessons in that particular skill. He had recently got out of jail and our house was the best decorated in the street and we boys got a bicycle, football boots and life seemed rosy. Bobbie Campbell was a known gangster having already served time for Bank Robbery and it was not unusual to have the house searched by the Criminal Investigation Department leaving me with a negative view of police officers. There was a lot of talk in the house one evening and hearing the word explosives, Tam Padden and fingers being blown off. The good life came to a sudden halt dad was arrested again and fitted up on false evidence for the hijacking of a whisky truck and armed robbery committed by his pal Andy Steele. Everybody knew who had committed the crime, even the police would freely admit it out of court, but Dad in accordance with the code of underworld ethics would never testify who the real guilty parties were. The code of silence was expected and respected in those days but there is also an unwritten code that if someone is doing your time then financial support occasionally should be dropped off to help feed that family. Dad was sentenced to ten years imprisonment and we were once again sentenced to abject poverty and deprivation.

My mother was a catholic girl from Fruin Street Possilpark who fell under Bobbie's charms and after the war they married. She had it tough when my dad was in jail bringing up children without a husband to help and support her. In retrospect I can now see how she must have struggled. My elder brother George whom we had never met but had heard of was adopted as a young boy. This also broke her heart. My mother was a broken woman who used to comment "Am living on my wits with you lot." It was not all bad. She clothed and fed us and if not a good upbringing, we did have her love. The Lord knows the crown of thorns he was forced to wear. My mother was entangled in the nettle bed of this life, maybe it will be a bed of roses next time around and we can get to know each other more. No sooner had dad gone back to jail than mother hit the bottle. She had seven children, which she brought up herself most of the time. Then unexpectedly my brother George knocked on our door, a young man of eighteen who had been sent to the isle of Tiree to live with a farmer's family. It brought a temporary happiness back to my mother. Her little lost boy had returned finding his own way and he was my mother's double. Now at age forty, she was without her man again and it broke her heart. My mother died three years later aged forty-two. A young woman who had her share of sorrow. I remember her telling my sister Helen these words "If you make your own bed you have to lay on it" so now these words ring true today with my own experience.

Back Then

There is nothing that could be called normal of the upbringing in the rat-in-fested slums of the 1950s Glasgow. Though 'the usual turmoil and madness seemed perfectly normal at the time my mother, of the Irish Catholic tradition, enjoying her wee dram, would often announce her favourite cheer to the household "Here's to the bird with the green wing, a free country and a Feinian king." All very well of course, while Dad was still in the jail for some bank robbery or other Dad, a Campbell of course, of the Scots Protestant tradition, would not exactly be chuffed to hear such open rebellious cheer in the presence of his children.

There seemed to no halt to Ma's moonlight flits with debtors hard on her heals. I recall being put into temporary child care and foster homes on more than one occasion during these periods. It was truly amazing for the like of us little Glasgow 'toe rags' fresh from the gutters of our streets of shame. Fresh air, sea and sunshine and, the food was regular too. Tommy was crying about his hands and face being swollen; in fact he was all swollen. His arms, shoulders, legs, everything. Believing that he must have contracted some terrible disease, we hurriedly sought help. "No! It is called nourishment son" explained the matron and apparently, we were all getting it. Tommy just kept on growing to become a tall strapping lad way beyond our other brothers George, Robert who was neither ginger nor orange haired it was simply blood red and the fiery spirit to match it. Where Tommy was big and beefy with a gentle heart, Robert would remain wee wiry even throughout his teens.

We lived in various places, mostly throughout the north of the city of Glasgow. Fir hill, Cowcaddens, and Possilpark then onto George St. in the city end. All of these places were just the standard post war red or grey sandstone tenement slums of the late 1800's we had no idea that there was such a thing as a bath-room until we moved on to or new house in Carntyne in 1960. It was there, for the very first time we had more than one room and the wonder of it all an inside toilet with wash hand basin and a bath. Furthermore, the streets were tarmac with broad pavements and gardens rather than the granite cobblestone with tramlines that I had come to know.

Being the sporty type, I played football for the new school team at Parkhead Primary, everyday passing the ground of the famous Glasgow Celtic. By then Dad was home from jail and things were rapidly changing. It was clear that money was coming into the household. I had seen with my own eyes bundles from some criminal enterprise or other. We were also more and more prone to police raids where the house would be torn apart in search of something that was never found we were all stuck into the bedroom out of sight on those occasions. More and more hassle as Dad and his pals pulled off more robberies. Dad was careful, we were never supposed to know, see nor hear anything about his activities but we could always gather the general gist of it from Agnes or Patsy or often Ma. I would say that we were financially well off then. The house redecorated and refurnished from top to bottom while we were polished, suited and booted like toffs. Half-boiled toffs my father would remind us. Finally, hence by the start of my teens I was already anti-authoritarian, in that the authority of the times being the police and they were not to be trusted. Nor likewise was I particularly impressed by the criminal element either. Ma died at the aged of 40 just a few years into Dad's sentence, which had broken her dear heart for the final time. My eldest sister Ellen was married with family of her own as with my other sister Sadie. This then left it down to Agnes at 16 years of age with a baby child of her own to look after another younger sister Patsy aged 15 me 14 Robert 13 and Tommy 12. My sister Sarah took Robert and Tommy and at fifteen, I moved in with my sister Helen. Just as I began my sojourn into the wild side of adolescent exploration. I was now at secondary school in Shettleston and it seemed I had acquired a 'bad attitude' as they say, yet when those opinions are that of authority figures such as school teachers, then those disrespectful attitudes soon come under the heading of 'Misconduct Reports'. I was there less than two years when such reports lead to my expulsion from Wellshot Road Secondary School at around 14 years of age. I was transferred to Dennistoun School where the famous Glasgow superstar Lulu was born and raised. It was also close by to the famous Dennistoun Palace dance hall where she danced the hucklebuck before going on to singing her anthem 'Shout'.

Living in Carntyne was my new free life beyond the sewers. While sport and football remained a passion, they took second place to music dance and girls. I would soon meet and team up with many more young and angry young boys of my age and ilk. We were to become notorious as the infamous Tiny Calton Tongs. No more than confident youth yet more able than most when it came down to aggression and the defense of our territorial boundaries. This by then included the Barrowland Ballroom on the Gallowgate. I along with Davie Cochrane, Rab McIntee, Gerry McNamara, Cabe, Kinny, Jimmy Johnston and many more would dance the afternoon away with the girls. I held the reputation as one of the best dancers and took my gift seriously, outstepping the mob and usually holding the floor a bit of a show off to impress the girls. Those days were yet dominated by the sectarian gangs such as the Bridgeton Boys and Garangad Shamrock, the Cumberland Street Mob. Maryhill, Ruchill, Possilpark, every area of Glasgow had a gang. Confrontations were never far away. It was considered a good night out if it ended in a brawl or a party or both. It was akin to living in a war zone with no brothers in arms. There is nothing odd in the way that we three brothers Campbell all ended up in religiously non-aligned teenage street gangs. Tommy quickly emerged as the undisputed leader of the notorious Carntyne Goucho Boys of mixed religion. The Goucho held alliance with the Calton Tongs with me and my other brother Rab running with them. Those were wild but good days even if it was only good luck and nimble feet, keeping me alive. Dad had taught us well, boxing our ears until we learned the arts of self-defense, the attitude it sometimes seems is ingrained in the psyche of the native Glaswegian. The motto on the Mercat cross for example reads "Nemo me impune nassasit." Which, in English reads "no one may assail me with impunity". In old Scots, "Wa nae meddle wae me" Simply translated in Glasgow to say, "Nae messing" but these were not my ways. I wanted out of this weary old town.

Part One: Shanghaied and Shackled
Chapter One: Ralph and Mary

I went to London in 1973 with a friend Ralph McLaren he was a tall handsome easygoing person and his girlfriend Mary was pregnant. They had decided their child would be born in Scotland and Ralph was returning to work in London and had a spare ticket going back. Having decided to utilise the spare ticket saying, I would join him to find a job. Telling my wife that as soon as work and flat or apartment was found she would join me with my infant son Scott. All plans do not always come to ruination. This one did. It was not long before Ralph and I ended up in Holland taking LSD and, hitch- hiked all the way across parts of Europe ending in Spain. Then returned home eight months later with a globetrotter badge, a ponytail, earring and an attitude now directed at legalising drugs. My mother-in-law, old Mary slapped me around the head, telling me "Away ye go and get a haircut and a job you lazy so a so ye are"

My wife was pregnant when I left for London and now, we had two sons and I would see very little of them as they grew up the irresponsible father still had big ideas driving me on towards new horizons. My marriage finally dissolved 1975 then returning to London and discovered the Velvet Underground punk New York bands and heroin. I met up with artists, poets, musicians, dope dealers alike. London was the most exciting city I had ever lived in besides Amsterdam. Squatting in Finsbury Park and my pals were Pappy, Frank and Vinnie Docherty, Peter Slowey Andy Mac McCarthy, all Southside of the city boys.

My brother Robert had a council house in Whitechapel east of the city and had married his first love Vonny McLaren and his pals were also mine Marsy, Robert Faulds, Robin Murphy Cool, all good dependable men from all over Glasgow. Our flats were always a mad house. All night music, all sorts of drugs and plans on how to get more. Frankie Miller, the great Glaswegian singer had a band called 'Full House' he was our local hero we saw him on many occasions around London and he became a friend to my brother Rab and the McLaren family and other Scots living in London. By 1976 I was off again to Holland selling student cards with a friend called Boatman from Glasgow we ended up in Morocco with a stash of LSD. Then in 1978, off again, this time to Saudi Arabia to work as a painter and decorator and had the job as interior designer for a company called Armco. With the money hard earned from that trip I went back on the road again and this time there would be no going back.

Chapter Two: Trade Route

It will always be a long hard journey following the Silk Road from Iran, through Afghanistan and Pakistan on into China. Even if you do sometimes, have the luxury of motorised transport. Marco Polo traversed this route by donkey, camel and on foot, is to hold a deep respect for the endurance of that intrepid traveller. Still to this day, many traders continue to tread these ancient routes where there remains a booming trade in all manner of goods. Yet alongside the usual honest backpack travellers and group tours you meet up with international nomads crossing the borders in Asia on the regular smuggler's trails. I would run into some of them repeatedly, at arrivals or departures areas in airports or border towns in Malaysia doing a visa run so as to stay longer at their watering grounds. I have met gold and gem smugglers, technology and data smugglers alongside drug and arms smugglers. Smuggling is more than a fulltime occupation for these people, it is a way of life, which I came to know and learn over many years of almost perpetual travel around these trade routes. You tend to meet, and travel with some interesting acquaintances whilst going over centuries of old mountain trails shortcuts into bizarre new worlds in pursuit of the rainbow's gold or in other people's case to get a photo of mount Trish Mir at sunrise or collect a healing stone or touch a prayer flag.

It is certainly interesting when you discover why some folk travel as for me having no direction in life other than just smuggling.

Then also my life went to the other extreme flying more air hours than pilots, getting free airline booze, sleeping in cheap hotels or brothels. After three months of this constant travelling buying and selling gold and technology would then rest a few months relaxing on a beach. This was, a pass time well suited for me preferring beach life to jetting over concrete cities to only earn money. There were many places to meet up with people in this international trade. Hong Kong was the central meeting point and I was having dealings in 1980 with a Chinese syndicate there.

On several occasions during that period smuggling gold and technology to South Korea, Bangladesh, and to Tibet Nepal and India. For example, my return trip prior to this one had been from Hong Kong to mainland China, Chengdu city then to Lhasa capital of Tibet, then overland stopping at towns on the way down to the border at Tatra Panni, then onto Katmandu in the Kingdom of Nepal. On my return then traveled overland back through Tibet, a barren dry land but with a charm to be experienced. Then eventually took a bus and train across China to Shanghai before finally boarding a ship to Kobe a port in Japan. It had been a long haul with cannabis resin but dealing in heroin was not my trade although more profitable and easier to conceal. I considered any form of THC acceptable and should be decriminalised if not legalised and so smoked cannabis every day. I was also inclined to smoke some heroin putting myself down the road to oblivion before coming around on a cycle of despair and self-loathing before pulling myself back up and out of that insane state of self-abuse. I had not yet worked out why I did this. Heroin is aptly named Nasty bringing delusion of tranquility to those lured to the dream only to be awoken with a serious drug addiction a short time down the road. While in Pakistan, I had built up a little tolerance with heroin.

Chapter Three: Reunion

It was 1990 and having my brother-in-law Billy Haddifon and my son Lochy travelling with me cycling from Katmandu to India enroute to visit the Dali Lama at his retreat in Dharamsala with his growing Tibetan community exiled there. It wasn't typical of me to go to a place just to say I had been there but never bought a tee shirt. It was because after our visit in Nepal to the lake in Pokhara and eating and talking with the displaced Tibetans we did find it a sorrowful state of affairs, yet they were affluent enough and intriguing to say the least. The respect they hold for their spiritual leader was humbling and all they wanted was their homeland to return to without communist interference.

I sold the three bikes in New Delhi and got most of my money outlay back it was hard work cycling and Billy wanted to wait for our return at the guest house in the Pahar Ganj area so Lochy and I headed to Dharamsala by train. I did not try to get an audience with the wise man himself knowing he would have other matters to attend with than two curious Scots. We ate well and enjoyed the scenery looking at the multiple Tibetan crafts that had a well set up little industry going on, money was here the tourist trade was booming by what I could see around me on travellers wearing Free Tibet tee shirts. On our return to Delhi, we discussed a future trip as both Billy and Lochy were leaving for London in two days' time. We spent that couple of days hanging around the swimming pool at the Imperial Hotel, Billy and Lochy drinking Kingfisher beer and myself smoking cannabis. I waved goodbye as they walked through immigration to board the flight from New Delhi to London with promises to do another trip together in the not-so-distant future.

I on the other hand had already purchased my cannabis upon arrival from Nepal from an old Italian hippy I met when first coming to India. He had never left and married a local lady from Manali up in the hills and her family-owned land and produced good quality hand rubbed cannabis resin it was now being moulded into a suitcase ready for Japan. After completing, that previous trip with Billy and Lochy my onward trip to Japan was a successful one. I had money to spend thus contacted my other son Scott via my brother in London. I had phoned and asked if Scott would like to join me. A few days later I called again and it was all arranged Scott would join me in eight days time I was delighted.

It was so humid that the sweat dripped from my eyelids, it was to be a special occasion for me, meeting up with my eldest son again. Scott had travelled with me before in the past age sixteen going to the Philippines, Thailand, Bangladesh, onto Burma and Malaysia. My son was now nineteen; it was great that the two of us were getting back together. Whilst waiting on his arrival inside Islamabad airport feeling my heart rate triple its beat at the thought of having him together with me on this adventure to traverse over some of the world's most awesome scenery.

When he finally, stumbled through into the arrival area I called his name. Scott turned opened eyed and smiling we embraced and shook hands before heading for the car and driver hired for me by an old friend. It was a relief to escape the usual airport hustle having the driver with me. During the ride to our destination, I was telling my son our first stop was Peshawar at the North West frontier. It would be good for him to see and experience dealing with people from another culture having visited the Philippines with me, a Christian country by majority.

I had contacted my old friend Attollah from Afghanistan he still had a carpet shop in downtown Peshawar. Attollah had secured places at a hotel for us to lay back and relax. I recalled having many a contented dream filled night at his carpet shop just laying back on the spread rugs and cushions puffing on a hash-filled hookah that would bring joy to any a weary wondering soul. My son would have no complaints this fine night. The drive back to Peshawar was a good laugh as I produced a few hashish joints in ready for my son's arrival and after a few puffs felt the ice breaking. At the entrance to the carpet shop in Peshawar Attollah's sons were among the group of raggedly attired children leaping and waving at us then leading the way into the building. We walked along a creaky corridor then upstairs into a huge welcoming carpet shop. Upon seeing us Attollah and his brother Hammed immediately embraced us with greeting from Allah for our safe arrival. Both these men had well lined and sun scarred faces. Although both men were younger than me they looked older. Planting our bags onto the floor, it felt like I was arriving all over again.

In this part of Pakistan, the North West frontier it is bandit territory. Peshawar is abundant with not only figs and fruits. It is also the most open display of weaponry and drugs in any town ever visited by me. It is a mystic place of exotic sights deep lined faced minority groups some with clear bright eyes peering over veils. It is also full of bearded Jihad Bandoliers strapped over shoulders and Kalashnikovs guns in plain view. I felt the sheer bustling, crowding; cramming of such grand phenomena can be overwhelming. Talk about 'culture shock'? This is a culture 'quake' shaking you to the realisation of what other people's lives are about in comparison with your own. Scott was beaming in the sheer joy of our welcoming. After Attollah showed gratitude once more to Allah in prayer for our safe arrival. We then settled down spreading our limbs and sighing in a contented anticipation.

Attollah's two sons Khalid aged fourteen and Aktar, 9 got on with the chores around the shop. Knowing these two boys well I loved to watch their antics, their exited enthusiasm. They knew my arrival always had a surprise in-store for them but they were to well-mannered and polite to inquire. It seemed to be a way with these children to get you to fall under their bartering traps. I watched, as Scott was enticed out of his goodies giving away cassette tapes, a tee shirt, as Attalla's lads tested the veracity of their trading prowess. Now feeling well settled my son and I smoked our first hashish hookah. We looked at each other and laughed till our heads did a spin equaling that of the mystic Persian 'Dance of the Whirling Dervishes' We snacked on some dates and nuts and were now onto smoking our second Hookah and both totally awe stricken by the sheer beauty awaiting us over the Karakorum Highway from Pakistan to China feeling literally on top of the world. The next part of our journey through and beyond China would entail catching a ship from Shanghai to Japan. Gaping at the magnitude of the road ahead sighing in self-contentment "Aye there's still a way to go yet my son" I said thinking out loudly.

Peshawar houses about one million Afghan refugees in shantytowns many, as if Attollah and his kin, still bear cruel scars from the Russian wars. Learning to assemble, load and fire, the standard Kalashnikov is child's play around here Attalla's sons were already busy teaching Scott till he could load and reload another clip. I had been trying to show Scott a difference from Glasgow hanging around street corners swallowing cheap wine and beer smoking low-grade cannabis. I had just wanted Scott to see other possibilities and to open up his horizons wanting to help him escape to freedom from the prison he and his brother were born into but do not even see. Alternatively, was it I who was deeply deluded?

Attollah had a spread of food fit for a prophet and laid it out for us sitting on the floor with a nice colorful carpet The spread was full with sweets from almond nuts, cashew, walnuts, and a few others unknown to me some sugar-coated others not, but all exquisitely aromatic. There was a range of dried and fresh fruits, dates and figs, and apricots from the Hunza valley, then goat and chicken kebabs, fresh barbecued, lamb, and stews hot Nan bread with fresh tomato, onion and yoghurts. My son and I ate well and were more than contented with our host. As we sat in bliss Attollahs visitors came and went about their usual custom while I nodded off in a happy food overdose. Scott on the other hand was having an adventure of his own deeply embarrassed and pursued by a highly esteemed homosexual Afghan agent. I could barely hide the smile as he sought refuge behind my coat telling me to tell him to "Fuck off faggot" it ended up a good night ablaze in Afghan pollen we smoked we laughed and had fun. Just in the wonder of those stars outside above those mystic mountains praise is to Allah.

Shot!
My son tries out his skill with a Kalashnikov.

Chapter Four: Miss Nasty

I had not told my son about filling my cigarettes with the devil's dust and I was still lost in delusions counting the Kali dosh, instead of the probable consequences. The reality was this me taking my son along on a drug smuggling trip. Taking him through dangerous terrain and where one wrong step could well turn to disaster. I had deluded myself with visions of living in my houseboat up the Mekong River going from Thailand to Cambodia, and Vietnam and was already drifting in paradise.

I get up most mornings with the sun; and immediately reach for some powder to fill a cigarette. I do this while awaiting boiling water for my instant Nescafe. Then once in my heroin daze usually took a shower. I dress in the local garb Shalwar Kamiz paying attention to the detail of stashes in the folds of my garb. Satisfied by the vaguely shabby, but clean impression that reflected back at me I set out to rouse my son. Going next door knocking a few times before it opened. They're stood Scott wrapped in a bed sheet looking the part as a Bedouin Nomad. That is always a good thing in these parts to fit in like the locals and learn to quote some words from the Koran.

Darra and Barra are tribal areas of the Northwest Frontier in Pakistan were large quantities of firearms and drugs are freely and openly on display and for purchase. While if you are prepared to buy the ammunition, you can discharge it freely all day at your leisure. This after all was tribal land and territory this was something Scott wanted to try out. I on the other hand was more fascinated by the weave of the colorful wall hangings. They just seemed to hang their abandoned to the weather like old billboards that no one notices anymore. Who had made these colorful weaves of art, and where are those people now? Scott taking me from my muse asked me when are we going to Darra Dad and I had to concede tomorrow. I also had been fascinated by those lawless areas and to return to have some gun firing practice again. "Ali Baba here we come" Scott whooped delightedly sparking up a hashish joint and confirming with me with a nod of his head "Tomorrow then Dad?"

Chapter Five: Fair Trade

I have always been an early riser once awake usually need to have coffee on hand or at least within easy access, thus, my arrangement was that the hotel night duty worker awaited my call to boil the kettle. Water delivered gives the duty man his first tip of the day. Fair trade is not robbery as they say. Having secured my boiling water and delivered with a smile plus getting a nod of approval for the tip. I sat back drinking coffee and smoking a powdered joint reviewing the plans for the day ahead having agreed with Scott that we would visit Darra.

It had been arranged that the Long-Bearded Jihad with bandolier gun and a jeep whom we met at Attollah's shop on Scott's arrival would escort us. We were leaving at around 9 o'clock this morning and I nodded off while smoking on the bed and lucky not to be burned. I showered and went to awaken Scott, holding a cannabis joint in my hand walking through his door and handing it to him saying, "Get ready its AK47 day" Scott was up in a split second, his boxer's shorts in a twist and headed to wash up.

We arrived at the rendezvous just after nine. Atollah was standing by the sidewalk deep in animated conversation with two turbaned gun-carrying characters. The sun was well up a hot haze had already begun highlighting the pollution in the air. A blue diesel cloud wafted by and the air hung oily. I approached Atollah and greeted him "Salaam Allium." embracing and shaking hands. I was introduced to our guides. Scott nodded hellos and we all jumped into the jeep. It was not a long drive to Darra, about an hour and the day was young. We were eager and keen to get about some shooting practice. The checkpoint was a simple wooden barber's pole across the road and guarded by tribal police officers of the Pathan clan. After an exchange of a few words with the driver, we were through. The first firearms shop was little more than two hundred meters from the barrier. We stopped and watched the men and boys at work huddled over untidy workbenches, filing, tapping, screwing the parts they had just made and assembling them into deadly weaponry. Our escort friends directed us around the back of the shops. Scott was out in front eager and ready. I stood at the back and watched as the two people fixed up their guns ready to fire. Scott braced himself and took aim on single shot. He was impressed by the lethal power at his fingertips blowing and puffing at the rush.

After he had discharged a few rounds, his gun was moved up to rapid fire. Scott jumped as if he had just been shot himself this gun gave the feeling to the novice that healthy respect for weaponry. It is the healthy respect necessary and required for survival in this region. This entire scene was being recorded from various angles as I passed over the camcorder that we had all would get on the film. It was a gift to Scott from my brother Robert in London before his departure. Looking every inch, the part of the freedom fighter Scott dons two of the bandoliers and casually hangs them around his shoulders with Kalashnikov slung low strap crossing over the bandolier at the chest. Then with seeming casual ease, he would stutter off a half clip of rapid fire, shouting "Free the

Glasgow two!"

I walked onto a small hill to take another photo angle all the while thinking I was a BBC presenter. Scott disregards the targets set out for him and blasts a hole in the sky on rapid fire. Just across the path was dope shops in all shapes and forms, pollen, hashish piled up to the rafters by the ton. In another shop raw opium and morphine in no lesser abundance. No wonder there were so many guns on hand and so many wretched souls lying around in doorways out of their long-bearded sculls, deluded, dysfunctional, dirty and disheveled. The contrast slaps you in the face with a cold shiver. There, on the one hand is millions even billions of dollars' worth of the best of dope. In addition, there on the other foot literally at your feet, are the results of that profit. I wanted Scott to see this was not in the tourist brochures. This is the down side and it has to be seen to understand that this is part of the harvest reaped from this trade. I was not just trekking merrily over poppy fields in a happy hippy trip. I was checking out the harvest where it is a means of living to farmers here. There were very little other crops or government substance to earn them money to eat. I had known some of the people they were once brothers in arms now returned to their valleys and their farms destitute.

Death did not scare me but how to die did. I did not like these sights around me but knew Scott had the picture. We decided we should make tracks back to the hotel. It had not been a bad day. Scott was excitedly babbling on about the balances of Karma. I was just glad we were on our way as far away as we could get from the shadow of death cast over those wretched lost souls who once were warriors. Shivering in the thought that for the grace of Allah I might end up like them addicted for life. It was late afternoon and we had only eaten watermelon during our stay in Darra so we were hungry. Atollah suggested that we do a detour to his home to rest and eat. Before departure I stood for a moment to take in the surrounding scenery but only seeing shadows in the fading light looking up at the strangest sky a mixture of purple blues deepening reds darkening yellows as the sun had started dipping. Its vastness made me feel small and somewhat insecure in my insignificance. It was a quiet trip to Atollahs place lost in dark thoughts of stretched skin stooped shoulders and heroin addiction.

Arriving after a twenty-minute drive we stood at the entrance of a refugee camp Atollah's house was here somewhere in this maze of walls built from mud. Some were better built with partial brick but most were mud adobe with corrugated tin roofs. It looked like a row of camels snaking across the horizon. A bunch of raggedy children immediately surrounded Scott. Some pale skinned with blond streaked hair a feature that made them stand out. Attollah's brother greeted us and we were lead through a hand dugout alleyway. It led to a small doorway into a well-kept back yard and beyond to the house living area. It was very basic in fixtures no television, no telephone and next to no furniture but it was warm and inviting. It was colourful with an abundance of scattered cushions, beautiful floor carpets and rugs. The kitchen was in one corner of the back yard where we had entered. The women of the house toiled busily beside a clay-baking oven, their heads covered and their hands nimble. We all sat down and were immediately served tea with sugarcoated almonds. Atollah was smiling a picture of wellbeing as he sat cross-legged on the floor packing small pieces of cannabis into empty cigarettes.

Scott was escorted and kept busy with Aktar displaying rugs in the other room; there was no closing time with these traders. It wasn't long before it was time to eat and we were served an excellent meal with mutton and a tasty sauce it came plenty of hot Nan and the evening hazed by just chatting and smoking hashish. Attollah was telling us about his new wife to be. I knew money would come into this conversation, and before long the trading began. I ended up buying $3500 worth of rugs to be sent onto London. I was to send the money once shipment was received. I liked that sort of trade when you didn't need to lay out first so we shook on it.

It was pitch dark when we stumbled stoned from Atollah's house. Only a slithered moon lighted the sky. Scott having done some trading with young Aktar now had a rug wrapped under his arm but he was minus one Sony Walkman another fair trade. Our guides drove us back to the hotel it was a good day out but now stoned and tired just wanted to get to bed.

We spent a couple of more days around Peshawar and changed some traveller's cheques at the local smuggler's bazaar. We visited the Peshawar Museum admiring some wonderful old carvings and learning a little more about the Buddhist influences here. I bought a postcard of the fasting Buddha. Gandara period Buddhist statues along with other such artifacts are readily on offer in Pakistan. On a previous trip I bought two small stone Buddha's in the market probably hacked from temple walls looted by thieves in Afghanistan during those warring years that never seem to end in this part of the world. I sent them to Scotland via Japan for safety.

It was also nice to stop in at the Dean Hotel for a cool beer a rare treat and watering hole in an Islamic country. Here you needed to have a permit before the purchase of alcohol. This was attained at the local tourist office in Islamabad, which I had acquired before my son's arrival. Scott certainly enjoyed a few beers after long hot treks through dusty streets. It was a pleasure just to sit down somewhere cool in the shade with a beer it gives your soul some cheer in Peshawar's hot dusty town mid in July. The more so since Scott was quite badly sunburned during these first few days and in danger of mild heat stroke. His neck was lobster red and it looked like he was about ripe to fry. I was keeping up the jokes and giving us a laugh even Scott managed an occasional ventriloquist dummy's smile. After a few more days around Peshawar, we returned to Islamabad gazing at the sublime sky by the outskirts around the Maury Hills... The colouring suggested such an inviting cool that you just wanted to swallow it up with your breath.

I had hired a taxi for the day so that we could do a bit of sightseeing knowing enough from experience not to waste precious hours or sometimes days in waiting for local buses stopping to pick up the goat etcetera. On our return to Peshawar, we stopped at the old fort built by the British and looked around that area, which now seemed had gone from grandeur to ghetto. It was 9pm before we reached Peshawar and needed a heroin top up. Whilst fumbling for my room key as I walked to the hotel Scott behind me. Getting to my door and just couldn't get things right dropping the key then turning it the wrong way till it nearly broke. When eventually inside the room I immediately packed a cigarette with powder and let out a sigh not having taken any with me when we had left this morning thinking to cut down. It felt like I had just got to the end of a long days walking trek all up hill, when in fact it was a taxi ride. It was a clear sign of desperation being without having my Nasty by my side. I'd been reducing my heroin use since the arrival of my son from the UK and was down to three smokes per day. I realised that I would soon have to come to do without this poison and whilst still in Pakistan. I had to clear my head, of the drug delusions before reaching China.

Chapter Six: On The Table

So here, we were years later my son was still an unfamiliar Glasgow teenager, who had managed all these years without my guidance. I still hadn't told him about my addiction still kidding myself I was in control. The subject of smuggling cannabis to Japan had been broached upon one afternoon as we sat talking during a beer at the Dean hotel. I had finally explained to Scott that my life in Asia was not all just travelling then outlining a brief history of my occupation. Starting in 1979 in Hong Kong and was mostly trading in technology buying a $300 US dollar seventeen-day round trip ticket to South Korea then onto Japan. I was selling the products on in black markets in downtown Seoul and was paid in Korean Won. I then would exchange this money back to US dollars. Having to scurry up some narrow-darkened side road to a faceless moneychanger located near the American military base at E Tae Won. I had visited a few American military bases in Asia it is where you find fast food, the red-light seedy massage parlors, and all the good old treatment for the troops on tour of duty.

Then I went onto Japan and purchased high tech goods at Akihabara Electric City, some items being cheaper there than at 'tax free shops' I would complete a ten day return with a stopover in Taiwan on the way back. This stopover created a loophole for people who wanted to visit the People's Republic of China. The reason being you were not allowed entry into mainland China if you had a Taiwan stamp on your passport. The British High Commission in Hong Kong issued me with a one-year passport to use for this purpose. I used it to go back and from Hong Kong to Japan alternating from one passport to the other to look like fewer entries had been made. Most smugglers would only stop off there to sell Korean Ginseng most would often opt to go direct to Hong Kong. Many syndicates would provide air travel and hotel expenses for backpackers plus $600 to $2000 dollars per trip for travelers prepared to carry gold. Not bad back in 1979/80 'The milk runs' they were known as and it kept the wheels rolling for the ever-growing population of semi nomads around the world. It also closed a heavy steel gate on others. I didn't need to work for someone anymore, had independent finances of my own, and could make a profitable return of about $1500 USD per ten days at my level just by trading in technology. It was great fun flying more hours than pilots but it could also become tiresome trudging around bars, brothels hotels and airports. I would mostly be meeting up with people in the same or similar trade as my own and that ranged from travellers on the milk run to more serious shady characters, I had met and knew a few.

I had secured 20kg of cannabis not fancy gold seal, just the fresh aromatic battered pollen and also knew the route through to China to take and, most importantly knowing these cannabis suppliers well. They were old friends of mine, Afghan refugees whom first meeting in the 1980 is when I had sent £5000 worth of their carpets given to me on credit onto my brother Robert in Bethnal Green, London. He had sent me the cash, thus indirectly assisting in the feeding of a network of Afghan families in dire need all along the north west frontier of

Pakistan. They were dependable proud Afghan people whom I had grown to love and trust.

I'd put my cards on the table with Scott outlining my full plan. I told him that I wanted to build houseboats on rivers from Thailand into Cambodia and Vietnam. It was my dream to live away from noisy cities and the rat race in general. I reminded him of the time when we visited Myanmar and sailed along Inlay Lake and how serene that experience was. Then going on to say that he didn't need to worry or get involved, but, just to tag along as an adventure holiday. "How can I help you carry the cannabis and not be involved?" Scott inquired. In addition, of course he had a good point. As we discussed it, further with me trying to reassure his anxieties and relieve any fears. Making it clear that if, in the remotest of possibilities, anything went wrong, never to acknowledge any involvement with these drugs. It was out in the open and the way ahead seemed clear. It was agreed that this venture would be like the two as one. Scott was now part of this smuggling enterprise and regardless of whether that had been part of the plan or not. Thus, the following day was spent buying travel supplies adding mostly dried fruits, oatmeal, nuts and plenty of well-wrapped dates, enamel cups, spoons, bowls, two tin openers in case one malfunctioned.

My first priority was to pack the cannabis so that it did not need to be disturbed until we reached a hotel in Shanghai. I had a nylon duffle bag with seven kilograms stitched inside the bottom I had had a suitcase made with the five-kilograms of cannabis completely concealed inside the lid and bottom. Then finally having another eight-kilogram wrapped up in towels and other clothing jammed at the bottom of a backpack. This was the most dangerous, least concealed, of the illicit cargo and the one for me to carry. I had little fear of being stopped and searched going through such remote borders and relied on dirty laundry and sharp implements placed at the top of my bag as a health hazard for other people to search and look through. As a result, they had never yet reached the bottom of my baggage.

Chapter Seven: Next Move

Atollah laid snoring head against a well-padded carpet cushion the lopsided grin on his face brought smiles to mine. Both his sons had camped down hours before and Scott now lay asleep on the floor stretched out his head resting on folded rug. I lay there curled up preoccupied in tangled thoughts psyching myself up for the oncoming of the inevitable heroin withdrawals. I then soon drifted off contentedly into a heroin nod. It was Atollah who woke me by calling out something to his sons and I roused immediately. Stretched a little, yoga being something I had practiced in the past, I was deluding myself now to break the vicious cycle of Heroin addiction with a few stretches, and controlled breathing.

Once Scott had risen and shook the sleep from his eyes, we made a quick exit from the shop having already said our farewells the night before. We all embraced each other one more time, with promises to return. We went back to the hotel to freshen up, collect our bags and go. I had already sorted out our money issue and had given Scott cash to keep aside for any misfortune that might befall us, or just in case we were split up or robbed or some other unplanned disaster not uncommon in these parts of the world. I had Japanese Yen, US Dollars, Chinese Renminbi, and British Sterling a mixture of currencies amounting roughly two thousand British pounds each. We said farewell to the hotel staff then we hit the street awaiting the arrival of our transport. Patan our driver would take care of our every need accommodation and food. He was another big strong character and a friend for many years to me. He was almost 60 years old now and kept himself very fit and well groomed. It was his his big bushy beard with mixed colors of brown, henna red, with grey streaks which really set him apart.

We took our final glimpse of the passing bustle of daily life in Peshawar. Looking at the people, the broken buildings on that parched and dusty landscape weather beaten faces and the cold harsh reality of the drugs industry the weaponry and the warlords. Welcome to the North West frontier of Pakistan.

It was time to move on. Patan had arrived and we set out on our journey. It was only several hours' drive from Peshawar to Besham, that was to be our first stop. I was smoking around one gram of heroin per day and having about eight grams of heroin to sustain me to the last border town. I would then stop check into a guesthouse for a week to wrestle with the demon of withdrawals. Having brought this on myself and would just have to suffer the consequences this I knew well. For every action, there remains an equally balanced reaction for every cause, an effect. That is karma and there is no escape. You deal with the demon you will pay the price in pain. I could leave Scott to his own devices exploration and taking in the breath-taking spectacular scenery whilst I would lie lost in the costs of my weaknesses crashing in stinking sweaty withdrawals on he dark side in some room out of sight of the glorious and magnificent mountains.

Besham is a small village where the air was clearer and cooler. The landscape was greener and more welcoming to the eye after the hot dry drive. I decided to cut the short sightseeing and just stay the one night in Besham before our next stopover in Gilgit. We had arrived safely and after a nice meal at a roadside hut had a look around the small town. We checked into a small motel then passed a quiet evening out on the veranda of the hotel before heading off to an early bed. I needed to have my nightcap smoke, and had enough for the next week, and was dreading the comedown.

The following day on the way to Gilgit, we stopped off at Taxila to visit the museum there. Taxila is still a center for Buddhist research, adorned with Gandhara art and other sculpture. It also has many archaeological sites dating back to 1000 years BC. We visited Dharamarijika dating back to 300 years BC and a well-known Stupa and temple there. We spent that night in the cool and calm, beautiful green, landscape at a lodge in Gilgit.

The following morning, we set off, we sat back relaxed as we headed up the Hunza valley. We would stay about ten days around Karimabad and I could spend that time recuperating from my self-abuse. Thankfully, Scott would get some sightseeing before our next move. Having told Scott about my addiction and he was deeply concerned and would keep a close eye on me whilst wrestling with the heroin withdrawals.

Chapter Eight: The Last Burn

I finally arose from my stinking pit on the sixth day having no more bile left in me to puke, looking haggard thin and smelling of bad odours. I could smell my demons in the discarded items strewn around me and took baby steps to the toilet in an attempt at overcoming my fear of water. I had been down this path before, taking a towel and turning on the water tap. My whole body turned to goose pimples the fear of purity when wetting my skin. Then gently rubbing my flesh and overcame the shock of accepting water. It took at least 20 minutes to wipe myself over having to squat down still feeling weak. Washing gave me the illusion that I had washed away my poisons and was clean on the outside, but I knew by past weaknesses it would take some time yet to feel clean on the inside. I was feeling better this day and walked a short distance around the room. The following day I ventured from the lodge once more out alone but not having the energy to deal with traders often trying to sell precious stones apparently worth many fortunes. It was the old too good to be true story so walked on listlessly out of earshot. This was indeed a beautiful land of calm serenity. Its people laid back, unhurried and easy going in their ways. Perhaps this then was the secret of inner peace and longevity or the results of it. Who knows? People seem to live long lives around here going into the hundred years of age and more it is common norm and was wondering why that was it reminded me of that book I had read 'One Hundred Years of Solitude.' It was something to do with finding peace wherever it is your heart lies. This was sure a lovely place even with my blurred and deluded vision.

Patan had returned from Peshawar one week after my last heroin burn. He did not want to sit around he told me. It was ten days on the Hunza valley then we packed our bags for the final part of the journey to the border. I was eating again and feeling my spirit lifting. The road was narrow, high and at times perilous, the jeep swung and swayed on the sharp bends and any attempt at bypassing a car coming the other way could be fatal. It was a sudden surprise for us when we were stopped high into the hills by the armed Pakistan police on foot waving our driver down. The jeep came to a halt "Now where the fuck did, they come from and where did that travel-hash-piece go?" I spoke to nobody in particular. This is just the kind of unexpected event we should have been ready for but were not. The tossing of the jeep had shaken my travel cannabis loose so that it had rolled onto the floor. I picked it up put it down the back of my trousers waistband. Our windows were open during the drive and just hoped there was no lingering cannabis aroma.

The pleasantly smiling officer in navy blue uniform popped his head in the driver's window. Scott opened his door and stepped outside onto the narrow road with myself at his back; Scott smiling away merrily. The paranoia was oozing from me just as the stink of heroin sweat had done the days before. Patan chatted away and the police became friendlier. It turned out that one even allowed Scott to examine his gun once the magazine was removed. Finally, they waved us on in good speed and we were back along the high and winding way.

Chapter Nine: Border Crossing

We finally reached the Pakistan Chinese border at Sust where we joined the general bedlam of people and traffic. The area around immigration was mobbed mostly with Pakistanis. Scott and I had said good-bye to Patan, before departure paying him two hundred dollars for his services and company and all was well as we embraced before he returned home. Having secured our immigration entry forms we sat by the wayside, I helped fill out some people's visa applications for them; we proceeded to fill in our own forms while those thrusting pen invaders impatiently awaited our help. It took two hours before we got through immigration and customs. I was nervous just in case something did go wrong but watched as my bag went through x-ray, sort of knowing cannabis didn't register. I still had that moment of uncertainty that it might go wrong .and that definite moment of relief when it doesn't.

We made our way over to a tea hut at the other side of the checkpoint now in China I let out sigh of relief audible enough for Scott to comment "Dad what's all the panic about? Don't worry." Hearing this did not make me feel any better at all. In fact, it set off alarm bells in my head. What was I doing? I wasn't used to having the responsibility of other people's risk and that this particular risk was one to my own son. I pushed those thoughts aside and was tired and feeling weak. The stress nerves were jabbing my neck, the adrenaline charge diminishing and a sense security now on Chinese soil.

We had the choice to catch a bus now or leave the following day, putting this option to Scott, he replied "If you're tired Dad, let's just spend the night here." It was late afternoon and we were hungry so with the use of sign language soon ascertained that there were no guesthouses around here but the friendly family offered us the comforts of their floor. It was agreed we would spend the night at the border in this tea hut we sat with a smile of gratitude on our faces and we ate in silence. The food was bland and tasteless but a few fried eggs helped the taste buds never the less. I was thankful to have something in my stomach and son by my side. Feeling the tension sweep over me as tightness in my neck stung like a dart. My nervous system goes haywire when I am stressed; pain shot into my lower neck. I slowly kneaded the muscles around the shoulder helping me relax a little.

The shifting shadows from the dull glow of the kerosene lamp seemed to dance reluctantly with the flicker from the fire in the stove. As if grudgingly combining in their light, or was I so God- awful fucking stoned? I thought to myself. What, in god's name, was I doing? That night as I lay on a matted rug my son sleeping by my side, I could see the outline of his face. He looked just like his mother and I slept with that in mind and not with the stupidity of sending my son through those hazards with so much dope.

The following morning early, we ate two eggs each and some hot baked naan bread, we thanked the family, gave them some money then got onto a bus lugging the twenty kilograms of cannabis resin along with us. The bus was full of border traders heading to shop in China. It never ceased to amaze me watching them barter and exchange money before even departing, great place to meet up you can be sure someone will now be able to find what you desire. Scott tried to keep a conversation going as we bumped along a desert road pointing out mountain ranges on the landscape, he had read up on telling me that the Chinese claim Mount Everest is in China. Then pointing out that "the Kunlan mountain range has moving glaciers Dad." I must have been unconsciously nodding affirmation but my mind was wondering down dark passages during that trip. We finally arrived and disembarked with the last few passengers at a place called Tashgurgan a dry and dusty oasis town. This was to be our second stopover in China, a desert oasis at best but at least we could have a room with beds and a shower. Now that is something to look forward too after any long dry dusty trip.

At the hotel reception, we had to show our passport open at the visa page and fill in a registration form. Scott and I sailed through leaving the mob of Pakistani people pushing more pens in our faces. Getting into the room and dropping our bags immediately, I started to undress, feeling the poison expel from my pores having an overbearing stink on me. The water was cold but plenty of it and just what was needed. Rubbing plenty of soap over my skin I washed those demons off me and then had a shave. Whilst exiting out the washroom Scott put a cannabis joint into my hand "Cheer up dad" he joked "you've got a face on like you like you didn't get any valentine cards this year!" I did not respond. My mind was preoccupied with what lay ahead.

Scott showered and dressed we took a stroll outside and bought delicious lamb kebabs with hot bread similar to a small naan. It was from a street vendor just minutes outside the hotel a pleasant surprise that the vender also had cold beer in a cooler under his stall. Scott purchased two cold beers and said "Cheers Dad!" raising our spirits with a great lip-smacking sigh. As we stood on a tree-lined dirt road smoking on the joint and finishing off our beer a contented feeling came over us before returning to the hotel and to get our heads down.

I awoke feeling refreshed after a good night sleep leaving my son in blissful slumber. Stepping outside and inhaling the cool morning air. There were several Pakistani people standing around the entrance smoking cigarettes. I went to look for a breakfast to start of the day but returned shortly with no result. Enquiring at the hotel desk for a menu and was informed that western style breakfast was available by room service. Having ordered two western breakfasts with extra toast then returned to the room and awoke Scott. It was a warm bright morning with the sun well up. Our bags were still packed from arrival so it would be a quick brush our teeth zip up and go.

The breakfast was somewhat artificial in its content except for the eggs, they were duck and tasted fine for me. The toast tasted like sun baked sponge cake, and the tea was green, but it was all consumed. There was a bus outside the hotel leaving soon Scott had paid our bill and we boarded and got seated. It was not long before the driver checked with the hotel reception assured every-one was on board before driving off into the desert oasis of Kashgar. It is known as one of the silk road's most famed and exotic stopovers.

I had been there on many accessions in my imagination, now I was going to the market there for real. I had a flutter of excitement charge through me, a feel-ing that I was going to meet someone I knew. The bus drive was uninteresting except for someone pointing out a herd of horsemen and a gathering of yurts. I elbowed Scott to draw his attention to it, and he mumbled he had seen them away back, and returned to his knees to his chest sleeping posture. I gazed out of the window until we arrived. It felt like that half the trip was already done when I stepped of that bus into that fame desert oasis.

Chapter Ten: Oasis

The journey into Kashgar was disappointingly sparse and uninviting, the architecture was mostly standard institutional communist block style. There were scatterings of local styled housing which almost looked out of place among the regimented rows of flats. We checked in at the old British Consulate building converted into the 'Chinibagh Hotel.' Nobody could miss nor mistake this building; it stood out like an architectural gem amid the mundane regimented blocks around it. I had secured a twin bedroom with toilet shower and a balcony overlooking the beautiful gardens of the consul's old quarters. At the entrance of the hotel a guard stood with a oversize uniform we smiled at him and entered the reception. We checked in and headed to the room dropping our bags with sighs of relief we cleaned up each having a shower changing clothes. We headed out to the open-air café just opposite for a cool beer. It was a busy little venue the tables were mostly occupied by other travellers. It is always an opportunity at these places to acquire interesting tips and advice such as moneychangers, best rates, and places to see, etcetera.

Scott managed to get a vacant table situated in the shade under a grape vine creeper, which arched and spiraled across a makeshift roof. Having ordered our beer, I was now looking around me for any old acquaintances but seeing nobody recognizable I did notice one person with his back to the restaurant wall preoccupied with rolling a joint, seemingly oblivious to digression. I returned back to the room and a few minutes later had a piece of hashish. The guy rolling before I left had now gone. Scott rolled up a few joints and passed one over to the three people at the next table. You meet people and you share, sometimes it is knowledge and experience. Other times it could be food or water now it was cannabis and conversation. We chatted for hours smoking hashish and snacking on hot bread and kebab, washed down with a local fine wine. It was now evening turning to night each telling tales of daring deeds, incredible happenings and close encounters. We all got so drunk I could not recall getting to my bed.

The following morning sleeping later than usual rising around 7am with a hangover, my mouth tasted like I had spent the night kissing camels. Taking a long shower, brushing my teeth and mouth washed a few times. It did not remove the fuzz from my brain but it did enough to clear my thoughts and head across the road for breakfast. Leaving Scott sprawled on his bed somewhere deep in Noddy land. The sun was well up and the easy dry heat lifted my spirits sitting relaxed in the shade drinking coffee. It was no surprise when a local person of Turkic origin asked me you need a guide sir. There are many minority groups of China's autonomous Xingjian region, earning a living by trading in local products. This part of China still had a semi open black market i.e., money exchange and selling hashish to travelers was a common sight. I bought a piece to try out the quality although having 20kg in my room. This was a different type of hashish however and had a lovely aroma similar to Lebanese hashish in colour that

I had smoked in the 1970s. It was good quality and cheap. Sabir as he introduced himself as sat down at my invitation and offered me to a free tour of the market place the following day. Kashgar market was something still to be seen for me. I first read it in a book tracing the footsteps of the intrepid Marco Polo along the Silk Road and had read about saffron and silks among other exotic spices, worth their weight in gold that had exchanged hands there, from as far afield as Europe and all the way to Beijing. I agreed to meet Sabir for the following morning.

That evening Scott and I attended a local dance. The night sky was clear and the air warm as we lounged in a beautiful garden bar. The surrounding plants matched the colour effects in my mind it was mellowed by the wine and cannabis we consumed. The place was busy and tables were mostly full of international backpackers consuming large quantities of good and cheap wine. Noticing two Asian women sitting alone and guessed them to be from Japan. I introduced myself to those two, somewhat bemused looking, female travellers. Saying a pleasant "Hello I'm from Scotland" in Japanese. To which both repeated in unison "eeah Scotranda" Introducing Scott as my son and suggested that we join them which they accepted. The conversation was basic about the abundance of the surrounding grape vines over our heads. The women smiled coyly covering their mouth as they did so, giving the impression of teenage teasing shyness. As the cool starry evening wore on with fine wine and laughter, you could see, their inhibitions fade to reveal the free and happy nature of these young women. Naomi was twenty-two, a vibrant energetic person and although her command of the English language was not too good; it was never the less enchanting and lovely to listen too. Her soft unpronounced syllable when she pronounced my name as 'Rocky san' would send a smile to my responsible side. Her pronunciation of the letter L would always come out as an R. Fate had it that we were housed at the same hotel. We spent most of that night talking about their travel plans and leaving out ours. I can't remember what my bedtime was but did remember leaving Scott laughing with the two Japanese ladies.

The following morning around 9am I got up and went across the street and sat at the same table as the day before. I ordered a bottle of water and a coffee for starters. Seeing Sabir with a couple of travellers, I waved, letting him get on with his business. Rolling my first joint of the day a ritual these years sat smoking cannabis and consuming sweet watermelon, which was put on the table complementary. Shabir came over apologizing for not meeting me that morning to go to the market." We can go now," he offered in amends. I asked him to wait while calling on my son and to enquire whither the Japanese women would like to join us. I went over and gave my son a shake and he got up immediately, passing the other twos door I enquired if they would like to come? Both ladies were ready so Scott Riruko and Naomi met us at the café within an hour.

We immediately headed off in slow progress through the throngs of people on the back of a donkey drawn cart. We took some romantic look at me pose with a donkey picture before deciding that it might be quicker just to walk. Sabir took care of the cart payment and we set off on foot. I have to say our advance was not that much quicker but we did embrace the vibrant energy all around us. We all were pointing out something exotic unusual or interesting. As we approached the market, we could see camels silhouetted in the distance and another feature amongst that market bustle was the uniformed Peoples Liberation Army soldiers most of the way along the route to the market center. It was Sabir who informed me that the people of Kashgar had some political problems with the central communist government. I was not politically minded and did not know what was going on in this region of the world but noticed his command of English sometimes surprised me.

We eventually reached the market stalls by the side of the road. Most of the stuff was cheap, Chinese copy of western styled clothing, household utensils, plastic plates, cutlery and toys. I also noticed a snow leopard skin, and furs of other endangered species, hunted, slain and skinned for a living where there are no sufficient state support systems. The local shoemaker shops displayed an excellent variety of finest quality riding boots and would make you them to measure. Sabir took us to his friend's stall where knives were displayed almost like in a kaleidoscopic show their handles encrusted with colored stones, the multipurpose blades in all shapes and sizes glittering and sparkling in the sun. We browsed and bartered until late into the day buying little souvenirs for the Japanese girls.

It was time to eat and Sabir led the way. It is a blessing to have a local befriend you and become your guide there is a fee to pay but it really does make a difference especially when you are invited into their home. Kashgar is populated with numerous ethnic minorities groups, many of them of Turkic ancestry to hear tales of legendary and historic warriors such as the Tajiks, Kazaks and the invading Tartars, not to forget the omni presence of the Han Chinese. The Islamic culture has thrived in this region of the People's Republic of China for centuries and continues to do so today, despite the propaganda of the communism's atheist ideology.

Looking around me within this oasis called Kashgar. The name always evokes visions of travels through these exotic lands; where those very harems of belly dancers, hash filled hookahs and eating like the Kublai Khan, are colourfully depicted. This place was not exactly, as the imagination might have expected maybe in times gone by but for now no. I had a strange feeling in my gut like there was something missing; or that I was missing something more than material, sensational or observational something transcendental. Then it dawned on me that there was no music yet the atmosphere hummed as if charged with ionic magnetism. We left the market area holding onto each other so as not to be separated. Sabir led us through a labyrinth of narrow mud lined streets baked red with the sun. When we finally reached our destination, he personally sat us around an ornate cast iron circular table. This was another garden restaurant well shaded by grape vines. Sabir ordered the food while Naomi and Riruko chatted excitedly in their own language. Scott was occupied by the rolling up of cannabis joints and my job pouring the cool wine that had been served. We ate excellent food and laughed happy in the shade. It had been an eventful day all round and as the evening shadows crept in; we said our goodbyes to Sabir. I paid him fifteen dollars and paid the food and wine then arranged a meeting with him for the following day.

On our way back to the hotel we half stumbled into another fantastic garden bar, this time with live music and dance. This place was authentic watching in amazement as the band of musicians switched to playing on two stringed instruments during the one song yet somehow managing to keep the harmony, which hypnotically drew you into the rhythm of the accordion and percussions. A slipping smile came onto our faces whether we wanted it there or not. It was late into that morning the four of us stumbled merrily, drunk and slightly hoarse, from the bar. We laughed, and cried with the elation of spirit brought on by the interchange of cultures. We had been a unconsciously absorbed into the rhyming of local life without expectation other than to be part of and enjoy. That's more like my visions coming to life.

Chapter Eleven: One Russian Artist

The following morning standing at the reception area at the Chinibagh Hotel was approached well-built man "Excuse me sir" he spoke with a mixed, thick, accent. "Can you tell me how can I get to those Yurts?" pointing to a map "Yurts?" I repeated, unsure of what he was saying and giving him a quizzical look. Then realized he was talking about the 'Mongolian yurts' we had seen en route from Pirelli to Tashgurgan on our first stopover into China. I told him about the bus and where he could get it. We then went over together to have some coffee across the street. Boris was born in Russia and was now living in New York and that he is an artist who wanted to paint something relating with a Silk Road theme. He had pointed out that the uniform of the hotel door attendant was a Russian cavalry jacket. In addition, had asked me take a photograph of him standing with the door attendant whom I obliged. We exchanged addresses he gave me a brochure of his past exhibition in New York and offered a welcome to each other should we ever visit each other's country.

It was time to rouse Scott from his slumber. Walking over to the hotel and gave him a shake saying enthusiastically, "Let's go camel riding!" Scott replied, "I thought we were to meet the Japanese women, they're leaving today." I evacuated the room calling back to him "see you in ten minutes across the road."

After meeting up with Scott, we escorted sat and had watermelon with Riruko and Naomi before going to the bus depot. It was bustling with Pakistani traders returning home with their wares. I knew that sitting space was going to be an issue here. First come, first sat basis. Your ticket purchased a seat but it did not guarantee bag space beyond a roof rack and that is not safe. We made a simple plan where we both would occupy space behind the women and stay until the bus was leaving making sure no open affection towards these women was displayed such as embracing before departure. Knowing this could be offensive to Islamic culture. Both women had already bought scarves and had covered their heads waiting in ready. We sat together placing their bags on the floor as footrests, easy access and safety. The occupants of the seats we were sat on arrived and we got up and stood by the window outside. It was a pleasant occasion spending time together as we said our 'good byes' and the bus pulled away. Scott, I and my other son Lochy had spent memorable times in Japan. The people were kind, cultured and adventurous.

Chapter Twelve: One-Way

After spending a week in Kashgar, we headed to Urumqi this is the capital city of the autonomous region of Xingjian. It is also the political, economic and cultural center for that entire region. We were only passing through to catch a flight to Shanghai and hopefully, the following day. After checking into a twin room at the Fulan Hotel equipped with the usual red plastic thermos bottle. It was with neatly wrapped green tea bags beside the phone table, with no connected phone line.

Scott immediately lay down and conked out on his chosen bed. I headed out to buy tickets for our flight, being soon reminded that we were in fact in China, and was hit by a barrage of red tape. It was sufficient to bind an angry rhino, and I left the offices of 'China Travel Services' without tickets and the solid assurance that there would be no available flight for another week. The next stop then would have to be the train station. I got into a taxi outside the China travel office entrance then pointing out where to go on the map I had. That much achieved, managed to reach the station and buy all three-sleeper tickets to secure the one private cabin for the following day departure. It would be a three-day journey overland through China. I knew stocking up with snacks and fruit was essential returning to the hotel feeling better for my meager accomplishment. Scott was easy about the change of plan and accepted the news of my harrowing ordeal with a yawn. That evening we strolled down to a small restaurant I had seen whilst mobile that day. It was an outdoors barbecue sort of affair. The evening was very warm and people strolled unhurriedly past us with children at their side. The air was thick with the sweet scent of blossoms in full bloom many of which had fallen covering the pavements in glorious colored petals. A beautiful atmospheric Shangri-La if you do not suffer from hay fever.

We sat outside with our backs to the sidewall and ordered sweet potatoes; lamb kebabs and hot freshly baked naan bread a little on the crispy side but still well appreciated. We sat by that roadside café until after midnight, just looking up at the stars and the sky stretching into infinity. Instigating a sojourn into the soul and coming up with what then considered as momentary enlightenment or still more justifications in the form self-delusions. The peace and tranquility of the moment left me with the false impression that all is and would be well with this world.

We took a taxi to the train station the following morning. It was crowded when we arrived two hours early. We wondered around looking for platform signs in English there was none after showing the tickets around we eventually found a spot to settle down to wait with our bags as backrests. The next thing I knew is Scott urgently shaking me awake saying "Let's go Dad they have started boarding!" Getting my brain back into gear, picked up my bags and began making my way towards the train unable to decipher the carriage numbers. A lanky scruff of a man eventually escorted us to our cabin. The poor soul appeared to be suffering some chronically infectious disease so I kept my distance. The cabin was small with the collapsing table and pullout seats doubling as a bed. We unloaded our bags and sat down Scott said "It looks alright here Dad and comfortable enough for two!" It was a treat to get away from the maddening crowd, I sat down and sighed. Scott pulled the door closed; it was going to be a long journey and many thousand miles to cover in three dawns.

Scott took control having purchased some beer we sat and had a couple to drink. I was telling the story again to Scott of how I had almost been robbed on a train traveling from Delhi to Dharam Sala to visit the Dali Lama retreat with his younger brother Lochy accompanying me. Wrestling with the knife thug and believing him to be some kind of crazed assassin. It was hours later realising that the waistband of my trousers happened to be slashed exactly where the money belt and travel documents were hidden. It was the metal zipper had saved me from being gutted and robbed. Going on to say such then were the ways of the ancient Thugge's the worshipers of the terrifying Hindu goddess Kali. They would relieve weary travellers of their earthly burden with a garrote around their necks that they may enter the kingdom of heaven unburdened Glaswegian's referred to such stolen cash as 'Kali Dosh.' In addition, if you stole theirs you ended in hell.

I unpacked a few things, toiletries, towel, clean underwear and socks, folded them and placed them beside my seat. There was no toilet in the cabin but there was one at either end of the carriage for sleeping berth ticket holders. Now settled in we both stared out of the window lost in our own private worlds of thought. It was the swaying of the train bringing me back to the harsh realities of Terra Firma. Scott was occupied looking through the video monitor and laughing and asked "What's so funny?" he passed the camera over to me. It was the scenes where Scott was firing guns in Darra Pakistan. Scott waving a gun above his head wearing free the Glasgow two tee shirts. I watched the film as we moved onto a small tour of the drug dens and cringed inwardly.

Not long after the train departed, we headed for the eating area and finally found space where we could sit down amid a band of scruffy men with unkempt clothes and dirty faces. The train engineers and porters I presumed, having ordered two beers in my limited Chinese we sat down. There was no point in looking at the menu I could not read but impolitely looked around me at other tables for anything to point at but could not see anything there even remotely edible. Scott managed to get the beers opened and finally to order omelet and rice. One of the Chinese people tried to start up a conversation but the only word of English we could grasp was 'Thatcher' whatever he was on about we didn't know and couldn't have cared less. Though unknowingly we should have for we had no idea that Thatcher's secretary of state for foreign affairs, Douglas Hurd MP was all over the news about his 'anti drugs' stance during his first visit to China that very week. As to us we sat oblivious to the world outside in the buffet area for several more hours drinking beer until growing restless and returned to the berth to make a joint. I decided to stand by the window in the passageway for a change of view and was approached by the ticket collector who was pointing to his nose. I gathered he was objecting about the smell of cannabis from my joint and dropped it out of the window. He seemed happy with that and departed. Returning to tell Scott about my recklessness and close encounter. I had that uneasy feeling again this time more justified. It was a dodgy situation feeling now half-drunk, stoned, and sitting on 20kg of cannabis resin. Scott looked concerned also and inquired if the person knew what I was smoking or not? 'Obviously' I thought, but uttered uncertainty, but still felt uncomfortable. Returning to the cabin and locking our door, we unpacked the cannabis from our bags except for the suitcase that was completely sealed. We decided to sleep the night on it and if or when the knock came to the door, we would have the stuff at the ready to throw out off the window. I had positioned the drugs so as to have quick access to throw from the window. I slept restlessly until morning.

Chapter Thirteen: A Bad Day

As sure as a new day dawn, this day was going to be a memorable one. It was around 9 am when a knock came to the cabin door. Scott was still asleep and I was not sure what to do. Not really wanting to part with my cannabis I opened the door. It was the same ticket guy standing there going on again about God only knew what. Having produced my ticket as if that is what my understanding of what he wanted was. To my surprise, he took my ticket and left. After awakening Scott, we decided to get off at the next stop then catch another train later. We repacked our bags. The cannabis that I would carry was not hidden very well to begin with and so wrapped it inside a bath towel then put it on the top of a small daypack. Then returning to the buffet area our bags already packed and waiting to be collected from our berth as soon as the train stopped. As the hours passed, we drank tea and discussed various options like throwing it out the window, except for the suitcase off course. Stashing it on the train to collect it, another day was a feasible option. In the past I had left money and gold behind at a couple of places on my travels to later retrieve. My ticket still had not been returned to me yet and the way things were going on in my mind, I did not want to see this porter person again anyway.

The train eventually pulled into a station called Zhi Zuo getting off we made our way towards the exit hoping to avoid the eye of the dreaded ticket man. Having no ticket to exit with was stopped. Scott had produced his ticket and I told him to walk outside and wait for me having an eye over my shoulder to see if the ticket collector was about. I was feeling shaken and trying to be calm. After a few minutes, another railway guard took my arm and guided me to the waiting room. Scott returned with me to a large empty waiting area with high ceilings. I immediately pushed the small daypack containing the hashish under one of the benches we sat on. We sat there for about twenty minutes occasionally getting up to peek out the door. There was an armed soldier outside my heart raced and realised that we were in serious danger. I tried and had to remind myself that our problem was merely ticket related although the rising panic in me screamed otherwise. I kept expecting this ticket collector to walk through the door sniffing like a hound dog directly to my bag. The paranoia was dripping out of me.

The train eventually departed and we both released an audible sigh of relief. Then it all came on top, as is usually the case, from the least expected place. Right there in that waiting room out walked a woman from a door behind us, went directly to where the guard stood outside, and started talking. We looked around puzzled, wondering where she'd come from. Scott strode over to the open door and looked in expecting that it may have been a toilet. To our surprise, it turned out to be an office, desk, chair, and other paraphernalia including a red plastic thermos flask. We sat back down and within a couple of minutes; the woman returned with a couple of khaki green uniformed armed men, either army or police as they all dressed the same. She strode over directly to me and pointed at the bag under the seat where I sat with my legs out-stretched, partly obscuring it from view. I ignored her and looked bemused. One of the guards came over and pointed under my seat again trying to ignore his gesture but, in my heart, knew this was trouble. I started briefing Scott on what to do and what to say. Telling him "Just keep it simple you're travelling with your father and you know nothing about any drugs." Scott was handling this well. I remained silent now and when the armed guard drew his gun and retrieved my bag neither did, we neither move nor object.

By the expression on the guard's face indicated that he had no idea what he had uncovered. A few words were spoken and one guard left the room returning a few minutes later and a few more words were exchanged. Still, we didn't know exactly what was going down until we were escorted to what could only be described as a 'torture chamber' The ones you see in the movies with chains and manacles on the walls bare damp brick "Fuck me! It's a fucking dungeon" Scott exclaimed in shock looking scared now as we were pushed inside. We sat there looking at each other dreading what could be coming next. It was only a couple of hours before anything did. Three civilian dressed men entered the scene at least one of them could speak English and introduced himself as a Public Security Bureau Officer. We were escorted from that dungeon and returned to another office in the train station. The English-speaking police officer asked me "Where did you acquired this substance?" pointing at the parcel. I told him that I had it from a man in Kashgar. He asked for more details and told him I did not know the people or their names, only that one was called Danni. That was the end of our interview.

To my surprise, we were escorted to a good hotel and booked in under normal hotel guest procedure except our passports were taken into the Public Security Bureau hands. We sat around talking in the hotel lounge between interviews for most of that day. I was ready to throw my hands up in despair, bewailing my stupidity for what I had done and plead for clemency for my innocent son. Then Scott pointed out that the camera in the bag told the full story on film. I had forgotten about the video camera and had put it into the hotel baggage storeroom. If they see that film footage Scott too would be implicated. In that film footage, was we firing guns and posing besides tons of cannabis and other heavy-duty narcotic substances? One scene had Scott firing his gun into the air and shouting, "FREE THE GLASGOW TWO" with the two of us wearing justice campaign T-shirts emblazoned with a bloody clenched fist clutching at a barbed wire St. Andrew's cross around the chest.

Thomas T.C. Campbell my younger brother was arrested and convicted of six killings in what was known as The Ice Cream Wars. His c/o accused Joseph Steele maintained their innocence and their plight for justice were still ongoing. It was such a national scandal with the fabricated evidence by the Scottish police force and their investigation tactics the people were taking to the streets in protest. If the PSB saw this film it wouldn't look to good on my or Scott's resume for court. I spoke a few words with the English speaking PSB officer that I needed medicine from my bag. I was really surprised when he nodded for me to follow him down to the reception. After extracting the cassette from the camera and stashed it while picking out some toothpaste along with other little bits and pieces. I zipped up returned my heart pounding, and sat with Scott we could not go into a room together but were allowed to sit outside in a lounge space. Lighting up a cigarette and mumbled using Glaswegian colloquial. "Give me a smother son" sitting for another minute heart pounding and dry mouthed before rising and strolling casually to my room controlling the urge to make a desperate dash. Not knowing were these panic attacks come from but they are difficult and painful to control. It was easier going through customs than walking to that room. With a great rush of relief watched the incriminating tape flush away down the toilet drain. That major problem now resolved felt at ease again with my Kashgar story. Sleeping restlessly that night but at least slept my conscience pacified that Scott would be free soon from this under 'house arrest' but with our bags full of cannabis down stairs that they hadn't yet discovered something would surlily arise.

Chapter Fourteen: The Outing

The following morning, we were escorted to the hotel restaurant and seated with the three plain clothes PSB officers. Being served a local styled breakfast consisting of a hot congee soup with steamed bread buns and a mixture of pickled roots and vegetable, which tasted great. My appetite had not been as daunted as my present self-esteem as we ate courses of buns with juicy meat inside. It was the best breakfast we had had since leaving Kashgar. After breakfast sitting back the cigarettes were passed around the table. We all smoked except for Scott. Having reminded the interpreter that money was needed by me to purchase cigarettes. "I'll have to change some money also or won't have enough to pay the food or hotel bill." I continued. The interpreter agreed he would personally escort me himself to the bank after breakfast.

It was all so casual, and I could have taken off at any time, and cannot say that the urge was easy to contain. Besides, to just leave Scott to carry the proverbial can and in reality, there was, as the song says. "Nowhere to run, nowhere to hide" At the bank after changing three hundred pounds I casually slipped my passport, back into my pocket in a vain hope for an oversight on my PSB guide who had returned it to me to change cash. It did not happen and handed it back over reluctantly.

On return to the hotel, we stopped to purchase watermelons from a street cart by the roadside. The interpreter took every opportunity to practice his English and I encouraged he by asking questions, what he thought would happen to me when the Shanghai police arrived? In addition, why were the Shanghai police investigating us in the first place? He smiled at that and said "Your destination was Shanghai" He went on to say that was why Shanghai's police is involved" He was clever enough in diverting my queries, but happy to tell me about watermelons being in season. Resulting in us, carrying two apiece back to the hotel. Scott was sitting reading through a book titled 'The Full Cycle looking up as we entered, he asked, "Change some money, Dad?" "Aye!" I replied simply and sat beside him. The interpreter sent one of the other people off for a knife. Upon his return, we opened two melons and passed the slices around. They were juicy and cold and a pleasant atmosphere was arising if only under different circumstances other than arrest for possession of an illegal substance. We were once again separated for questioning and the police tactics had changed now saying that we were now both being accused of involvement in taking this cannabis to Shanghai. "Your son has confessed," they told me. "I knew the present Pope when he was an altar boy!" I responded. This remark off course went over their head and asked me to repeat myself. I simply smiled and replied my son did not confess, and emphasised the word 'confess' and told them the whole story again: I met a person in Kashgar who offered to sell me some cannabis whilst sitting in a café. It was a true story after all but not the right one or the same cannabis. That he offered me a large piece for my own personal use if I took his parcel to the Seaman hotel in Shanghai where this person called Danni would call to collect it. Telling them having refused that offer more than one time and that was not tempted till a few days later when he approached me again. Finally agreeing after he would make me an increased offer of a piece weighing 300gms for personal use. Having explained that my son had no knowledge of what my doings were telling them that my son he did not smoke at all himself.

The interrogations were becoming repetitive and I would sometimes resort to sarcasm to ease the monotony using the lowest form of wit going way over their heads in their limited and humourless command of the English language but was achieving nothing. It was only my facial expressions revealing my contempt for their allegations about my son. That evening we dined out and letting the interpreter order the food. It was a traditional styled circular table designed so that the various dishes revolved around to you. Scott called for two beers and who could object. We offered a glass to the PSB people but they all declined. Scott going ahead we raised our glasses to each other, then to our lips. The food was served in what seemed like a never-ending procession. Soups, meats, fish and a wide variety of fried and steamed vegetables along with heaps of steamed white rice and many small bowls to use. This was not like being under arrest at all staying at a hotel and eating out. Scott bought six more beers to carry out and a bottle of local liquor and off we went to get drunk. One of the PSB people called Lee spoke the clearest English and was enthusiastic about boxing. Scott asked him about Bruce Lee but he had never heard of him. "Bruce Lee the Kung Fu master" I tried to clarify but he still had no clue then Scott asked "Do you know Lee Munro?" Being surprised by that one, I also and asked who he was. Scott reminded me of his good friend who had boxed for the British Commonwealth team "You know his dad as well" Scott said "Bertie Munro." That was Scott he still had his humour even under these circumstances and we sat and chatted easy with each other in a kind of friendly manner giving us a sense of security. These PSB officers were very humane outside their investigation mode. Probably just, want to practice their English I thought, rather than admit to myself that they might even be decent people. Lee conversed tirelessly and myself never short of inquiries as to his opinion on the consequences regarding the possession of this illegal substance.

Later on, that evening, Lee accepted a drink from another bottle Scott had just opened thus initiating our first communist party. By early evening, the beers were downed and the liquor polished off. Lee himself went off returning shortly carrying two more bottles of a powerful concoction called Mai Tai and with another bottle opened, glasses raised, drinks were downed and a party atmosphere was created. Chinese and Scottish songs were sung in unity while getting drunk and sang my own 'made up' version as I went along. 'The Proclaimers' "And I would walk five hundred miles…" topping my vocal range. Temporarily forgetting the dire situation, we were in.

Lee ordered snacks consisting of dry shredded squid and other dishes of various kinds arriving in separate bowls. The alcohol was taking its inevitable toll.

Lee's face had become reddened and his eyes looked bloodshot. By late evening, we were all ready for bed getting up drunkenly and saying goodnight ready for sleeping. Scott downed his glass and the other two PSB people who had not indulged in the night's booze up accompanied us to our separate rooms.

The next morning Lee informed me that the Shanghai PSB would be questioning us that very afternoon. Still hung over and had a bit of a headache and by the look of Lee and my son's faces, they were not any better off. I showered and shaved to sober myself up a little then went for breakfast with the usual entourage on a beautiful sunny day. We ate at a different place this fine morning soaking up the sun eating outside well and supping on delicious watermelon for another short while before returning to face the opera of our new interrogators.

Chapter Fifteen: Shanghai P.S.B

Whilst lying on top of my bed in the hotel three scruffy dressed Shanghai Public Security Bureau officers walked into my room. I sprung off the bed onto my feet. "Sit down" the one with the rumpled double-breasted suit said walking towards me like something out of an old black & white B movie. He had a cigarette poised in his hand millimeters from his mouth whilst busy chewing on a tooth pick. "Hold on what's going on here I inquired? You are now under the investigation of the Shanghai Public Security Bureau," they informed me in unison. They had commandeered office space and they manhandled me into it all three suited agents eager to impress their professional seriousness upon my psyche. This was to be yet another ball game all together. Scott, apparently, was being interrogated in another room and my demands to see him be ignored. Asking if I could speak with Lee the local cop, keeping my tone civil but that too were ignored. On the other hand, maybe he did not understand my English so repeated my request. The B movie actor simply ignored me and introduced himself across the table as Alan he was in his late twenties and obviously educated on roaring 30s American movies. He started of by telling me he studied American English. Then he explained to me as if talking to a pupil, "It's easier to speak and understand". There is only English I said. "Listen to the word, it's English. Was he having a dig at my Scots accent it crossed my mind? So, what's this American English you're talking about?" I threw back at him. He obviously thought to take over from Lee as the more qualified interpreter but was losing face for the fact that he had never experienced an accent like mine and was having some difficulty if I choose to apply it. He hesitated, considering his reply but he was to slow and interrupted his chain of thought by interjecting. "Chinglish" You speak Chinglish" then explained its meaning to his deepening annoyance.

The other two PSB people now seated themselves astride and flanking me. The questions came fast. The old routine, going on and around the same repeated questions. I had been going over the same story as told to Lee only this time it was being recorded on tape. I asked for my cigarettes left beside at the bedside in my room. Alan cocked an eyebrow in what he must've thought depicted western cool. There was a slow arrogance to his movement as he leaned over the desk and produced a packet of 555 cigarettes. He offered one to me before placing another in the corner of his mouth, lighting it and puffing smoke in a contented show loudly into the air. I wondered if this guy was really writing his own movie script or something. I knew the story regarding foreign imported cigarettes in China they are a status symbol in many parts of Asia. After examining, the cigarette commented that I use to smoke this brand also that seemed to make Alan smile. He went on to tell me that he got them as part of his police rations but because they were foreign cigarettes, more expensive, he got less. Laughing at use of the word 'rations regarding 'cigarettes' He looked at me puzzled "cigarette rations? I was showing my finger turning on a crazy head intending to indicate government cigarette rations seemed crazy. This unintentionally, seemed to have knocked him down a peg. One of the other people smirked, produced a packet of Marlboro Reds, and offered me one from his pack maybe they did have a humane side after all. This first interrogation was not as bad as I had expected it would be judging by their intrusion into my room that morning. I had expected that it might be a little more physical once they had me alone. That evening I met up again with Scott this time accompanied by six Shanghai PSB to dine with. It was not the relaxed atmosphere as with the local police so we ate in silence before heading off to bed.

Scott and I were reunited again at breakfast in the sitting lounge area eating rice soup and steamed dumplings. Scott started telling me what was going on with him but one of the PSB people spoke out "Don't talk" Taken aback, we ignored his statement and then asked Scott if he had stuck to the script. Scott assured me that he had. It was getting heavier and the pressure taking its toll on my nerves and still had the far greater bulk of the cannabis in the two bags that they had not discovered yet and might just stumble into at any moment. We now had six PSB officers around the table with us and thoughts of 'Midnight Express' were flashing through my mind.

Perhaps "Detained at the Desert Crossing" would have fitted more apt in the present situation. If they were treating us like major criminals now, what would they do if they found the rest of the cannabis stash. Alan had something to say and the table listened. There were new conditions laid down. No more going outside to eat no more alcohol. Also, Scott and I could only get together during meals and in the evening after interrogation sessions. We were back on the tragic round again.

The interpreter, Alan, held my passport open and flicking through the pages with a smug smile across his face. He noted the counties I visited and the time I had spent there over the years. One part of my story I told them my job was exporter and importer. Alan was not having any of that and suggesting it was my involvement in international crime. How all these short visits indicated that I was part of an international smuggling network? Alan had noted which countries I'd visited and when pointing out to me the shortness of stay at the stopovers in some places concluding that I'd smuggled drugs in or out of these countries. He was closer than he knew and to close to the bone for my liking. He was only wrong in detail. Looking at him dumbfounded in his ignorance of those places; he was effectively accusing me of the equivalent of smuggling coals to Newcastle. Alan had it a bit back to front but I did not enlighten him on that. I was in fact a fulltime smuggler but not of the ilk he proposed and not usually, nor often, with drugs, and never with class A narcotics.

Chapter Sixteen: Train Drain

The two PSB people accompanying me ensured that the entire luggage from the storeroom was retrieved. Thoughts had crossed my mind to simply leave it behind but now that plan was off and would not have worked anyway. Feeling shaky and my nerves rattling, I would have to take that yet undetected greater bulk of cannabis with me into the Shanghai police headquarters. I might still have the chance to dump some from the train hanging onto any hope of getting rid of this other cannabis. Talk about 'The Lion's Den'. This was more like the Dragons dinner, and I was about to be served up as the meal. Scott carried the suitcase with 5kg of cannabis resin professionally concealed together with his own luggage. The Shanghai PSB would carry the other captured 7.9kg as their evidence. I had the badly concealed dope with me. I only was hoping that Scott was safe and out of incriminating range, but that remained a slim hope as we carried our bags to the awaiting transit van.

My heart was in my mouth by the time we reached the train station. Then Scott freaked out, "Dad that bastard's filming us" he shouted looking around me but I could not see anyone with a camera. Scott pointed to the PSB officer behind me. "Look dad, that briefcase is a fucking camera" and then saw the briefcase the PSB cop was carrying but still no camera. The next thing I know is Scott flying through the air and landing a Kung Fu kick on the side of this person's chest, sending him and his briefcase spinning across the platform. Stunned, unable to believe my eyes as pandemonium broke out. The other two officers leaped on Scott. One gripping his neck in a strangle hold while the other gripped his lapel and tripped him. Scott kicked back and they all went down in a tumbling heap rolling around the ground. I dropped my bags instinctively leaping into the affray, kicking and punching till sufficient space was made for me to grab hold of the PSB officer with the strangle hold on Scott. I gripped his neck. It got back into some form of order quickly and no one was touching us now. I had let go and stepped back panting. Scott was shouting, "Who the fuck do you 'think you 'are? James Bond or something"

Little did we know then that this was to be but the start of a perpetual battle for me and a gradual downhill slide into chaos. It was also the introduction to their reward and punishment carrot and stick system and I was not to be given any more cigarettes they informed me. Scott was also separated in adjacent cabin. My bunk position was placed on the top and I stretched out. It now was at least one hour had passed before asking for access to my cigarettes. The PSB guys had been blowing smoke in exaggerated sighs into the air I asked for my cigarettes again. Again, Alan refused. "Is that right?" I said sneering into their faces as in the Glasgow challenge style, depicting imminent physical confrontation. "Fuck you," I added raising my voice and my arse off the bed. Alan mumbled something rapidly and the Marlboro man handed me a smoke. Thanking him and laid back down to savour and enjoy that condor moment and let my mind wonder free on nicotine high having nowhere else to go. During the journey,

Alan had told me that we could go to jail for up to seven years. I was calculating remission in my mind would be free in four years maximum not a pleasant thought. I'd been on the road in constant travel for a long time and was growing quite alarmed and psychologically disturbed by the realisation of my present predicament. It was like some kind of cosmic 'jet lag' and I really needed to land before crashing. Meditating on my breath winding my psyche down to a minimum peep as the arrest realisation landed in me with a thump.

It was lunchtime before coming back from my mind wonderings. Scott joined us again in the crammed cabin he was fine and we both ate heavy heartily. The constant bump and grind of the train at every stop was mind numbing and my head was splitting. Constantly coping with the PSB did not help matters either. It was as if these people felt a need to regain lost face before reaching Shanghai. Their constant attempts at intimidation intensified as the day dragged on and on in endless screeches until I just wanted to scream out in pain with the steel wheel grinding on my nerves. It was in the middle of the night before we pulled in at Shanghai station.

We disembarked and stretched grateful for the space and air. I had not any opportunity to dispose anything from my bag so had nothing to pack. We were escorted from the train station this time handcuffed together both of us stumbled with every step trying to manage our luggage. While yet another team of Shanghai PSB with camera, crew at hand filmed the entire event. It was unbelievable something else was going on here something we did not know about yet. What we did not yet know was that we were all over the Shanghai news as part of a gang of international smugglers whilst Douglas Hurd the UK Secretary of State was on his trade negotiations visit to China. The Hurdy Gurdy man himself and was not singing songs of love but was here urging the Chinese authorities to clamp down on the illegal drugs trade.

Chapter Seventeen: The Barracks

The road had very little traffic; the sirens wailed their international tune, "Get off the road we are coming". It had been raining and the oil slick reflected colors of melancholy in my mind. We were driven to the detention cellblock and seated in a large conference room. They filmed us with the cannabis at our feet. Scott, ever undaunted beamed a wide smile saying to me "Told you Dad, we're movie stars now" But my heart was thumping and my mind racing this was serious, very serious indeed. Why would so many high officials come to meet the train at this god-awful late hour of the morning? My brain was bursting mostly in fear that they would not accept Scott's story never mind mine and was trying to blank out the thought that both of us would end up in jail. The fear continued to haunt me. Just picturing what his mother and all the family would be thinking about me now. They most certainly would be far from pleased. Like the towers of Babble, everyone was talking at the same time the noise was painful to my brain and irritating to my ear. We were being ignored except for the filming crews who kept busy on us. Not a word of English was spoken and no idea what was going on? We both sat with our heads down looking at the floor.

Finally, we were escorted through a door and out onto a cobble stoned courtyard what appeared like an army barracks. Two armed guards stood at each door we passed through until we entered the reception of a jail block building. Here Scott and I were separated. It felt like being parted from my living breath. I was escorted to the property check section and Scott somewhere else. Standing in front of the high desk, behind which sat an old officer flanked by the two interpreters and one-armed guard. I had to take every item from my bag while it was noted down on official format. I was inevitably getting closer to the bottom of my bag where the other yet undiscovered cannabis just lay loosely wrapped. Eventually retrieving everything except the package the bag partly collapsed empty. My chest had a minor death rattle an instinctive alarm to warn me that it was nearby. I straightened up they had all my clothes and other items documented. Then casually I started putting my things back into the bag again almost choking in my panic. Folding some items and replacing them back into the bag. It felt like my whole being was transparently exposed. The interpreter told me to remove my toothbrush and soap before eventually zipping it up. To my utter disbelief and part relief the bag was removed and taken into storage. The sight of that bag being carried by the PSB seemed so familiar. I had seen this scene before, it was Deja-Vu, I just knew it would be found, I didn't know when, and now wasn't the time for contemplation nor confessions.

Chapter Eighteen: Shot In The Head

I was escorted back across that cobbled yard into yet another annex, through more guarded doors and finally into a large office with a film projector. They sat me down facing a group of khaki uniformed officials. There was a lot of chatter, in the room all alien to my ear. The lights went out except for the projector the only other light glowed from their cigarette puffs. It reminded me of the fireflies on the beach at old my place on Boracay Island in the Philippines. If ever in need of a cigarette, it was now but just knowing nothing would be forthcoming surrounded by eight male PSB officers and one female.

I watched in disbelief as the scenes unfolded it were three army trucks going down roads, the camera operators just following their route. I was not able to understand the commentary but the message soon became clear. The trucks came to a stop at the entrance of a football stadium; the camera zoomed into the back. I saw faces of men and women all with the same expression. It was a look of sorrowful finality in their downcast eyes. The stadium gates opened and the trucks drove inside, circling the grounds as crowds cheered. The trucks finally coming to a halt outside the center circle. Six soldiers disembarked with a prisoner bound in rope crisscrossed over their chest and held by the noose at their necks. Each prisoner had a placard on their chest with Chinese writing on them depicting their crime. These people were being humiliated before their peers as part of the punishment for their crimes before being executed. I had heard years before that it was not uncommon in China for these public mass executions. It depended on your crime it was just the first one I had seen and not by choice.

The memory of that film will always be with me leaving me often pondering the meaning of the word 'humane' in relation to east -V- west interpretations. In China, the Government administration regularly shoots people in the head after a short period of appeal time ten days being the quickest on serious crimes against society. It is usually within three months from passing sentence sometimes within ten days in more controversial cases. I am not sure if twenty years on death row is any the more humane or crueler. I am only happy that the decisions of life or death are not mine to make. Although my instinct tells me to choose life and would rather live. Then again not being in that position yet do not know where the truth lies. The policy of public humiliation in China was yet another matter and did not like that system. I was now directed onto a wooden chair secured to the ground, like a barber's chair only with an extra arm folding over my lap to lock me down. It reminded me of an electric chair. Not liking this one bit.

The Film had been shown again with English commentary by my ear. Alan who had come into the room was now translating the Chinese placards on those people. Leaning over and saying softly. "Mr. Campbell, I hope you can see the trouble you are in." He then explained that those offenders who were shot were drugs dealers. I replied quicker than probably should have saying "I'm not a drug dealer" and in the living reality, was already trying to talk my way out of being shot. The film had really shaken me and "what then now thinking of Scott?" and was trembling in outright fear. I was now escorted to a cell and told by the ancient warder interpreted by Alan to think on it overnight. Alan escorted me shuffling and deflated, up two flights of stairs. The jailer was a very thin man with exposed gums and decaying teeth who smiled at me continually.

The cell door was unlocked and I was pushed inside. I stood there facing eleven seated men in an overcrowded cell. One person rose and came towards me holding out his hand and shook mine. He stood by my side while I looked on at ten other faces. This must be a temporary holding cell was my first thought. The person at my side said Hello, and smiled, I smiled back then telling him my name was Lockie and asking "What is your name?" "Mr. Cai" he said. "Sit down please" he replied in much accentuated English like a Benny Hill spoof. The cell was about 9 feet by 12 feet with a 1 foot raised concrete platform about one square meters in size. It had a squat toilet pan, and above that was a narrow but long window.

Around the walls were painted Chinese characters, which were explained to me as numbered allocation spaces for each prisoner to sit and sleep. Mr. Cai then allocated me number 12 by the door next to him, and letting me know he wanted to be called Charlie. The people sitting at numbers one and two were two hard looking downcast men in leg irons. Charlie explained they were scheduled for probable execution. The others were all seated with their backs to the wall, heads down in their chests at their allocated floor space saying nothing at all.

Once seated and not taking my eyes from the men around me while Charlie told me in his broken Chinglish that he used to work in Hong Kong. Charlie's English was very limited but having a good understanding of Asian spoken English. I put my communication skills and sign language to work. I encouraged the speaker to continue confidently by smiling and nodding my head and could usually gather the gist of their meaning. Consistently going over some points until it got through to me, but still just could not take in what he was telling me. It was not his lack of communications skills but the content of what he was saying that baffled me. I sat there open mouthed in astonishment thinking 'This guy must be a nut case or something.' He was saying that he personally had been in that detention block for the past three and a half years and hadn't been charged with anything yet. Did I hear him correctly? Surely, this could not be right, could not be true. It was true all right and yet the worse was still to come. As I looked around me squinting in the dull light, hesitating to make eye contact, I thought it very strange and unusual that nobody was speaking. Surely the sight of a foreigner had not shocked them so much. In my ignorance to the rules of detention tried to ask some questions. The first one being "Do any of you speak English?" One little guy spoke out and said "Mr. Cai is responsible for this cell if you want anything you must ask him for permission." "Permission?" I repeated,

"Permission for what?" Charlie came over beside me and said, "No speaking" but inquired further, as to why there was no talking. I had been here less than an hour and already in a verbal battle for my freedom of speech. My brain was somersaulting and was struggling to grasp his full meaning his instructions were as follows:

No talking unless it was to Mr. Cai if you wanted to use the toilet, you have to tell Mr. Cai." He then instructed me to the towel rack and the way the towel is to be neatly folded and perfectly in line. Charlie seemed to me that he was being friendly but still couldn't understand why no one else was talking, even amongst themselves. This somehow made what Charlie was saying a little more sinister. This was not exactly what was needed under my present circumstances. Charlie pointed out the written black Chinese characters around the walls and the concept of allocation of floor space. I was thinking that could not be right; it is impracticable, unperceivable, and impossible for people to conform to this but the sight of these men was convincing me otherwise. They all but one had their heads and hands resting on their chest in total submission. I was not grasping why nobody spoke up and Charlie had not told me anything that I fully understood.

Lying awake that night my brain kept returning to rats they would draw the police to my bag in storage. It would uncover my lie to the PSB and probably get me shot. I lay tense all night trying to think of ways to get out of this the last draft to hell. Hearing people getting up in the night to piss it kept my defenses ready, in case they tried to murder me in my sleep. Twelve people in a cell size twelve feet by nine feet were only enough to lay a row of thin men sideways along the walls. There wasn't even enough room to swing a cockroach in here never mind a cat. Looking at my situation couldn't even begin to feel sorry for myself thinking of Scott and how to maintain order in an overcrowded cell. How had all this started cannabis instead of technology and gold? Then recalling a night out with a few smugglers in Tokyo, we were drinking hot sake at a bar called 'One Lucky' in Ikebukuro San Chome. It was a favourite hang out with travellers. Good food and cheap alcohol. The owner's novelty was taking photos of customers and had racks of photo albums dating back years for the clientele to browse through. If you returned the following day, you could see yourself in the new album and buy a copy. This particular evening was the first time that nobody in our company had any cannabis. This was something that had never happened before. The pursuit for THC was on and we did eventually find some in the early hours of that morning in a nightclub called Club 69, a Reggae joint near Shinjuku San Chrome underground station. On entry to this place could not believe my eyes at first. It was full of Japanese Rastafarians, dread locks and the whole 'Rasta man' vibration. Reggae music blaring out in that crowded smoky, wonderfully happy place. It is where also I first realised the dire expense of cannabis in that country. I had just paid the equivalent of thirty English pounds for two grams of tourist shit you would get of the streets of Delhi or

Bombay for three dollars. It was not good quality at all, and it did not take long for the mental calculator to work out the figures in the rate of exchange and for me to decide on a change of preferred commodities for my return trip back here. My first step though, was to make the connection here before making the trip.

That came later upon a chance meeting with a young Japanese lady called Riruko. We met whilst on an outrigger boat from Boracay Island in the Philippines where I had a house and diving school called Jocks Rock. I was feeling somewhat puzzled by the idea that she might be playing footsy with me on the way over to Panay on the mainland to do some shopping at the market there. Soon however, Riruko was telling me that both she and her husband Lou, a photographer, had just arrived for a holiday, going on to tell me they were returning to Japan from the UK after six years of living there. Riruko had worked for Japan Airlines in the administration department. Lou her husband was a freelance photographer and he was going to take photos at the cockfighting there. It became a wonderful meeting for us all in more ways than one.

Chapter Nineteen: Daybreak

The sun finally dawned to redeem the cold harsh light of the living reality. Finding myself trapped in the legendary Chinese 'Dungeons and they were very, real. Feeling the sense of unadulterated dread, dank and death was overwhelming. I just wanted to cry out how sorry I felt. I would swear to God, with all my heart and soul that I would never dream of ever doing anything wrong ever again. And, really mean it.

I could hear the sound of someone walking in the corridor outside the cell then the sound of metal striking metal. I lifted my head and looking around me saw that a couple of guys began to sit up myself then following suit. Whilst rubbing the sleep from my eyes I watched the little guy who spoke to me in the better English the day before as he did some sort of breathing exercise. Standing with his legs apart and performed some Tai Chi breathing for around five minutes until the sweat dripped from his forehead. Once he finished, he immediately sat down in the squat position on the toilet. It was a six-inch high concrete slab with a hole in the middle. For the next few minutes, the sound of his loose bowel movement and the stench of excrement fouled the air. As one person finished their bowel movement, a word from Charlie and another would squat. Then each would fold their blanket and stack them by the door wall in a perfect block shape. One by one, we got up, shit, and dressed folded, and stacked the bedding.

The cell door had a square six by six-inch hatch hole cut out near the bottom where the water food and was pushed through to us. The water came in through the spout of a garden watering can, which arrived about thirty minutes later. Prisoners would fill a plastic basin, again in turn by their floor space numbers; then they laid their water basins in a row along the back wall. Charlie stood close to me quietly mumbling in Chinese while all this was going on. Once everyone was finished, he beckoned me over and as I had no basin, he handed me the one he hadn't used. When I had finished washing, be beckoned the others to begin. The two guys in shackles did whatever they wanted no rules applied to them.

There was so little space to move around that without the rota system there would bound to be chaos and violence. It was just a pity they could not organise an air filter. The stench of putrid excrement and rancid urine was thickened by the scent of sweat and fear choking and stinging to the eyes. My head was having difficulty taking in this morning's routine it somehow seemed like temporary accommodation following some great flood or firestorm. It was unsettling watching the two people in leg irons it seemed so odd. They performed painstaking Houdini like antics just to take their trousers off at night and put them on again in the morning. It was another half hour before the breakfast came through the hatch on the door. It arrived in aluminum boxes about ten inches long by three inches wide and four high. Charlie allocated the job to one person who slid the box along the floor for each in turn to take theirs with steamed bread rolls stuffed inside. I had no cup and thus nothing to drink from Charlie shared his cup of hot water along with the story of his arrest again with me. I listened closely occasionally asking the other man for clarification on a meaning with Charlie's English. This quiet guy was much better but he was obviously not very comfortable with my questioning him, and he mostly looked sidelong at Charlie for affirmation to speak.

I got up and walked around the floor, asking this Mr. Charlie bloke more questions on the subject of bail procedures and such general 'need to know' issues. Charlie asked me for an explanation as to exactly what was meant by the word 'Bail' But the concept of paying money to get out of jail always seemed to be interpreted as 'Bribe' to Charlie "No!" he exclaimed "No pay money" It was the Tai Chi man who came to my rescue with Charlie's permission explaining that there was no bail system in China. I felt a strong sense of eternity right there in that cell as the chill of confinement walked through me.

Later in the afternoon the cell door opened and me taken downstairs, shackled, for interrogation. I had never been shackled at the ankles before, and was only glad that I had not had to sleep with these things on through the night. They were very rigid, rough and difficult to walk with. I had seen it in the movies and noted that the prisoners always appeared to walk as if ashamed and humiliated. I now realised that their appearance was nothing to do with humility or how they felt. It was more to do with how to cope with the shackles physically. You soon learned to adapt to walking with a shuffle to avoid painful tugs on the chain. You kept your head down, not out of shame but to watch you are every painful step. Having only to wear them going to and from interrogation sessions considered myself fortunate. Every step and every session thereafter only added to that pain. I watched the death row men they showed me how to wrap them but that was for those who had them on constantly. At interrogation, I would be strapped into that chair again and shown more sequences of film people with placards around their necks being shot for various crimes, mostly drugs. Some of these killings were very impersonal, at least in as much as the camera made it appear so by showing close up is of people before a soldier raises a rifle and blasts their head.

The accusations are presented as statements of fact and the questions as simply seeking your confirmation in confession. "No 'ifs' no 'buts' this is what you did and what you are" and "if you do not confess you will be shot." Confession is the only thing that can save you in accordance with their law. All my efforts could only say that I wanted to see the British Consul and that was entitled to see the British consul. Trying to resist and keep my mind where I wanted it and not in the hell where they put it. I was looking at other things and my mind was escaping into daydreams it was the small red glows from their cigarettes taking my mind back to a time when often had watched the fire flies dancing in the starlight on Boracay Island in the Philippines. Then I was shocked back to my present nightmare by the popping sound of recorded gunfire. Gritting my teeth as it repeated again and again. Then with unintelligible babble coming from all around me being deeply unsettled by those gunshots to the head scenes, trying to blank them out of my mind. Mr. Campbell a voice spoke from somewhere close to me and a new, hard faced, PSB officer introduced himself. "I am Fan Zhiyi from the Justice Bureau" he said, gesturing to the ever-present Alan to escort me from that room to another where again was placed into one of those restraint chairs. Fan Zhiyi exuded a powerful aura of self-confidence, iron control. He spoke clearly, almost as if with parental care to a wayward child. Not telling nor trying to convince me but simply explaining that. "True confession is the only way to gain leniency in the Peoples Republic of China Mr. Campbell, if you do not confess you will be shot. His manner convinced me that he was not playing games but simply that he was obliged to inform me of the facts before carrying out the sentence. Like the police are obliged to do in the UK in their 'caution' before charge. Only this one starts with the presumption of guilt and the sentence already passed. You have a right to confess; if you do not wish to enforce your right you will be punished severely.

Shot dead! His voice echoed through my mind to the popping sound of gunfire and bowed heads. "Consu, visit" I said repeating myself part mumbling "I am entitled to see the British Consul" and was told by Alan that they have been informed but he expressed it in such a way as to make it seem irrelevant and impotent in the circumstances. My ass began flapping like a choking goldfish. "Mr. Campbell," he went on "China has suffered and was manipulated by foreign drug barons. Our national dignity stripped and our people trapped by addiction. You must confess now" The pitch of his voice rose considerably. "I am here to give you this chance, confess now" he insisted, summoning Alan over and spoke a few words. Alan rifled through a desk and handed over a few sheets of A4 paper to me with a pen. "What's this?" I inquired? "This is for your confessions write it down." Alan handed me the paper taking it from his hand asked for a cigarette. They both looked at me. Alan spoke first saying "When you confess you will get cigarette." "I've already confessed, and admitted to having the cannabis." It was falling on unsympathetic ears. This is not what they wanted to hear. Handing the paper back to Alan but keeping the pen and told him. "No written confession until my lawyer comes." Fan barked out a spiel. Alan interpreted "You will confess." Looking up at him I asked for a cigarette again. Alan said something then his cigarette packet was produced and was given a cigarette from Alan's foreign pack smiling up at him as he lit it for me. Inhaling the smoke like a dose of medicine cherished it like a badly needed fix and immediately felt more relaxed and at ease. Even in the realisation that this was a point of negotiation here. Yet what did I have to trade with other than my soul in confession. Scott's soul was his own and not for me to barter with but maybe I could spark up negotiations of my own in trade for Scott's release?

I started to open up and tell Alan a bit about myself drawing out the interrogation, playing for time and another cigarette. Alan had said" The Consul has been informed," my only trump card so far so took the opportunity here and requested to see my son. Going on to explain the law in Scotland and the principle of the presumption of innocence and how that would entail the right to see my son. Fan, the PSB man, however, had heard enough. He stood pointing his finger at me like a gun, leaving me with a stern warning. "You must confess or face the consequences Mr. Campbell" So ended that day's interrogation.

I lay that night jumping from one mad thought to another. I came to the conclusion that even in the direst of situations your mind can still get filled with silly ideas. It must be a safety catch instinctively kicks in and changes your perception to adjust to the present environment.

Chapter Twenty: Day Two

The following day Alan had a new interrogator with him, a small person around five feet six in height and slimly built. He introduced himself as Mr. Chang I was to listen to him go over some points from Alan's notes. He asked me questions regarding how we encountered the person who gave us the cannabis. Weary as I was of their repetitious questioning, I then retold the story of how I and not we met this person Danni in Kashgar. Chang went on to tell me China treats drug smugglers as counter revolutionaries' intent on undermining their government. They were not content with catching the 'courier' but more intent on the supplier as a threat to their national security. Chang had made it clear; if the buck stops with you, then you are either the main man or you are protecting him. I could not very well turn round and tell them the truth having had crossed the border with it myself. My destination was actually taking the cannabis to Japan." It was their manipulations and sly maneuvers in trying to implicate my son that just was not going down well with me at all. At one point being so annoyed by it that I let loose with a mouthful of unpleasant Glaswegian curses. That only resulted in no more courtesy cigarettes for me. However, after signing a couple of papers from a statement I had written in English, confessing to possession of 7.9kg of cannabis. I was then was returned to the cell. Chang reached down opening my leg irons Alan asked me if they were painful ignoring his comment, he knew well that these barbaric restraints caused pain. He was just having a fly fucking dig at me below the belt in that polite and civilised oriental manner.

Entering the cell in a storm of a mood the room was silent as usual; everyone except Charlie was sitting with his or her heads bowed. I could see the look of dejection written across their faces. The cell door slammed behind me and was still fuming as I looked around me, deciding there and then I was not having any more of this subservient shit. It was only my second day here and all around was these hard-faced criminals and two opposite me, scheduled for death, and were all afraid to talk. I simply could not fathom it at all and started pacing the remaining cell space quite rapid and irate with the events of the day. Charlie told me to "sit down" and the anger rose up in me. In my best impersonations of 'No!' that I could think at the time but shouted it unconsciously reverting to my natural Scots accent. "NAW!" my face up close to his, invading his space, while thumping the palm of my hand against the side of my head. Indicating plainly to Charlie that I'd had enough of this crap and would remain on my feet and continued pacing. Charlie began walking with me thus forcing the other detainees to draw their knees in closer to their chest. There just was not enough room with two people pacing the cell and I could not get into the stride nor fixed mindset. Charlie was obstructing me by trying to walk and talk two abreast causing a lot of fidgeting and discomfort for the others. I eventually just sat down leaving him standing. I distrusted everything here and already detested the regime and this Charlie character I did not like the way he ran this cell. The "No Talking" for example. That was the weirdest experience yet, locked into a cell with eleven other Chinese men and the only noise you hear is an occasional body shift. It was uncanny at times to say the least. The afternoon meal distribution was much the same procedure as witnessed in the morning. This time when the food came through, Charlie took to dishing it out. I noticed he removed the meat from two plates before he passed their food to each in turn. Watching as everyone hunched over his or her bowl with no complaint or comment. The food rations were minimal at best Charlie's plunder of these rations would leave two people hungry. It disturbed me and seeing my scowling look he handed over a piece to me and gave the remains to the other two people with shackles. I held up my hands saying, "No Thanks" and would not tolerate any bullying or take part in the spoils. The fact was I was actually boiling with fury then interrupted Charlie to speak out and ask" Why did you take their meat? What do you think you are doing? Charlie explained that these two were Moslem and did not eat pork. That shut me up. I began to realise that I had carried the trauma of the interrogation into that tiny little overcrowded universe where one person's paranoia could wreak havoc in a free reign. Grudgingly giving ground I ate my food lost in deep dark thought. I had read the situation wrong again and resented Charlie so much for imposing this 'No talking' regime. I couldn't understand how he got away with it. I wanted so much to ask these detainees so many questions. Charlie had told me none of them could speak nor under-stands English, but did they? What was happening to my mind? I just couldn't focus on keeping a tight rein on it there was just so much nervous energy running through me and must have radiated like a microwave. Sitting down with my back to the wall I stretched my legs and started doing some breathing exercise. I was inhaling deeply through my nostrils trying to bring my heart rate down and calm the storms of energy threatening to explode into madness or heart attack. I put my thumbs onto my neck and massaged my muscles gently. Charlie sat down beside me and began telling the story of his arrest again. I was not much interested in listening to his Chinglish for hours on end. I had my own problems preoccupying me and which needed desperately to be dealt with. Charlie chattered on with his story anyway. He and another person had set up a business importing Kodak film from Hong Kong. He went on and on about how this happened I did not really listen and was somewhere else dealing with my own worries. Then suddenly standing up and interrupting his story and asked if he could get me paper and a pen. Telling him I needed to write notes for my lawyer you no lawyer, "Charlie replied I know that" "but when one comes, I'll need some questions answered" Charlie told me you cannot have a pen or paper until the next day's interrogation.

Everything and every communication were like an interrogation here. I left it at that sat down again and psyched myself up for another night in detention. The Shanghai Sheraton five bar hot hell was the only pit option for me this night. I had been interrogated two times daily since my arrest. I didn't know what was really happening. I didn't know what Charlie had told me was real or not. How could it be someone held three years six month without being charged? I was very suspicious, and the thought of Scott going through what I was suffering haunted me all through that restless night.

Chapter Twentyone: Cell Hope

Now, one week later, awaking on the morning of my seventh day and feeling optimistic and hopeful that this would all soon be over. The reason for this optimism stemmed from the discovery that Scott and I was simply under investigation and would have to be charged or released in ten days from our arrest in China. I thought maybe we would not even be charged. Maybe we would simply be deported as Charlie and Tai Chi had both indicated was likely. I allowed myself to cling desperately to that illusion that it may really happen. It was usually in the afternoons when interrogations took place, the humid temperatures rose over 120 degrees on the outside. It was more than that on the inside of this hate factory. My skin became very sensitive and sore, developing red swelling under my arms. It constantly irritated me and I just wanted to suffer in peace but that would never be allowed. At interrogation they used the same procedure with me most days. Alan would escort me to the film room and they would start with the execution scenes then onto accusations, and demands for confessions beyond my statement. Always they tried to have me implicate my son. You would think they would get tired of that tactic. I was certainly bone weary, sick and brain fried by it.

The film execution message had certainly sunk deep into my psyche no matter what I tried to do to block it out. Even laying in that cell at night it would come back. That public execution at the stadium and the sound of gunshot echoed and ricocheted around my scull through each night reminding me that death remained immanent and closes at hand. Feeling the fear stick to my skin like sour body odor and tried to hide it. But knew I could die here a statistic in these desperate places. The ones who knew they would die had nothing to lose. It would be enough just so long as Scott would go free. What was happening with Scott? That question already haunted me on that hot and howling August night in Shanghai crying in my shame and despair. The rain battered at the prison roof that night splashes coming in through the bars in warning that the typhoon season was on its way. I lay there in that crammed cell hot, and sore with sticky itch. The swelling under my arm had developed into dumb boils and it felt like my brain was infected with poison puss.

The following day during interrogation sweat was running from behind my ear down my neck. This interview proceeded as usual in the barber's chair and ended up with me surrounded, yet again, by high-ranking Chinese officials. Alan did most of the interpretation telling me these younger PSB officers were from out of town. They are training in Shanghai he went on where he was proud to be born, he said. I was thinking is this a fucking guided tour group or something these words screamed in my head to release the tension but remained cautiously muted as they goggled on at me. They asked me questions such as "How much money did you earn working?" Moreover, "How much wages do policemen get in the UK?" I gave them their place, showed interest. I answered their questions politely. Using that form of speech normally used with children.

Speaking slowly and nodding encouragingly for them to continue with confidence. I could not have done to badly as along the way I had managed to get several cigarettes and a cup of coffee. I have always enjoyed the pursuit and exploration of that twinkle of interest perceived in people's eyes. These 'out of town' PSB officers would be gone tomorrow, carrying their little tale of their confrontation with the foreign devil drug smuggler.

I was left alone again for a few minutes still locked into the Sweeny Todd barber's chair. Then in came Alan again with some X rated Red Guard renegade of the old school he was raising his voice, trying to impress me with fear again but he failed at imposing his outdated interrogation tactics upon me shouting his anthem "Confesses and you will be leniently treated" Alan didn't' have to think about his translation. We both knew it by heart. By the time the show was over returning into my cell brain in melt down.

It was yet another surprise when the cell door opened again and was called out again. This time escorted and without leg irons. That blind optimistic hope rose in my heart again led just along the landing to the guard's office, shown my chair and handed a cigarette. What next thinking like a kid at Christmas my smile could have split my ears. A Chinese prisoner appeared with a red plastic thermos flask like those at the Tashgurgan Hotel and that office the woman exposed us at the dreaded train station. He also had Nescafe, milk and sugar whilst inhaling the smoke like the lord of all I survey; sipping coffee, thinking the best has still to come. There was just the one guard who had opened the cell and one more sitting with me in the cell converted office. The guard smiled and started to talk to me and could only smile and nod. Feeling awkward because not having a clue what he was saying but did not want to interrupt his cheerful flow. Whatever it was it sounded okay with me whilst in receipt of this rare treat. The nicotine rush psychologically settles my head; a momentary illusionary recharge. The guard at the door walked away, and hearing another cell door opening and a Chinese prisoner came into the office and stood beside me. He too was also handed a cigarette, and we were all sat around the table. They all spoke and the prisoner who had just joined us turned to me asking. "Excuse me sir do you support football," He said in very clear English." Yes" I replied. The next question followed "Do you support AC Milan? "No" I told him. Then asked him a couple of quick questions which he answered slowly but clear enough so that I felt confident to ask him if he could put my request over to the guard to see my son Scott. There was another exchange of words and I was handed another cigarette but told that "The chief says no, you can't see your son." I sat in silence for five minutes then was returned to the cell.

Charlie wanted to know everything, especially "Who speak English for you? You have cigarette. How many? You go home tomorrow" He concluded, and then Tai Chi spoke up Mr. Campbell you have been here ten days tomorrow they will charge you or send you home" I told them exactly what had been said in the office explaining about the coffee and cigarettes. The retelling made it sound so good, like a big day out or something. Charlie said they "Wouldn't have been so kind if they weren't letting you go would they?" That night sleeping in vigilance and prayer looking for a ray of light, some sign from on high to confirm that we truly would be going home tomorrow.

Chapter Twentytwo: Don't Pass Go

I now roused each morning and going through my daily ablutions before anyone else was up. I sat lost in thought of what today might bring as the 'Gate fever' ran high. Could my son and I really be getting out of here? We could and should be released maybe a fine and deportation. We had suffered more than enough for my stupidity. Yeah! Stupidity is what it was reassuring myself. Thinking after all, it was only cannabis we were talking about here, right? Not as if it was opium, heroin, cocaine or crack but simply cannabis. It is openly promoted in the West. It was No big deal. Thinking of all those songs and artists such as the Legendary Bob Marley and the 'Legalize it' campaigns. Thinking of the number of legal paraphernalia on sale and around the world cannabis culture was being accepted. It was openly for sale and on public display in parts of the civilised world.

I was taken from the cell early that morning without the leg irons and sat in front of Alan. This was it then it was going down and it was looking good with the freedom of movement. Alan spoke with a sparkling glint in his almond eyes, both his hands running over each other as if in exited expectation. Then he spoke, you will be charged today with possession of 7.9Kg of cannabis. The pit of my stomach fell digesting my futile delusions of freedom. Alan handed over a piece of paper and told me "Sign here" It stuck to my sweaty hands and I uttered mournfully "But this is written in Chinese" I stared confused and alarmed at Alan feeling to be sick all over this place, what about my son" asking him and dreading to hear the worst. Alan said that is another issue. You will be investigated next by the Prosecutor's office who is now handling the indictment procedure of your case. This is our last time seeing you until court. Alan's statement passed over me like never hearing it and could not take in the full extent of what I had just heard. My head was spinning in confused panic and exclaimed "But what about Scott? He's done nothing wrong" Alan reassured me "You will be informed of everything this afternoon" and again asked me to sign the papers in my hand and cooperate. I wasn't signing any more papers until seeing and speaking with a lawyer of whom we didn't' even has one yet. Alan offered me a cigarette and began asking me questions regarding my feelings about my treatment by the police. Had I been treated unfairly? Looking directly into his eyes and answered squarely "Yes you have treated me unfairly not being able to see my son. You won't let me see a lawyer or phone my consul and I need to contact my family they will be worried about Scott" I began to lose the place a little as pent-up emotions let loose. What is going on in this fucking place?" raving on. "I'm untried, not a convicted prisoner and should be allowed to see a lawyer or make a phone call. Then pointed my finger at Alan do you think I do not know what you people are up to in this place? I know your keeping guys here for years without charging them. I also know that people are shot in the back of their head for what I considered ignorant of law crimes. Spitting out a few of the horror tales I'd heard from Charlie over his years of being here.

Alan didn't' look at all phased by my outburst but simply smiled and pointing out to me that I had cooperated with the police by confessing and accepting having committed a crime from the very start. He said that I cooperated fully with the police in exchange for leniency and expressed my shame... Listening to this, it sounded like he was mentally ticking off a list in chronological order. Like ticking off all, the right boxes for me to qualify for something, I did not exactly realize it then but that is exactly what he was doing. Being returned to the cell I handed Charlie the piece of paper, which I was supposed to sign he read out. Hearing a few sympathetic sighs then sat down putting my hands to my face and head on my knees. It was late in the afternoon before the cell door was opened again and I was escorted downstairs to the office. I assumed that this was because of not signing that paper given me but was in for another surprise.

Chapter Twentythree: British Consul

I was being led across a courtyard and escorted by two armed guards while Alan and another official from the prosecutor's office walked in front. I was taken into a large room with a thick red pile carpet fitted throughout. A large wood carved table at the center. There were four large desks and counted fourteen carved high back red velvet cushioned chairs. I sat there looking around me at the old flock wallpaper with the gold patterns. The ceiling had a center rose and surrounding cornice. It gave an impression of past glories but did not' quite come up even near to standard. On the back wall, there hung a large framed painting of the Heavenly Gates in red and gold were five stars of the Central Committee of the Communist Party. My heart was racing as trying to put some order to my priorities of questioning. Scott being first on my list but everything else seemed to get cross-wired and confused. Having took a deep breath and closed my eyes, willing my attention to focus on a dreadful situation we were in. Hearing their voices before seeing them I stood up excited, and was finally going to have some issues sorted out. Maybe even acquire some inkling of my own fate. Ian was a large well-built man in his late thirties he offered his hand and introduced himself. Then he introduced the consul interpreter as Miss Jet. We all shook hands and were seated my first enquiry was as to Scott and his well-being. He had not seen him personally Ian told me but that Miss Jet was with him that morning going on to say that he was fine and they would see him again later today.

Ian was a non-smoker but did bring a packet of cigarettes with him very considerate. I could light up at my own pace during the visit and did not' need to depend on handouts from the PSB. Ian also handed me a list of lawyers. The guard for inspection immediately intercepted this document. Ian then asked me if I was being treated fairly and I told him about the living conditions and pointed out my arm infections. Taking notes, he next enquired whether there were any urgent messages needed passed onto my family. He produced a newspaper with the headline

"Scotsman May Face Execution In China"

I gulped Ian assuring me this would not happen to me or Scott. Alan reached over to have a look but Ian pocketed it smartly. I pursued other avenues of inquiry seeking out anything that might help gets us out of here now. Ian made it clear that his office could not interfere nor be involved with judicial matters and issues. That area would be covered between the Chinese authorities and my solicitor. I asked Ian can he recommend a lawyer from the list. Ian replied that a committee of executives recommends those named. I have no dealings with them personally. Whomever you choose will enlighten you in regards to what can be expected in relation with Chinese criminal law. Ian went on to say "From what you have told me you have made a full confession and our office has been told you have cooperated. You have not caused any trouble since being here that should make things go easier and more smoothly." There never seems to be enough time at these visits but we managed to stretch the official thirty minutes into forty. I still forget to ask many questions before it was time to depart. I shook both the interpreter and Ian's hands asking when they would return to see me again. "Anytime in emergency." Ian replied. "Ask the police to call this office." He handed me his name card. Alan reached out and plucked the card from his hand. Ian continued "Otherwise arrangements for another visit next month and brings you news from your family." Whilst departing Ian called out "Take cares of yourself Lauchlan and keeps your chin up, Bye for now." and they were gone. I watched them leave the building leaving me in that room with the flock wallpapers doodling with patterns in my brain.

Chapter Twentyfour: Living It

It had been over a week since the Consul visit and no other interrogation sessions within that time. I had not been out of the cell and had not seen a doctor yet. Nor indeed, had neither bath nor access to one since arriving here it was all just a body wipe. I had lost weight through dehydration my skin itched and my face unshaven was irritating, with this humidity. I now had a spate of boils spread under my armpit. I had asked to see a doctor when the third lump appeared now there were five. I had already asked Charlie to call through the cell door again, to the landing short term prisoners. They were employed as the warder's gofers. Their foremost duty was to tend to the warders every instruction and their every need. Then their next priority was the food and water distribution to the inmates. 'Laodong' means 'worker' in Chinese. When someone calls from their cell, he would attend to it and not the guard. Charlie passed on my request to see the doctor.

It was evening before the cell door opened to reveal a guard accompanied by another man. He looked as if he had just been dragged out of bed and still wore his rumpled pajama shorts and dirty string vest. His thin shoulder length stringy hair straggled about his face and snagged in the wisp of a goatee beard protruding from his ever-averted face. The guard spoke and Charlie in turn translated for me saying "This is doctor and to show him" I opened my shirt up and holding it there to show him. The doctor spoke a few sentences. Charlie informed me something relating with "You infection" and that I would get medicine tomorrow" "What about painkillers for now?" I asked. Then more words were exchanged but "Tomorrow" was the best he could do. Feeling pleased enough that some potential resolution might have been achieved to help ease this pain.

The following afternoon with no medicine forthcoming, thinking, there was not much point in me accepting this situation quietly. It seemed to me that I had nothing left to lose. Getting up I began shouting through the steel door. The gofer had come on several occasions yesterday but wasn't appearing now. Being pissed right off now and shouting, "It is not acceptable. No doctor, no notepaper, no pen. Charlie said to me that the senior guard was on duty and it would better be asking tomorrow. Charlie spoke pleadingly "He not like being disturbed" Fuck him I want my rights and shouted over Charlie's head at the cell door. The guard returned accompanied by a small flat-faced guard. He asked who was making all the noise. As if he couldn't' tell my voice from the locals. Charlie with his eyes averted down, explained about my past Consul visit and that I was told could receive paper and a pen. He then went on to say about not having any medicine. The cell door was locked again and five minutes later, the gofer passed me a pen and one sheet of paper through the food latch. Sitting there on the floor sticky and wet with sweat, going over repeatedly in my head exactly what I'd said during police interrogation. Not having told the real story of the cannabis, but the story I told was an accurate enough account of a similar happening. I felt satisfied that I had given a good enough account, although partly exempting myself from the full consequences of my actions. It was more important to fully exempt Scott from any responsibility. I had already admitted my crime of illegal possession of cannabis but had not accepted that I had come to China with criminal intention.

I had chosen a lawyer at random, as they were all unknown to me. Charlie and Tai Chi seemed as much in the dark regarding lawyers as me. I had also requested a legal visit so to get some inkling as to what the future may hold for me. Charlie did mention a lawyer's name 'Li Guo Ji' but could give no contact details. Having wrote the name down for the next consul visit when Tai Chi added that Li Guo Ji was the best lawyer in Shanghai and that he stood up against the government. I didn't' take that literally, though later however would. It had been a very eventful day and feeling better for having taken things into my own hands to better results. I began to relax talking more now with Tai Chi, much to Charlie s obvious displeasure.

Then Charlie was called from the cell one day and Tai Chi sat closer to me telling me in perfect English that Charlie was a resident informer. "What! How do you know this?" I asked excitedly. He looked around nervously, saying that he was afraid to speak and that I should be very careful not to speak about my crime. Not to trust Charlie or the police, that they would trick me into confessing and then punish me severely. He told me never volunteer to speak about my crime he repeated and I should keep my mouth shut when dealing with the authorities. When Charlie returned, one of the other people started speaking. I watched Charlie take off one of his thick, hard brown, plastic shower type sandals. He walked over to Tai Chi, who had stood up with head bowed, and Charlie whacked him a full-on slap across the face with its sole. I tensed in shock and astonishment but when he moved to deliver a second whack to the unresisting Tai Chi. I jumped to my feet and gripped Charlie by the offending arm. I shouted, "What is going on and was promptly smothered by bodies pulling and punching at me. Pummeled under a pile of bodies and could not breathe with the overwhelming pressure upon me I blacked out. When opening my eyes again, I lay spread-eagled on the floor with my head resting in Charlie hands. Everyone else sat back against the wall, hands folded, heads down, eyes averted and silent. Picking myself up from the floor still breathless, asked Charlie "What do you think you're doing?" Tapping my finger to my temple to illustrate 'craziness' The others stirred restlessly some to their feet, but with an offhand wave from Charlie they promptly sat back down again. Tai Chi sat nursing his jaw, which had developed into a thick red welt. In simplified speech I asked Charlie why he was an informer. Pointing around me saying, "Look at these people Charlie, why are you helping the police? You've been here for years and you should know better" Charlie merely smiled wistfully and nodded slowly; with a casual sweep said, you no understand. It was a clash of cultures and values. It is fundamentally wrong and erroneous to presume that one's own cultural values are universal and or morally superior. I didn't' have a clue here.

It was Chinese to me. It seemed to me then that Charlie was a tyrant, bully and informer and he was not denying it. Whereas, where I come from no part of any of this would be tolerated in the least. I was having difficulty getting it into my head that my standards and values were not universal and that this was, after all China. Then the paranoia began thinking had I revealed anything to Charlie? Nevertheless, knew that I had kept the secret of those kilograms of cannabis in my property so close to my chest I was afraid to even think about it. My brain was going into overdrive again and overloading. It was so fucking hot in here that all were constantly wet. Lying down, which was against the rules but I ignored them feeling exhausted and closed my eyes.

Wang was a handsome bloke age twenty-seven he had been given the death penalty on August 26th. 1991. I was thinking back to when I first arrived at this cell. I had watched him do his Harry Houdini by taking off his trousers with the shackles on. He never once getting flustered or irate about it but nonchalantly went about his way. He had what the Chinese consider a feature of beauty. His nose was long, not flat. I had spoken a little with him; it was Tai Chi interpreting for me. I learned that he had fought over a girlfriend and stabbed the other person to death. He had accepted from that moment and without complaint that he would to be executed. I called him 'Sing Song' Wang simply because he would just start singing right out of the blue. No one would ever object or complain, although I never understood a word. It never the less sometimes was beautiful to listen to and everyone enjoyed when he sang. On the night before Wang went to court for sentence to be carried out. He was handed a pen and a piece of paper to write a final farewell to his family. Tai Chi, with the tears running down his face, read Wang's letter out to everyone in the cell. It was the first emotion seen since coming here and it was the tears that burst the dam. Nearly everyone was crying some softly in silence and quiet dignity, while others simply sobbing their hearts out unashamedly. Tai Chi then translated the letter content for me. Wang's letter of apology to his mother was seeking her forgiveness for the trouble and pain that he had caused her, He asked that his mother remember the days when they visited his grandparents in the countryside. Describing the scenery and the happy memories, they shared as a family. Wang's sister should take care of Mama and not to let her work too hard. Tai Chi said he could not translate anymore; it was too emotional. I understood well enough. I had a lump in my chest crushing me.

It was quite a surprise to hear a rustle and to see a pack of biscuits produced by one of the prisoners. Suddenly, like the 'Loaves and Fishes' of Jesus, Goodies were appearing from everywhere and passed around. Something was going on everyone moved around and chatted away freely together. Wang himself was chatting away merrily munching biscuits as if without a care in the world. Sitting down with Tai Chi beside me, he patted me on the shoulder and smiling said it is a different cell today he said. I enquired as to why that was. Tai Chi explained that "The death penalty inmate has a free day" Which entailed that you could talk and if Wang wanted to eat packet noodles, then the Laodong would provide the hot water for our cell. I glanced over again, to where Wang sat, he was enwrapped in conversation and I felt humbled at the thought that this guy sitting opposite me would be soon dead. Thinking of those extremes brought me to think of how little my problems where at this moment but how extreme they could become if I did not get things straightened out. I had written down all my points and queries for the lawyers' attention and would sign the contract from the list that the consul had provided. Legal fees were to start at seventy American dollars per hour. That was a lot of money by Chinese rates where a monthly salary for a tradesman was thirty-pound sterling. The only other option open would be a court appointed lawyer assigned to me for a lesser fee. I decided to pay the higher fee my reasoning being they must be very good at that sort of price.

Gradually sliding down the cell wall, hot groggy and wet with perspiration that nobody could afford to lose. My new red stripped boxer's shorts were tied in a knot at the waist to keep them up and were strangling my groin. Shoe Laces, tiers, belts, they even took the metal clasp to fasten your trousers, zips and things were strictly forbidden here. Probably to prevent people from hanging themselves before the authorities could get the chance to shoot them.

Chapter Twentyfive: The Triad

My thoughts were interrupted by the cell door opening and waited in the hope of a cool breeze that never came. I did not even bother to lift my eyes or care anymore. We were all exhausted, drained and dehydrated. Many like me suffered from skin infections and nasty rashes in every extremity. It was the clatter of shackles that caught my attention and shook me from my stupor. I could hear the muffled grunts of pain. I quickly sat upright just as the cell door slammed shut. Jumping to my feet in shocked reflex at the sight of the badly battered and bruised man standing there at center stage. I pointed my finger to where he could sit down and saw his jaw drop in shock at the sight of me. Perhaps it was that my beard was red and which always seemed to get a stare around this part of the world. Charlie went about telling the guy to put his things down and I went back to my attempted escape from this heat into sleep.

Later that evening Tai Chi told me that, this new person was one of the 'Triad' leaders of a chapter form Northern China Dunbae Tigers. They were a fierce and infamous clan with a wide reputation. This intrigued me and I asked Tai Chi to enquire further regarding the 'Tongs' and as to whether they were a big Triad mafia in China. After an exchange of just a few sentences, he answered we have not heard of Tongs. I explained about the movie I had seen in Scotland as a youngster. Once more, they exchanged a few sentences. Tai Chi said the Chinese word Tong has many meanings, one of which being extortion. That sounded okay to me and I was off into some fantasy telling the people back home about my encounter with a real Tong in China. I had a feeling I would get along with the person whom I had named Triad. He also brought news of other foreigners being held here. How many I asked? Flicking open my fingers, "One, two, three?" Tai Chi said he had shared a cell with one German man who was with another man somewhere else in the building. It may seem strange and perverse but somehow it was a sense of relief to know that one is not alone. Yet it is a fate you would not wish upon anyone. I recalled my younger brother TC Campbell, when he was sentenced to a ten-year incarceration for street gang related offences. He had told me about how his hands had bled as he had carved out a poem on the stone solitary cell wall with a bedspring.

Five years done now, two more to do,
Six months in this digger for assaulting a screw.
May get another year, may get two,
So remember there is always someone worse off than you.
But if that's any consolation,
You are a creep.

Yes, it is true. There can be no happiness nor is consolation at neither another suffering nor that do they suffer along beside you. To me it was just the hope of the opportunity to speaking and exchanging stories with another European who was already here.

Chapter Twentysix: Being Ousted

The weather just got hotter and hotter along with the tempers and tensions in the cell. You could feel the violence sharpen through the thick tepid stale air. There was some kind of storm rising in the psychic atmosphere of this miniscule world. I could feel the static buzz crackle from one glance to another. It was becoming obvious that the clouds were about to break. I had no clue what so ever just what was going on. The eye of the storm seemed to stem from around Triad who seemed perfectly at ease, while unconsciously exuding an aura of natural power. It was time for some changes to be made. Many things had been going down that I had not known about and simply cannot understand everything from body language alone.

However, it later emerged that Triad had been making moves that Tai Chi had been to frighten to mention to me. Charlie was receiving torrents of softly spoken abuse from Triad every time Charlie spoke anything at all. That evening when the food was delivered pork fat with rice, everyone seated awaiting the go ahead from Charlie. Triad stood up and walked from his floor space to where Charlie sat. Then he calmly reached down, picked up Charlie's food container, and smashed it hard across his face. It was then utter pandemonium erupted food and blood splattered everywhere as almost everyone in the cell attacked Triad. I leapt into the affray intending to drag people off the pulverized Tong the next thing was me right in amongst it. It seemed to that everyone in the cell was letting loose their pent-up pain it was terrifying, as if all hell had broken loose and I was fighting for my very survival. I started kicking with all my might and ability just to get some room around me to gasp for air. The only thought left in my head was for air to breath. Suddenly there was loud shouting and the cell door crashed opened. In pure and utter amazement, I realized that nearly everyone was sitting back in his or her places. Charlie had a wide-open wound on his cheek he quickly stepped towards the cell door holding a towel to his face. He had not finished whatever it was he was saying before being frog marched out of the room. Tai Chi then spoke up and, after a few more words the guards face turned deadly serious with a tight-lipped expression. He pointed his finger at Triad, cackled something rapidly and slammed the door closed again behind him. No sooner had the door slammed shut when Tai Chi said to me "The boss wasn't happy being disturbed during dinner" What is going on here I asked has everyone gone crazy or something?" Tai Chi uttered a few words and everyone starting eating. They were still waiting to be told to eat this was definitely a nut house. He then sat back down and told me 'this problem' had started from the moment Triad had come into the cell. That he had felt a deep sense of shame at being in the same cell with a government spy. Tai Chi translated the Triads whom he associated with were known to kill informers or spies without hesitation or mercy.

Soon after we had finished eating the cell door was opened again and Tai Chi and I were called out. It had been some time since being last out there. It had been some time since being last out there. It felt spacious. It felt like a privilege in that weird way that sensory deprivation distorts your appreciation and perception. I was being closely questioned they seemed more concerned with regard to how badly hurt I was than they were with anything else. We sat there for over an hour. Tai Chi and the guard seemed to be getting along well as they sat chatting and drinking tea. Tai Chi was a non-smoker but he managed to slip a few cigarette butts into my pocket before we were returned to the cell. Tai Chi explained to me what he had just told the others that he was to take charge of the cell and would interpret for me. He then went on to tell me in detail what Charlie did here at the detention cells. That he was a full-time spy. Not quite KGB or CIA. What Charlie did was to trade the information with the PSB, which allowed him to be planted into whatever cell the PSB wanted to gather information. In return, he got food parcels brought in and sometimes a visit. I was to learn much more about this treacherous trade in the future. Charlie and Triad were removed from the cell giving us more space to sleep for now. I lay thinking about Charlie and his dastardly game then dreamt that night that I was sitting astride a massive American Bison looking onto an endless landscape. Then I awoke to the cold harsh light and the now familiar sound of the jailer's keys.

Chapter Twentyseven: Good News

I had lain here wasting away in this god-forsaken cell for over one month. I was now being escorted down to the visiting room. The consul was here and I looking forward to that with some relief. Sitting there in that same room with the outdated flock wallpaper, happy enough just to be outside that dungeon. Ian had a smile on his face upon entering the room and as he shook my hand and we sat down. "How is Scott?" I enquired, anxious for news of my son. Ian replied "Scott has sent you one thousand pounds from Tokyo". Looking up shocked and certainly surprised asked what? Those words could only mean one thing. Scott was free and had taken the suitcase with the cannabis resin with him to Japan.

The sense of overwhelming relief almost floored me. Scott was okay and free from this hellhole that was the main thing. When was he out of here excitedly I asked? Actually, Lauchlan he was released on the tenth day of his imprisonment here. The same day you were charged but it hadn't yet been confirmed when seeing you the last time. Ian couldn't tell me how Scott had reached Japan, only that he'd flown from Shanghai to Hong Kong, after that he had no idea. We discussed a few issues and I handed over the signed document for the hire of a lawyer the visit passed quickly. Ian told me that he would not be returning here to see me as he was moving post to the U.S.A. but that another consul member would visit me soon. We shook hands and once again watched them depart. Hearing the car engine fire up and they were gone. I was returned to the cell and sat thinking about what Ian had told me. Scott was free and in Japan, he had sent me money, that could only mean that he had taken the case with the cannabis with him. That only left me still holding the bag my stash had not been found this far. The odds were that it might never be found at all then. I lived on hope and a prayer and slept well that night knowing Scott was okay free from this hellhole. God blessed you, my son.

Chapter Twentyeight: The Glasgow Header

The following day, things were back to the normal stark madness and were all out of adrenalin. Old Dong was a country bumpkin, no education and no family to bring him anything. He usually got along by doing the local boy's laundry for miscellaneous items. He was a harmless old soul inoffensive and always keen to oblige. So, when seeing one of the local Shanghai tough nuts slaps him hard across the side of his head and sending him reeling. I sprang to my feet outraged instinctively reverting to my natural Glaswegian colloquial 'fighting talk' "Here you, fucking bam" growling stepped up to him. I grabbed his hair bent my knee to give me more spring and head butted him a perfectly executed 'Glasgow Kiss' full on the mouth. I felt his teeth against my skull and he was on his arse at the other side of the cell. His hands held to a bleeding mouth and spitting out teeth. I knew he was well out of it and I was in a fucking rage but left it at that and turned away ranting. Whom the fuck does these people think they are Fucking Shanghai Gangsters think there better than everybody else does, fucking bullies. The only outcome of that incident was they removed the bully to another cell.

With Charlie gone the cell was totally different over the weeks I had observed men like old Dong making decorative objects like lighter holders, picture frames, out of nothing but scrap paper wrappings. I saw them make these amazing executed men with a collapsing head. Seeing detainees make chess pieces, and playing cards from scrap paper and rice glue. The art of origami really thrives here but more as an underground movement. The chess and playing cards would be confiscated if found by the guards and this would also entail a penalty imposed on the entire cell. This was set up to encourage people to inform and co-operate with the authorities. It never seemed to stop anyone in our cell and they always made a spare set bye bye Charlie.

One day whilst asking, help to roll some tobacco from the cigarette butts I had saved from the guard's room and Consul Visit. I had no lighter to fire up. I then watched a guy take some stuffing from his quilt and spread it out roughly into a twelve-inch square. He then scraped soap shavings onto it and rolled it into a cigar shape. He then took off his shoe and forcefully rubbed and rubbed the sole over the cigar shaped object. He then broke it open and blew into it until smoke rose it became tinder and our cell had a good smoke that night as we cheerfully passed around the rolled-up cigarette butts. I also experienced another time another person attached a piece of cotton, rolled partially with silver paper. He then fixed it unto a toothbrush. Climbing up onto another's shoulders he removed the light bulb and inserted his device into the open socket and came away holding a flaming torch. What some people will do only to have a smoke being one of them I was ever grateful for their ingenuity and fearlessness.

Chapter Twentynine: The Lawyer

The months passed and the weather grew gradually cooler as summer faded into fall then into winter had I been forgotten? A bright winter sun had started the day having just finished eating lunch when the cell door opened. I was called upon to go downstairs, expecting that it must be a Consul visit. But it wasn't then got overjoyed when it turned out to be the lawyer. I was just as glad to see somebody, until he told me that I was scheduled for court the following day. The lawyer handed me my indictment written in English. It was the first time reading my charge Possession of cannabis. The charge under that article read seven years maximum. I was still confused and unsure whether to be glad or mad. I hadn't had time to discuss my case before he was about to leave again. I hurriedly went into my story, asking questions along the way about my defense. Mr. Ho raised his hand to halt me in my tracks, telling me that I did not need to worry. He explained to me that I had confessed you are guilty you do not need any defense was his reply. Did you bring cigarettes? I asked? He produced a pack and lighter. Then ten minutes later Mr. Ho stood up and took off on his way. I left that meeting having a strong feeling that my lawyer was a government agent. Then after listening to stories from Tai Chi I was not sure if the lawyer was wholly working on my behalf. That night sleeping fitfully dreaming about my lawyer wearing a Judges wig towered above me poised to slam the gavel down on my head.

Chapter Thirty: Court

I was up and out of bed at the usual time. Then being handed a plastic disposable razor through the hole in the door to shave with but could not shave my face with this length of beard. I would need to have it cut off with scissors or electric shaver first. Tai Chi saw the look of bewilderment in my eyes. I asked can you get scissors by any chance. He looked downwards as if humbled and said Mr. Campbell sorry you can't have those things" Why the fuck not? "I persisted aggressively and said I can't be expected to shave this off without trimming it first. Going to the door I called for the guard. The gofer came shuffling along; and could hear servility in every step. Tai Chi interceded as the person got to the cell door, he said a few words and the gofer was off at a run again.

Finally, the slot on the cell door slid open again and a pair of manicure scissors was handed into Tai Chi. He asked me to sit by the toilet that it may then be easier to flush away the hair. There was a sudden babble of chit chat as I collected my basin. Tai Chi was having a good laugh so what's the big joke then?" asking with a grin. What is going on I asked? Mr. Campbell, he struggled to control himself these countryside people want to keep your hair. I had been using the toilet first nowadays for the sake of my health and hygiene. I then just sat there as the cell went through its morning ablutions process. Not exactly, a sight you would choose to remember but when you are living it, you become part in it. Tai Chi went onto explain, "They believe it is lucky. Gold hair brings good fortune to their home and families" Guess I had heard of such things before but who would have thought of finding it here in this god has forgotten place.

Some people meditate, others in prayer implore, some people use healing stones, crystals, or quartz. Others carry a piece of cloth taken from a Shrine, Mosque or Temple. Still more bathe in the Ganges water, or carry sand and stones home from the Holy Land. God is certainly great and works in wondrous ways. Who was I to object? I left the matter of my hair distribution to my barber, whom I could have garroted that morning as he tore the face of me with a disposable razor. It doesn't matter how close you get with scissors you really need a couple of Gillette new blades to get off a beard. The job was done though, leaving my face feeling like a well-slapped ass.

Now ready for the day with great expectations of getting a smoke or two. The craving for a cigarette temporary occupied my mind more than the predicament now in or what I was about to face today. It was hours that had passed before being summoned and escorted downstairs to a large room where three other Chinese people stood. Two were linked together in leg irons the other was handcuffed and was stood opposite me. The Chain Gang stared at me like some kind of rare species and they started chattering excitedly. I had no clue as to what was so exciting but they sure looked dangerous. My Scottish hackles did not arise as fear entered like a cold jag to my spine nor did I like the odds by look of this pair. Soon we were on the move and somehow that felt safer. Now looking out of the police transit van window at busy streets full of life, it was seemingly unperturbed by the blare of sirens as we weaved through the morning traffic swerving around bicycles, and all sorts of bundle carriers. I saw stalls abundant with fruits that I would have loved to eat. I was away again into the daydream land making desperate escapes to freedom before the reality kicked back in. The wonder of imagination...

We were speeding through the entrance of the court with the Tiananmen Square Heavenly Gates emblem on it. The People's Republic of China flag blowing in the breeze high above. I glanced at a plaque by the gate entrance 'Shanghai Intermediate People's Court. I was then escorted into the building and slammed into a small single cell about one meter square with a built-in concrete seat against the back wall where I sat down. The guard came, handed me a cigarette, and lit it for me. I was pleased the wait for court would not be without a smoke. It probably was only some hours but it seemed like all eternity to me before entering the courtroom flanked by two PSB officers. The lawyer was there and a representative of the British Consul that could not be identified. Nodding to the lawyer and was happy to see no foreign press. The court lay out was similar to the British system only there was three Judges presiding here and not one.

I stood erect as the court proceedings began, and remained standing until lunch. The charge against me was read out first in Chinese; then again in very poor English. That you Lauchlan Campbell, a British national being apprehended at (such and such a place.) Moreover, having acknowledged your guilt, stand today charged with possession of cannabis. It took ages for all this to be read out and it was difficult to try to keep a straight back and solemn face. I let out a few nervous coughs so that I could turn my head to look around. I noticed the full proceedings were being recorded by cameras set up at different points around the courtroom. I was direct in front of the one behind the Judges. The woman from the train station waiting room was there to identify me. The train guard ticket collector, whom I had first encountered when foolish enough to have a joint on the train. Which had started this entire show rolling was also there and identified me. Apparently, this was all standard procedure. The PSB team from Zhizou came in my nod to Lee was ignored. They too went through their encounter with me. Then they were asked to identify the substance, which they had found in my possession. It lay on a table in front of the Judges. It was a painful enough experience emotionally and by lunchtime, my head was splitting. My back was breaking with standing there for more than three hours straight. I was pleading guilty for Gods' sake!

The court had a lunch break and once locked up in the Dog box again requested to see the lawyer. He had not said a single word yet then thought nor was he given any opportunity to do so. The guard did not understand anything I was saying, and after ranting on for five minutes he presented me with my lunch. It was a steaming hot plate of rice with mixed vegetables. Then another dish with a whole fish covered in a sweet and sour sauce. Forgetting my headache, forgetting my lawyer, and ate into that hot tasty food like a man possessed. This was followed by hot nestles coffee and a cigarette. Now sitting back sighing contentedly as the life force flowed back into me and the tension oozed out. It was all somehow not so bad again. I would probably be given a heavy fine and deported for Christmas just eleven days hence. That would be a nice gift for the family and me, I dreamed on. The cell door was opened suddenly rousing me from my reverie as two PSB guards filled my vision to escort me back for part two of the trial process. I was left standing again while a few more witnesses were called to confirm and identify me. Then it was my lawyers turn, in plea of mitigation, he explained how I had confessed and co-operated and that the substance was a category B class, non-addictive drug. He went onto say it is often smoked and acceptable in many western countries where it had been decriminalised. I thought he was doing well and putting it across plainly. He spoke for about thirty minutes before proceedings were closed and the trial was over.

I was now returned to the cell where was soon visited by the consul rep and the lawyer. The consul enquired as to my views on the fairness of the trial and I could only tell them that, as I was guilty, and therefore, it did not matter and was just awaiting sentence. The lawyer intervened to tell me "You did very well Mr. Campbell. You kept a straight back and showed no disrespect" So what happens now?" I inquired anxiously. The lawyer said that I would be called back to court within a month. Then asking what kind of sentence he thought might be meted out now that he had heard the proceedings? His answer wasn't very reassuring "I already told you Mr. Campbell, the maximum sentence under this article is seven years but am confident that you won't be getting that" What about deportation?" I asked the Consul. The lawyer intervened I don't think so Mr. Campbell" and went on to tell me about another British citizen whom he had recently represented. Going on to tell me he had been sentenced to four years and fined £5000 when caught boarding a ship from Shanghai to Japan with cannabis. That caught my attention as this was the route, I had intended to take small world sure enough. I then thought but his charge was smuggling and he got a four-year sentence and a fine. I whereas was charged only for possession and may yet get less than four years. I would just have to live with that thinking to myself as they departed.

I sat for another hour or so until the three who arrived with me returned. Only this time two were bound with rope crossed over their chest and held firm from behind by an armed police guard. They had just been to court for the final time and were off for execution. It choked me to see that. I remembered one person in the cell making those executed men ingeniously from paper wrappers it had been this morbid pastime, which had prompted me to ask about the death sentence in more detail. Tai Chi had explained the system to me. If you were shackled you were a potential death sentence prisoner. If you had rope bound around you then you were scheduled for execution that day. I had looked into the eyes of these two men as they were being led away on a rope leash to be shot in the back of the head. The interrogation film was one thing but to have brushed up against and sat in the same van has left indelibly marked scars deep in my psyche. The law states their family would be billed for the bullet that would kill their kin. The system here is people who have committed no crime and who are often ostracised, as result of their kindred's execution. Some sick human somewhere in the administration has thought of this uncivilized procedure and everyone else has followed obediently. Whoever that was should be speedily retired if not yet long dead and that act repealed. The lawyer was direct to the point regarding the outcome of the trial and I would just have to accept it. There is not any other choice and would be going to jail for about four years. "Fuck it" horrified at the full realisation.

Once back in the detention cells I told Tai Chi the story. He was always eager for details and conversation to improve his English. We chatted until lights out. The other men rolled up cigarettes from the ones I had pocketed at court. We would keep them in store for the next couple of days then suffer withdrawals until the next puff come our way. I could not sleep for the court session running through my head like a fast forward and rewinding cassette tape. My mind leaped from one court scene to another and would not slow down. Having visions of those two people being led off to be shot and was counting my blessings. I give thanks to the Lord for showing me the sufferings of others before dozing off into sleep at some point in the night.

Then the morning came bringing a new day as we sat around the cell. I was a little more at ease now that a massive pressure was lifted, now that the trial was over and I still had that lingering hope. The other person, the Englishman had gotten four years for smuggling 7.2kg of cannabis. That is a serious international offence convincing myself whereas mine was not as serious. It was I slipping back into my delusions. I was off again into my safety net remembering passed encounters and recalled the occasion when I met up with a Japanese couple on Boracay Island they were great company and we ended up very intimate friends. We meet up again in Tokyo where, once upon a drunken night, it was suggested that we all do a trip to India. We could take the video cameras and other duty-free technology and return with some cannabis. Everyone was up for it quicker than I had anticipated. My limited experience in this ancient land had only taken me either into Duty free shops or bars and little contact with the cultured people whom encountering at shrines and festivals. I have found however that all sorts of people, all the world over, are open to take risks for new adventure. This couple was certainly two of them. We went to India and our little venture succeeded.

That night just before lights out, another new person from Shandong Province was put into the cell. So, Shandong is what I called him. A very hard-faced young man and when he spoke, he looked fierce. His story was he and his brother had been working somewhere in the city of Shanghai without the proper permit papers to allow them to stay or work. In China, you just can't up and resettle into another city without getting police registered I.D. card with photo. You also need permission from various other bureaucratic offices to work. The story was one evening some local people broke into the room Shandong was sharing with his brother and another friend from their province. The intruders were waving large bladed knives. Fearing for their lives they defended themselves. Shandong's brother was killed and he his friend badly injured, and seeing his scar that he too was stabbed. He was thrown in jail for not having the right papers. It all just seemed a little bit over the top to me. Like as if the authorities have not the slightest respect for the common people and are intent only on adding to their pain and their burden. The people just seem to take it all in their stride as if they never would have expected anything else.

Chapter Thirtyone: Merry Xmas, Coming Home, 1991

It was a miracle coming on December 21st at around midday. I could not contain my joy. The cell door latch opened and a folded A4 envelope had been pushed through to me. I opened it with cautious apprehension, and then scanning the perfectly worded English document content carefully. I read that line again; then again to be sure was reading it properly. Case withdrawn from Public Prosecution, under article 131 of the Chinese criminal procedural act. I handed the two pages over to Tai Chi one was written in Chinese I stared pacing the cell, kicking up the sand from the imaginary beaches that I'd soon be strolling on. Tai Chi read aloud the Chinese version and soon I was being hugged and my hand shaken by the people in the cell. I wanted to laugh with relief but also to cry for those poor bastards who were all smiles and happy for me. My emotions were chaotic, swinging from euphoric to manic sadness. Having heard so many of the prisoners tell me over these months that being a foreigner would be treated better, "You pay money, you go free" "British treated better you go free" I'd found this talk gave me an uneasy feeling difficult for me to live with. As far as I was concerned was treated exactly the same. We all shit in the same hole ate the same food and shared equal cell space. That's was that full stop. I had no idea of how the Chinese system worked it just seemed to me to be a fucking shamble. Even if only part of what I had seen and heard was real had realized a long time ago that corruption and bribery can often create an even balance. A bribe can pay the wages and feed the families whilst simply cutting out the red tape and formal documentation of a sometimes lesser fine.

I started to allocate my property to the neediest, my woolens blanket everything possessed right down to the clothes now wore. I could almost smell the mold from the hash in my bag picking out my clothes for the journey ahead. They would take me to the immigration holding cells this afternoon and would probably spend the night there and be deported as an undesirable in the morning. It would not be a nice stamp to have on my passport but better than any alternative. Besides, that could be easily remedied. By the time the evening food arrived I was mentally and emotionally drained. It was like just another of their mad Chinese puzzle games again. Every sound heard throughout that day had me up and ready in anticipation of liberation. On the other hand, was it just that ghost of freedom wailing in my brain? By evening knowing I could not be going anywhere until morning reluctantly put my head down nothing ever happened at night. I lay tossing and turning the long lonely night away desperately willing the hours to move into day should be off in the morning. Even as guilty as sin began to think that I was being unlawfully and unfairly detained. Has some anonymous bureaucrat somewhere filed my release order in his overcrowded 'in' tray and had not gotten around to it yet? Don't they know how important my life and my freedom are to me?

Holding out until lunchtime the next day when the food was being passed through, I could not contain my expectations any longer and called the guard myself. We were taken into the office and Tai Chi asked the big question for me. "Mr. Campbell wants to know when he will be going home" They exchanged a few words. In my mind translations, the guards were saying "Oh! Any minute now" As it turned out the actual response was that he didn't do the prosecutor's job, how would he know?" He did tell Tai Chi that the PSB were re-investigating my case and we returned to the cell with me deflated, deeply worried and scared. The arrogance was kicked right out of me and could not even eat lunch. I sat with my back against the wall stretched my legs out then pulling them up to my chest and began to rock back and forwards. My mind was gone my life was gone and I was psyched up on the verge of murder. I had asked Tai Chi to explain exactly what was meant, in this country by 'Re-investigation' by the PSB. His reply was that the guard on duty does not really know anything. He just shifted the responsibility to the PSB so he will not be disturbed. Mr. Campbell you are going home Tai Chi said. That succeeded in perking me up for about ten minutes till off again down into those dark and dangerous labyrinths of my mind.

'Gate Fever' that dreaded Gate Fever blues had a hold of my heart and was tearing at it over the next two weeks. Day by day waiting in expectation for that door to open and set me free. They would call my name and send me home. "Any day now, any way now, I shall be released" Bob Dylan perked up my stamina, as his song rang through my head. Waiting for that door to open, waiting, at any time. I would not care if it were a slow boat from China or a fucking pushbike. Just get me out of here. I tried to relax and create the mood of Christmas. Therefore, in my imagination invited Billy Connelly to China. We sat around the cell and he was telling the old Crucifixion yarn from the Glasgow point of view Tai Chi was doing the translation and by the response, it was hilarious. It was great to see these people really laugh everybody laughed. Chinese people do laugh yet it was a sadly rare commodity in these dire surroundings.

Xmas day passed just like any other. The only difference being me singing a Christian hymn and Carols "Away in a Manger" I sung as "A wean in a manger" the way we always sung it as children. No crib for a bed, the little lord Jesus lay down his sweet head. The song always takes me back to the stark poverty and hunger wrenching days of my early childhood and felt a little nostalgia choked up but my voice did not crack. Christianity has not much pull in China not one person in that cell cared a hoot about the man who walked on water. Isn't it so true that when you are far from home and having a good time, you tend to forget everybody else? But when anything goes wrong, you expect family and friends to run to your rescue?

Boxing Day, Hogmanay, New Year's Day, all just another ordinary day with no festivities attached prison truly is severe here. I couldn't let the guys in the cell down on New Year's Day so invited my family over for the day and sang a Scottish ballad with emphasis on the chorus "For he would never dishonour the Tartan of his Clan" and even got up and did the jig with my hand on my hips holding my imaginary bagpipes blowing proudly and fiercely patriotic. Dancing around the cell like a maniac getting louder by the moment O Flower of Scotland, when will we see, your likes again? Then put more emphasis on "Who fought and died for, your wee bit hill and glen and stood against them Proud Edwards army, and sent them homewards to think again. Now psyched up and ready for a fucking war with these Chinese PSB bastards but was interrupted in mid madness by the cell door opening. The room went uncannily silent and I was called to the office and questioned as to what was wrong, and why was I shouting and disturbing everyone? Tai Chi explained about my traditional New Year's Day celebrations. That in my country it is customary to bring in the New by singing out the Old. The guard seemed to like this idea and the cigarettes came out. The guard asked if I had celebrated the Chinese New Year. I told him about my first encounter with those festivities in Hong Kong. The guard insisted hotly that "Hong Kong is China" as if he expected some dispute from me. I did not disagree, and never picked up on his patriotic vibe. But was rapidly discovering just how much the hatred and resentment for the British is imbedded into the Chinese psyche. The British are the top of the 'We Get you bastards back charts' here in China. I had a couple of cigarettes while Tai Chi and the guard spoke. Tai Chi said we were to be quieter once returned to our cell. Lying back that night in my cell still trying to fathom out what was going on hadn't seen my lawyer or Consul since court and felt abandoned and deserted. January had slipped into February still no lawyer, still no Consul still no one was opening the door to send me home. Still, they could be coming; finally, they did come, bearing their new indictment.

Chapter Thirtytwo: Death Sentence

I was handed a new indictment on February 7th 1992 the charges read the same as the first one with the exception of two words. This was obviously an upgraded and more serious charge. The word transporting was added thinking it must be a translation error. Yet according to their acceptance of my confession, I had never crossed any border maybe that is why they have not used the word smuggling nothing was ever sure here it had been confusion since day one. Returning to the cell still baffled handed Tai Chi my new indictment he scrutinized the Chinese version carefully before delicately pointed out to me that there were now two new changes.

1. 'Possession' was now 'Transportation
2. Cannabis was now 'Cannabis ester.'
So, what was cannabis ester? I could not make heads or tails of it and was just so furious that I was not going home after all.

The next outing from my cell came quicker than anticipated. It was February 15th and it was my lawyer. As soon as my ass got on the seat, cigarettes were the last thing on my mind this day. I was absolutely boiling over with questions, I handed him the withdrawal from public prosecution' paper asking what it was all about. Then I said have you brought cigarettes. He produced a packet and I sat listening intensely to his explanation of the meaning of "withdrawal from public prosecution" You, would think that it could only mean what it said. Not according to him, it did not. It felt like as if it now meant that it was no longer public but 'personal' or something against the people. How could this be happening? Moreover, would swear to God that lawyer he was a government agent. It was when he read from the Statutes book exactly what the sentence for my new indictment entailed. I sacked him on the spot." You are a treacherous bastard," I shouted at him. They had led me along the garden path only to spring their evil trap. He called the guard as my ranting raged in a torrent of vile abuse until they had to manhandle me back to the cell in a state of total manic insanity.

He had just told me that the new indictment carried the death penalty. It could not be real and I could not believe it. Sweet Jesus Christ suffering is it not known here in this godless land. Standing in the cell purple faced and cursing everything, this was my belated Christmas gift from a Godless Land. The daydreams were over with a rude awakening. This was Shit Street Shanghai Sheridan and this new indictment carried the death penalty. There went my visions kicking up the sand on a beach. It was appearing more like pushing up the fucking daises. From the prospect of going home to, spending a few years in jail staring down steel barred corridors and concrete cubes, to staring up the cold barrel of a gun quite a turnaround of events. I had used all my reserve just surviving, learning to accept and to cope with the day-to-day close confinement of my immediate predicament. I was now clinging desperately to sanity against the thought that maybe to spend maybe even up to four long years in these dismal places of despair was better than being shot. Hearing the clanking of keys and slamming of cell doors and could still hear the voice of the lawyer saying that the new indictment "Carries the Death sentence, Life sentence, or Fifteen years minimum imprisonment." I now sat listlessly on the floor as the words echoed and re-vibrated through my pounding scull. It was as the cell was my head and somewhere in there was deep despair but also something else was stirring and awakening. It was some kind of outrage against this system. First to make me think am going home by withdrawing the prosecution case against me then dragging it out and dragging it out till I'm almost on fire with gate fever then tell me that am being indicted all over again. What kind of administration is it that thinks that it is okay to do this to anybody? In addition, why do these Chinese people tolerate it?

Despair could only give way to rebellious outrage there was nowhere else to go. At the end of the weary day, it was my own stupid fuck up that put me here. But that does not mean to say that anybody deserves to suffer this kind of torture under this kind of system of so-called justice. I was being only charged for a bit of cannabis for goodness's sake! The cell was silent, everyone sensing something bad had happened. I found myself in the fetus position trying to disappear into the void of nowhere ness but couldn't escape. I did not eat that evening but just sat there staring into the far distant space beyond the bars in front of me. My neck and head cocked to one side as if trying to find the angle to squeeze through. Not this night though all the shadows churned unsettled in darkening stormy clouds not in sympathy but in disharmony with my soul.

Chapter Thirtythree: Another Frame Of Mind

I roused the following morning automatically going through the same routine like a mindless zombie. Making inquiries about long term prisons with Tai Chi and he asked around the cell. The feedback neither presented relief nor hopes to cling to. It all sounded quite horrific unless you were sent to a farm. The farms I was told though where mostly full with criminals to do hard labor. Or officials fallen foul of the party but still had the contacts and financial power to buy their way there. Everything would be for sale there including illicit sex it sounded better than this Shanghai PSB. 100% party line policy puppets.

Now waiting to be called for reinvestigation over the next few days but it never happened. Finally, when the cell door did open for me, it was a visit from the British Consul. They handed me another list of lawyers while I explained the latest shenanigans. The 'Withdrawal from public prosecution' papers and the new indictment with altered substance and wording that put my head on the proverbial chopping block. Jim Short, the new vice Consul, wasn't exactly enthused about the procedures himself but couldn't offer assistance other than ensuring that proper legal representation would be forthcoming" Jim went on to say that, he had only received notice of the second trial this morning.

I nearly swallowed the cigarette on my lip and inhaled in shock. "Second trial when I asked 20th February Jim replied. But this is already the eighteenth" stuttering in disbelief. Jim Short had thought I was aware of the date and was quick to suggest that we could try to have it postponed in the circumstances. We discussed that possibility but my main worry was the conditions of confinement here entailing reluctance to prolong that unnecessarily. Considering the shortage of time left available, appointed another lawyer named 'Ma Yu Min' and signed the papers for the Consul to hire him today. Jim said expect to see the new lawyer soon we shook hands and said our fare wells. Returning to the cell with my head thumping by the time I had explained it all to Tai Chi I was thoroughly exhausted and ready to bury my head in the sand. I did sleep fitfully through that night but slept.

The following morning, I could not get up from bed. I felt I couldn't face another day but eventually sat up with my blanket wrapped around me and covering my head like the Grim Reaper or something Grim Weepers more likes with this forgotten bunch surrounding me. I was feeling deeply depressed, turning in on myself, gazing into the void that gaped before me. Sitting like that for hours until the cell door opened and a lot of shouting in Chinese shook me from my stupor rather abruptly. The guard was pulling at my bed cover, holding on to it and he pulled me to my feet. What is going on turning in confusion to Tai Chi who explained a senior communist party member is inspecting today and we are to clean the cell up, and also for you to get up and fold your blanket. Fuck off was my response and sat back down again huddling in my blanket. Whatever interpretive skill Tai Chi utilized, the result was that the guard turned and left slamming the door behind him. What is going on? I asked again. Everyone

Everyone was shuffling about fixing buttons on their jackets with excited chatter. Tai Chi explained that sometimes a visiting committee would inspect the place and that they were expecting a visit today. It was all so pathetic it was almost comical every time any sound louder than a fart was heard, these people quickly straightened their backs and re-examined their buttons. I could not make heads or tails of all this fuss and proceeded with the day as usual. Not that this amounted to much more than shifting my arse into a more comfortable position. Nobody visited the cell anyway, yet these untried men remained ever ready and dutifully upright until suppertime that evening. I had a lot to learn.

Chapter Thirtyfour: A Buddhist Lawyer

On the afternoon 19/02/1992 being taken down to have a meeting with my new lawyer Ma Yu Min. We shook hands on introduction and held on a little too long to the delicate hand of his lovely secretary. Mr. Ma then explained that the second trial would be no more than a formality. There would be no witnesses recalled. "But I thought this was to be a retrial" handing over the withdrawal from prosecution document and asking, "What is this and why serve me with this document?" There was just so much to ask but foremost in my mind was this withdrawal document. It was doing my head in it just didn't make sense that one minute I'm being set Scot free and the next I'm indicted with a death penalty charge. What was the difference Possession Transporting? It was on my possession when going from one place to another that is nothing new. So, what is going on? Persisting. It was the way he replied that was surprising for me he informed me that it was also his duty to disclose any information obtained from me that may help solve this crime. I could not believe my ears; this place is insane and vented my outrage on how fucked up a system this place was. Mr. Ma calmly reminded that "Your indictment carries the death penalty" and I quickly replied "Do not try to intimidate me Mister. It is cannabis we are talking about here, not heroin" and was really pissed off now seeing this as no more than another interrogation. "Mr. Campbell," he went on smoothly in a voice that would make a Buddha smile. "This is China and our law punishes according to the crime and how the offender cooperates with the investigating authorities knowing all that" and interrupted adding that my I had made a confession. Then went into another verbal outburst of how bad the living conditions were here "What sort of system is it that only allows your lawyer to see you on the day before the trial? The last lawyer moved my charge from a seven-year maximum to a fifteen-year minimum with a death penalty hanging over me like it could happen. You tell me it is all a formality, all done and dusted so what am I paying you for? Raving on and left the visit with not a bit of hope in my bones.

I was naive to expect anything other, or anything else from a screwed-up system such as this and was definitely snookered now it was just a small matter of how far they wanted to blackball me. That night's sky was quick in coming down due to the changing season. Most people now sat around wrapped with a blanket. It was cold and there was no other internal heating other than the human aura as we huddled around. It was the only time we all really bonded together as a group as if bonding together against the harshness of the winter cold chill with a smell of the grave. It was court tomorrow it was to be a mere formality. My crime now carried the death penalty but for this moment, we would have the freedom to huddle.

Chapter Thirtyfive: Appeal

It was another day with much to look forward to the cell door opened taken downstairs to await my escort to court. This time it was only me and three guards in a police car. I was handcuffed and placed in the back seat. The sirens wailed as if in mourning as we speed through the usual trade traffic and bustle. I lost myself in mindless daydreaming to distract from the reality of my situation. So strange how people go about their daily routine oblivious of other people's extremes. Would my look be desperate and dangerous like the others I had seen clad in chains and shuffling woefully to their death? Our arrival at court was uneventful, almost mundane now put into the same box cell that I'd previously occupied, again was given lit cigarettes when requesting for one and looked forward to lunch, remembering how hot and tasty the last meal here had been. The court was finally called and I was escorted to the rail where I had stood before. Again, standing for hours too listens as they went on about the past trial. It was just confirming that all the facts remained the same having accepted my guilt in confession. I was the only one left standing and again my back ached and my mind screamed. By lunchtime was close to collapse; my head was spinning amid the babble around me which seemed to kind of taper away into the far distance. It felt my legs were giving way beneath me and nobody was paying attention. Couldn't keep this up and only the pain to remind me to try stay upright and erect? Now returned in the dog box, I let out a sigh of relief and was eternally grateful for the small mercy of a seat and cigarette blowing away all my aches and pains with each glorious puff. When the food arrived was not disappointed either with the same dish as served up before. I had two large steaming hot dumplings with meat stuffing. It certainly helped me relax enough to doze off for an hour of blissful oblivion.

The afternoon session was much briefer and finally they asked me if I had anything to say and thought they were asking me how I plead and replying simply "Guilty" The court waited in silence myself also wasn't sure what was going on so stood silent too. My lawyer stood up and said something briefly then produced a placard with Chinese characters written on it and explained something regarding the substance possessed. The court was dismissed and was returned to the cell. The lawyer came down to see me almost immediately and asked me why I had not spoken up seeking the courts leniency and replying, "I didn't know it was expected of me to speak again being guilty. I did not hear much by way of a plea of mitigation from your end Mr. Ma." "Mr. Campbell," he said wearily, "it is my job to help you tell the truth. Not to defend you or your actions" Come on give me a break, it's your job to submit mitigating circumstances to the judges with a view toward a policy of leniency the explanation given that, as a foreigner and not acquainted with, nor understanding the Chinese law and acted in ignorance and not out of malice or disrespect for the law and customs of this country. I already explained all this to the other lawyer and hardly had a chance to speak with you. For some reason, probably blind presumption just had not expected to be going over the whole thing again with this lawyer. There was no point to this anymore it was finished and no going back to try again. We said farewell and he said that he would visit me again before sentencing. I could not have cared less what he did having a headache and was just glad that it was over and would soon know my fate. That night Tai Chi and I were escorted to the office and seated facing that ever-smiling faced guard with his khaki uniform. He wanted to tell me that my case was very serious and that should expect a prison sentence. No matter how I tried to fathom out why he would take the time to tell me this, but just could not relate with it any more. It may be that he was trying to give me the good news that the word was not to be executed. It all just went over my head at the time. Just nodding my head politely as if grateful for his every word while in fact was only being nice to have more time out the cell and more cigarettes. I am not normally that shallow on some occasions it is an easy escape from thinking too deep into those darker extremes. I slept surprisingly well that night and did not awake until Tai Chi gave me a shake next morning. We spent most of that day teaching English to the people in the cell who would roll around in peals of laughter when I tried speaking Chinese. For the moment, at least we had escaped into some kind of life.

Chapter Thirtysix: Money Matters

On March 18th 1992 being visited first by the procurators office they told me to transfer my personal funds from the consul office into my property at the detention holding cells. I asked as to why I should do that? And was informed that it was to pay a fine, my suggestion was that to pay the fine once it has imposed upon me. That comment only resulted in that stern threatening look and a warning that non-cooperation would not bode well for me in the circumstances. Not needing other reminder that I still had the death sentence hanging over me. I wrote a short note there and then to the consul requesting to have my money transferred to me here at the detention holding cells. My next visit was from the lawyer that very same day. He had me sign his legal fees bill and permission for the British Consul to pay him from my personal funds. It seemed to me that everyone was suddenly in a big hurry to grab as much of my money as they could but before what? I told him about the visit from the procurators office but he already knew. I tried to get some hint from him as to what the future may hold for me but could not get another word out of him now that he had been paid. He merely smiled and left me with a couple of cigarettes as a consolation. Then returned to the cell where all were keen to hear of the latest developments. Tai Chi translated what had just happened. This was all apparently not new and unusual in China it was considered normal procedure. They all babbled in speculation still sure the money would buy an air ticket and I would be deported home. All the conclusions were positive and, in my favor, but you would not really expect these poor people to conclude that the prosecution was only emptying my western pockets before jailing me.

The consul visited me on March 22nd and I signed the money over from their account to mine. The money had been sent via the foreign office by my brother Robert in London specifically to pay legal fees. The Consul could not tell me any more about the procedures nor the possibility of a fine. Soon the visit was over and I said thanks and goodbye.

Chapter Thirtyseven: Criminal Verdict

The following morning after my consul, visit when the cell door opened, I was shocked and surprised to be told to get ready for court. Feeling excited in the deluded hope of paying the money as a fine and that would end this horrible existence. I was escorted down stairs to the now familiar rigmarole to wait. Then other detainees entered the room. I was surprised to see two westerners with their heads bowed. I asked them which country they came from. The smaller one of the two replied simply without looking up "Germany" Then a third foreigner appeared through the door. I asked where are you from and he said "Wales" "So we're all from the same planet then" I joked, and nobody laughed. Just happy to see someone and I immediately started asking questions.

Within minutes we were traveling towards the court all handcuffed and seated together in the transit van. The guards kept telling us to be quiet but we ignored them and talked about the other British person getting four years for smuggling 7.2KG cannabis to Japan. My thoughts were to expect the same, saying nothing about my fear of possible execution. The two Germans were charged with possession 3KG of cannabis between them. The other British person was charged with supplying the two Germans and possession of 400 grams of cannabis and another 1 KG found at his girlfriend's residence in Kashgar. I was expecting that he would probably receive the heaviest sentence due to his charges of trafficking drugs but did not say so aloud.

The sirens sung their usual wail as we came to a halt at the court and were escorted into the building where we were immediately separated. I could not see anyone but we could still hear each other if we called out. I was still having difficulty with the thought that maybe having to serve up to four years imprisonment here. I just kept pushing that nightmare to the back of my mind and had somehow managed to blank out the very idea that my crime carried the death sentence. I maintained the delusion, in my reasoning that, as the other guy was charged with smuggling and I wasn't. Therefore, could get a lesser sentence. I was off in some far place in my mind when the cell door opened and it was time to face the music in court.

Standing there before the three judges my knees were shaking as my head flashed from execution scenes to boarding a plane a deportee. There was silence as the Judge read the verdict and sentence in Chinese. I looked over at my lawyer for some indication as to what was going on. Then the court interpreter repeated it again in bad English. I didn't quite catch it all there was the numbers fifteen and three thousand but nothing about what that entailed. I was still very much in blissful ignorance when returned to the holding cell by two grim faced guards. It was only minutes later however, the lawyer enlightened me when handing me a copy of the English version of the verdict and sentence to sign. Shanghai Intermediate People's Court Criminal Case No. 24. 1992. It was then the realisation struck me as if a sledgehammer sentenced to fifteen years imprisonment and $3000 dollars confiscated from me. Fifteen years in prison.

It echoed and ricocheted around my head as if trying to find a place to land or to fit. Nevertheless, it was not wanted there and it did not belong and could not quite take it in. Simply disembodied data did not have any real meaning and did not apply to me. Then hearing the other detainees return and shouted out asking what their sentences were. The Welch guy who became known as Bull shouted, "Eight and a half year and a 10,000 RMB fine telling him my sentence and after a pause he asked how many people did you kill?" The two German people had received eight years and a 10,000RMB fine each. We spoke on the way back and trying to reassure them our sentences could not stand up in the face of the other British person only getting four years for smuggling 7.2kg to Japan. I was really trying to reassure myself, trying to apply logic how it could be that one person gets four years for smuggling 7.2kg strapped and concealed on his body and the Germans get eight years for smuggling 3kg and me getting fifteen years for possession or transporting of 7.9kg? No way! It just could not be held up to be right convincing myself.

Of course, in my ignorance had failed to take many other factors into account like the kind of press received. Thanks to the Douglas Hurd mission and the press blitz in association with my Brother TC Campbell's dire situation back home in Scotland. Thanks to the press, I was the head of the international crime Clan Campbell but I was the only one here who did not know it. Not a lot more could be said after the initial shock set in. We sat lost in our own personal shattered worlds quietly contemplating the future. We were immediately separated from each other on arrival at the detention cells. It was agreed unanimously we would all appeal against severity of sentence. I was taken directly into the guard's office instead of the cell and was given a cigarette. I sat for a few minutes in silence, as the guard just quietly looked me over. I felt numb Tai Chi entered the office and looked at me as the guard spoke. Then Tai Chi translated saying Mr. Campbell the officer wants to know what you think of the sentence"? Fifteen years, fifteen fucking years for a bit of cannabis, can you believe that?" letting my anger speak "Mr. Campbell the officer says you return to the cell and rest now"

Once inside my cell I felt the inmates so wanted me to get away with it so they too might also have some hope. I told them about the other foreigners, their oriental eyes opened wider with interest, and they all started babbling as if in heated debate about my news. The cell sounded like a busy market place where nobody listened to anybody else. The noise only stopped when a key rattled on the door. I was thinking fifteen years with five-year remission still added up to ten. God's sake it doesn't even make it sound any better. I was still to discover that it really and truly wasn't any better in fact, China doesn't do remission, early release schemes, or training for freedom programs, hearing this from Tai Chi. I couldn't eat anything that night but did have a couple of smokes and began to be worried about the guy popping the electric socket for a light. What if he gets electrocuted just to light an illicit smoke? Would it be me made an accessory for supplying the smokes and then dragged back to court again? We all could certainly do without that at this time but it did not stop us smoking. Tai Chi had underlined some Chinese characters on my charge and verdict. He told me that my problems all came down to the change in the naming of the substance that I had been originally indicted for 'Dama' the Chinese word for 'Cannabis.' However, the 'Verdict Sentence' stated that I was sentenced for 'Dama Zhi' i.e., the equivalent of cannabis oil. After scrutinising the Chinese characters underlined, I could see that they both looked the same except for one added character. Not being able to understand this until Tai Chi explained that 'Zhi' the added character was a chemical compound in Chinese and not a natural substance. On the English version, it only used the word cannabis i.e., Dama yet the Chinese version differed why? I would have to inquire about that when the next consul staff member arrives.

The next day Tai Chi unexpectedly disappeared and never returned again. I enquired about him and the guard said that he had been sentenced to five years. Shanghaied? or just listening walls? or one more PSB plant I didn't know.

Chapter Thirtyeight: A Dangerous Man

Everything was much more difficult without Tai Chi and his diplomatic translations. He was such a straight and intelligent person and really missed him. From
that point onwards, everything became even more difficult and confusing with
more and more conflict arising in all areas. Another new guy arrived in shackles
and scheduled for death. He named himself Fenzi which translates as 'Crazy.'
From the very moment, he entered the cell he was pointing fingers aggressively
and shouting commands of some sort. Old Dong the farmer plus a few others
mostly curled in fear. I just sat and just quietly observed.

The proverbial last straw came with the arrival of yet another two new people into the cell the following day. This would bring us up to fourteen people to
sleep. It was already a tight squeeze with twelve but space was quickly allocated. I still kept my place secure at the cell door there was no doubt in my mind
that Fenzi was in fact crazy. I could see the desperation in his eyes perhaps
understandable seen as he was already scheduled for death, he was obviously
dangerous.

One of the new people, a practicing Moslem from Xingjian, insisted on washing his hands before prayer. Fenzi in shackles grabbed hold of him by the neck
and started to throttle him, shouting some kind of obscenities. Everybody froze.
No one would intervene to stop him killing this poor person. Thus, I took action
grabbing hold of him by the neck and pulled him backwards towards me. Then
held him in a stranglehold, forearm locked tight around his neck as he struggled
to free himself from my grip. The more he struggled the tighter my grip until he
finally relaxed in submission. I could only speak to him in calming tones breathing heavily close to his ear in English. Nobody had a clue what was said. "Take
it easy pal we're all in the same boat here, just settle down and you'll be fine."
When finally releasing my grip he was keen to shake hands but it was not long
before he attacked someone else and was forcefully removed from the cell to
God only knows whatever hell. It was strange and particularly odd that the cell
door had not burst open the way it usually would when any fighting broke out.
It was becoming apparent that we were being singled out for a hard time by the
guards. It was on 27 March 1992 being taken down stairs to the visiting area
for a surprise meeting with my lawyer. I had not expected to see him so soon.
I could not wait to ask about those Chinese characters that Tai Chi had underlined for me. As I spoke about this my lawyer was quick to respond that he too
had noticed that. This substance, 'Dama Zhi' or cannabis ester is not what you
had possessed Mr. Campbell" he was quick and keen to agree. He went on to
tell me "There is also the quantity to consider" So my appeal then, according to
the lawyer, was to be based upon two points.

1. The erroneous renaming of the substance involved in the verdict and sen-
    tence.
2. That there was not a clear definition in Chinese law as to what would con-
    stitute a 'large quantity' of cannabis.

The law states those caught in possession, with 50 grams of heroin, or with 500 grams of opium or other drugs in a large quantity. This charge carries the sentence death, or life imprisonment or minimum sentence fifteen years" I had been indicted in English for cannabis the Chinese word Dama. The Chinese court had sentenced me for Cannabis Oil in Chinese Dama Zhi. Which I did not have and which entailed an inference of a higher concentration in the substance per weight. As the lawyer left, he told me he would return again next day. It was not like before the trial when only allowed one quick visit in all those months of waiting. This appeal visit had lasted a couple of hours and the lawyer would return as often as needed. I returned to the cell feeling perked up and a little chirpier for our meeting. I couldn't explain to anyone what was going on without Tai Chi but they knew as soon as the smokes came out that I'd been to a lawyer or consul visit.

The following morning, I got up feeling good in the knowledge that I would have another visit that day, also hoped, and expected to see the other foreigners at the appeal. Especially as the Welsh guy as he was using the same lawyer as me. Being called down to the visiting rooms around two o'clock. Mr. Ma was already there with a smile and file of legal papers, smokes, chocolate and fruit at the ready. We went over the verdict again in more detail and realized for the first time that the money was confiscated as 'Illegal Earnings' that could be easily proven as untrue through the Foreign Office who had made the request for legal fees to my family. This was noted. Then I asked about the difference, the legal or statutory definitions and implication, between 'Transportation' and 'Possession' For whilst the cannabis remains on my possession, whither I'm going from A to B either on foot or riding a train, I still haven't crossed any borders within China. He took notes on this for further research. Then we moved on to the main issue the substance itself. The lawyer had explained that the Chinese character Zhi translated, as Ester in English but that did not mean much to me. In my interpretation, he was saying that the cannabis was a chemically produced substance condensed into oil, and not a natural one. Mr. Ma said he would research more into that. Then the next point was; How to define 'A large Quantity' under Chinese law. There had to be some statutory definition or case precedent references to research. I said the Englishman carried about the same or similar amount to me but he did not come under this act. Going on to say the quantity then must be down to the alleged condensed purity and there has been no such evidence. The lawyer left with a promise to be back on Monday 31st March. Feeling alive again, something was being done to sort out this dreadful mess of administrative errors I was entangled in. Now allowed to have a pen the lawyer had asked me to write down all the different names for cannabis. Names like hashish, or hash, pot, ganja weed and could now keep occupied with making notes for questions to ask my lawyer at the next visit.

On Monday morning waiting impatiently in expectation for my legal visit, I was listening out for every remote sound of feet coming towards my cell. It was late afternoon before the cell door eventually opened and was off for my visit. It is such a relief to get out off that cell, even for the shortest of time it is a godsend. We went over a few legal points together his manner detached. The lawyer had already marked out the guidelines for my appeal. The main point would focus on the type of substance possessed. I gave him my notes and those on cannabis names. Letting my lawyer know it is decriminalised in many countries and legalised in others. Also pointing out that it is culturally acceptable in parts of India the West Indies and declassified down scale all over the world from B to C. Whereas cannabis oil was mainly classified as A.

My next visit was on 9 April 1992. The lawyer produced photocopies of a drug classification chart from the American Library. He had circled the words 'Cannabis Oil' and underlined Dama Zhi in Chinese. This, Mr. Campbell, is not what you had in your possession when you were arrested, he informed me forcefully as if I didn't already know. Or as if it was my mistake for getting me sentenced for the wrong thing. Having explained all this to him at the last visit but now realized that he had not a clue about drugs and would not just take my word for it but would rather carry out his own impartial and objective enquiry. Obviously, this man was of independent mind and may not take to being told anything. Therefore, I asked him why my English version of the indictment had stated simply cannabis whilst the Chinese version states another substance other than that which I was arrested with. He did not have any answer for this question but still wanted to hear him confirm that this could only have been a deliberate deception and fraud upon me and wanted him to say it. He thought for a long time before saying that he would point that matter out in court. I asked him about the other British person who had four years and that surely this was a precedent? That less than 8 Kilo of cannabis could not be considered as a large quantity seen, as he never came under that article on his indictment. He was able to say to me that the other British man who got eight years six month was appealing also but would not say more than that. I shook his hand this time before saying goodbye. Something I had avoided doing ever since my first encounter with the dodgy Mr. Ho. However, felt better each time discussing the appeal with this lawyer. It seemed like we were working the completely tangled mess out and were given the time to do it.

Mr. Ma visited again on the eleventh and fifteenth of April. It had all been fully discussed and the preparation for the appeal was complete. We would be ready for the Appeal court on April 21st. I had gotten a fresh new white shirt and tie but for some strange reason, no change of trousers was allowed. I'd worn these ones on and off for months and they smelled awful. This place really is red tape China and sought help from the consul. I even put my plea for clean clothing in writing but nothing was forthcoming and finally I had to borrow a pair of trousers from a guy in my cell. He had not long arrived and was wearing a suit.

Chapter Thirtynine: Not A Pleasant Surprise

Ready for court once more was taken downstairs and it was not a pleasant surprise it was more of a shock. When the van door opened to admit me there sat another Westerner. I knew this one well and could only nod an acknowledgement keeping my eyes averted not wanting the guards alerted that we knew each other. Like me, he was a professional and full-time smuggler. I had had a fall out with this person on more than one occasion in the past. I knew that he had been bust before so now wasn't the time to acknowledge each other. During the journey he asked me a few questions, what sentence I had gotten and I told him and about my ongoing appeal. The guards told us to be quiet but we continued talking until we drove into the court parking area. We were both escorted into the building and separated.

I was called within an hour of arrival and listened to as much as possible as the court went through the procedure of a second hearing again. It still meant nothing to me until my lawyer took the floor. He held large written Chinese characters up for the court to see. Then he went onto explain the difference inherent in these characters in relation with the substance possessed by me. Then moving on to show the characters relating to the substance I'd been sentenced for. There was a clear error between the name of the substance sentenced for and the actual substance arrested in possession with. I had a natural substance, not the chemical compound as alleged on the sentence and verdict. It all came down to that the charge should not have been upgraded for the second trial and that I should be re sentenced under the articles of the first trial, which held a maximum of 7 years imprisonment. This was all spoken in Chinese as we had discussed these details and I knew what he must be saying He did explain some of it in English for my and the consul representatives' benefit. Besides, I knew the consul would have their own interpreter anyway and should be able to get a copy of the translation so had little to do but listen.

It was all over and I was returned to the basement cells by lunchtime. The lawyer came down to see me and told me the hearing had gone well but that we would not have the outcome for another few weeks. We shook hands and said goodbye. I had lunch at the court holding cells, before heading back to the gulag. That old acquaintance of mine, Cranky sat opposite me. So, what happened at your appeal?" he asked. I was telling him what the lawyer had just said. He let out an exasperated gasp saying man!" as only an American makes it sound and knew he would be curious. I told him the story of the case being withdrawn and the subsequent substance error to a higher charge. He had been bust with cannabis too. Cannabis oil in fact, just over 2 Kg inside a thermos flask. It was not the first time he had gone down with cannabis. I knew of him leaving Manila to Hong Kong and being bust with marijuana and once again in South Korea smuggling gold. I knew this person well enough. We were in the same trade although he had not arrived on the Asia trial until the middle 1980s. I knew his good friend Fred from Colorado. He was an old hand doing overland trips from Hong Kong through the Chinese mainland onto Tibet. Then down into Katmandu with gold. I did it myself a couple of time. It is a long road to travel but when you are being paid to see parts of the world you want to visit. Who could complain? Cranky told me he would read of my arrest in the Hong Kong newspaper. He also knew about the other British person whom we had not met, and had got four years for attempting to smuggle 7.2kg of cannabis to Japan. "So why did you get fifteen years?" he inquired, suspicion in his voice as if disbelieving my story. I could have said that it was because mistakenly charged with Oil but simply replied with God if I only knew" It was time to say goodbye, good luck and hope we never meet again in these circumstances. Back to the usual cell and the usual hungry eyes, the usual illicit cigarette butts the lads got to their usual rolling it least felt like one more night of getting one up on the enemy.

I waited three weeks before my next legal visit and by then was really pissed off. I would become dependent and expected a visit at least every week. What was I paying him for? When entering the visiting room my heart was racing in expectation that he had the result of the appeal. I lit a cigarette, inhaled deeply and asked "Any news?" and was actually trembling inside. The visit was only for me to sign over cash for his fees and tell me the results were due that very week. There was nothing more to say on that then. We sat and used up a full hour just chatting anyway. It is so good to talk in your own language in a strange land. Mr. Ma was a kind faced old man and told me he was a Buddhist. He had not joined the communist party and was not a party member.

On May 18 1992 I was called downstairs, sat between a Judge and a prosecutor, and handed the appeal verdict. I read the English version and it said simply, "Appeal Refused. Verdict Upheld" Four simple words to collapse my world and blow away my deluded hopes of commonsense and justice prevailing. What could be said? Other than "I want to see my lawyer"

The British consul visited next day, they couldn't interfere with the verdict, so there was nothing much to talk about except to asked them to pass on information to my family. I then asked about the prison I would be going to, if they had been there to visit the other British guy eager for any information of what might lie ahead. They had in fact visited the other prison and commented that the conditions were appalling. I inquired as to my lawyer's whereabouts and why hadn 't he visited. The consul informed me that Mr. Ma was no longer under contract with me. The lawyer had not told me this. Mr. Short went on to explain that once your case for appeal had reached its conclusion you no longer had the right to legal counsel. What if I want to petition or take my case to a higher court I said? It was neither a fair nor an accurate decision and asked Jim Short can you raise this issue with Mr. Ma? Being assured by the consul if the lawyer delivered any news to his office, then it would be forwarded on.

Chapter Forty: Moving

I had been kept in that same cell for ten months until May 29th 1992 when my cell was door opened and I escorted to the office and told that I would be moving cell to join the other British person from Wales. Thirty minutes later and was now in a cell that had a bath. You could not believe the difference from my last cell to this one it had a fucking bath in it. It also had a western design toilet pan and only housed four people. I sat down and exchanged stories with Bull, so named for his bullish bulk. He told me how he had met the two Germans and, it was obvious he was upset and angry with them. Bull explained that it had been they who had informed on him and his girlfriend a local woman from Kashgar, and she was still in custody here at this same detention center.

I told Bull my story and he remembered seeing me in Kashgar and told me that the PSB had shown him photos of me asking him if he knew me, "I can recall seeing you also I said one time drinking and smoking with other travelers we chatted easily. I was nodding my head towards the cell window and could see that this cell with a view was something special. Asking Bull how long he had been here and was surprised to discover that he had been here since his arrest in November. He also had extra food stores and bottles of chili paste. I just could not believe the contrast from this cell and the one I had just come from. I asked Bull about the two other Chinese people in the cell. One was around thirty the other forty. The eldest was charged with dumping waste into the canal. It was shocking but not surprising that this was considered a very serious offence in China and could warrant the death penalty depending on whatever environmental damage ensues from that crime. The younger person was in for bribery. He was well educated and spoke some English he was expecting to go to jail but for how long he did not know not having his indictment yet.

I settled into my new cell by having a semi warm bath and enjoyed the extras offered, such as hot water to make tea or noodles etc. It gave me a sense of suspicion to say the least. Like why has Bull been so much better treated than I have? What is it that I do not know? However, never did find out nor reach any conclusions, either positive or negative about the vast difference in treatment. It was quite a treat to be watching television and snacking on biscuits that night.

A few days later, all the Western prisoners were called to the main office and told that we should pack our things from the cell. We were moving to the main prison, Tilan Xiao, the following day, June 2nd 1992. On that day we were escorted down to the area were my baggage had been stored hearing my heart pumping, pure paranoia ripping out of me in cold sweats in expectation of another death sentence indictment. I still didn't have any idea what bag Scott had taken with him but could only guess that they wouldn't have given him the one checked in by me. The one with the cannabis hardly hidden inside and could be in for big trouble like as if fifteen years wasn't enough. It was when seeing that my son had actually taken the chance and had taken my bag. Praise then is to Ali Baba and the forty thieves letting myself breathe again in an audible sigh of pure relief. It was never ever expected by me to have such a break. That then only left me with the completely concealed suitcase with the last 5kg securely hidden. I wanted to cry out and shout with pride and joy but the death sentence scenes flashed through my mind again thus gulped, swallowing my pride instead. Then carrying my luggage confidently said to the heavens, God blessed you, my son.

Chapter Fortyone: Tilan Xiao Prison Shanghai

The detention interrogation room was now full the American had joined us his sentence fifteen years and 10000 Renminbi fine the equivalent to 2500 us dollars. We were handcuffed in twos and put onto a transit van. The jail was located downtown Shanghai and the police escort took us right along the waterfront along the Shanghai Bund. It was the equivalent of driving down to Piccadilly Circus in London, only we were handcuffed in these Chinese police transit van taking us to God only knew where and for how long. The drive only took about twenty minutes we sat in silence lost in our own thoughts. The jail entrance wasn't any different from any other prison. It had those large gates and two unwelcoming military guards standing armed and ready at either side. This jail was right in the city center and built to isolate and contain. Cranky had copped a fifteen-year sentence for his cannabis oil. "Fifteen Years man" being sarcastic at times parroted him when he'd joined us. We were very much in the same boat now. Both of us in our forties and heading for sixty by the time we got out of here.

We disembarked from the transit van shuffling nervously inside the prison grounds. Everyone's eyes turned in our direction as we were met by an old guy dressed in a grey prison uniform called Jin Feng. He had blue and white stripes running down the outside leg and a stripe across the back and front of the prison jacket. A very stern face guard, who stood with him, directed us into a large reception area and we were seated. I clutched onto my suitcase like I'd just snatched a 10-million-dollar heist. Each of us was given a prison number on a plastic card holder pinned to our jackets. I was number 13499. We were given a brief introduction as to what was to be expected of us. Such as not to get out of line while going to our cell block. On the way we passed a few very large prison blocks and could see that the exercise area was a basketball court. We entered cell block eight now being able to read the Chinese character and walked up to the third floor. Passing some guys on the stairs, smiling to show them I was friendly but got no response and continued to our landing where we had a meeting. Parking my case against the stool where I was told to sit on by Jin Feng. Then seeing the other English guy walk towards us his hands outstretched. He looked as if he had just seen man Friday as we all shook his hand. Then Cranky, Bull, and I all at once started asking him questions about the place but he didn't get a chance to answer. Jin Feng called us to sit down and listen. A slightly build man in his middle thirties addressed us as Jin Feng gave us the English interpretation. "My name is Captain Yu I am the leader of the 8th brigade third floor and want you to know that our system of reform is through labour. As foreigners you will not need to work. You will be given intellectual status and a study program." He went on about Chairman Mao and how great he was. We were not to associate with the Chinese inmates. The meeting was over, Jin Feng called for us all to stand up but only the one person who did was Grad, the obedient lad.

Chapter Fortytwo: An Oxford Grad

Grad from England and had an Oxford University degree; he was quick to tell us. He also had a four years sentence for smuggling 7.2kg of cannabis strapped to his body whilst boarding a ship bound for Japan. He had also been given a fine of forty thousand RMB. Around five-thousand-pound sterling. He was to be our group leader he told us. I didn't think so. Oxford degrees don't automatically qualify as leader where I come from.

Walking into my cell for the first time and lay on the floor and put my head against the back wall. Looking up, I cannot see any electric light on the cell ceiling. Reaching out my arms I can touch both walls. I then calculated that it was around 8feet by 4feet. No window and iron barred cell door. There was a wooden bucket that was for the toilet. This was going to be a problem there would be no way my skin was touching decade's old damp urine and shit stained wood. Smack in the center of the back wall was a poster with large written Chinese characters on it. Later translated it read.

The Ten Don'ts
Don't oppose the four cardinals.
Don't oppose the teaching of the Cadres.
Don't step over the warning line or leave the group.
Don't trade in food or try to manipulate others.
Don't fight or train kick boxing, make weapons or gamble.
Don't conceal money, explosives, or poison.
Don't keep contact with people outside of the prison without permission.
Don't bully, beat, abuse, or insult or frame others.
Don't hide contraband in your cell.
Don't sabotage production, slack off at work, or steal nor damage public property.

It was decided that the three British prisoners would share the one store room and be allocated a space there. The two Germans and Cranky would share another. Grad informed us that if we wanted prison uniforms, we would have to write a report requesting them. He was wearing his own civilian clothes. It was unanimously decided that we'd wear our own clothes, at least, for now. Securing the suitcase in the store room still with a flutter in my chest then wandered onto the landing to look around my new abode. Being met by the translator Jin Feng who told me his English name was Joseph King. "You're Joe king?" I said laughing at my own wit and was pleased to see Joe King laughed along with me. "So, what shall I call you" asking him "Jin Feng or Joseph?" He said that the guards wouldn't like me using his English name but after giving it some thought, shrugged and told me to suit myself. I asked Grad where to have a shit. "In your cell" he replied then inquired as to how he managed to sit on that wood without protection and he soon enlightened me. Seeking out Jin Feng asked him to get me a set of bucket pads made. It was a simple twelve inch long by four inch wide padding a bit like a shoe insole one side marked to identify were to place them. That priority sorted then spent my first day getting to know the other tales off arrest and hearing their views of our new surroundings. We passed most of that morning exchanging stories when telling my own left out several of the pieces of course omitting what Scott had done and my narrow escape thanks to him taking the dope out from the detention cells for me. Nor, of course, did mention the case full of dope in our storeroom right beside us. Crank's story was a bit iffy to say the least according to him his girlfriend was being held hostage in Tokyo. She'd been snatched by some guys whom Cranky had done some deal with but it all went wrong and he was blamed for it. The guys wanted their money and they wanted it quick. Cranky agreed to do a run to Shanghai as part of a pay back. He was to check into the Peace Hotel and pick up a parcel. If he returned with the goods his girlfriend would be safe and he would earn some money to clear his debt. According to him, he simply did as he had been instructed but was busted picking up the parcel from a hotel room. He claimed it was a set up from the beginning and believed that the cops were just waiting for someone to show up and it was him.

When introduced to another little Chinese guy with several fingers chopped off and could see only stumps on his left hand. I immediately thought of a Japanese Yakusa victim for bad service to his boss. It turned out this little guy was the guard's gofer. It was his job making their tea, washing up and laundry. Not a job fancied by me but the Chinese prisoners didn't have a choice especially ex-communist party members gone wrong like this little guy had done.

The landing was quiet when we arrived most cons were out on work detail. We were squeezed into a tight space here; the walking area was only three feet wide. I got quite a fright when an ear shattering bell rang and the entire area filled up with guys all shouting over each other to be heard old men, young men, all shapes and sizes, and within minutes were all seated in silence. One Chinese con stood at each table and called out something, it was a head count. Then they all started babbling again, a pandemonium of sounds not all alien to my ear but already disturbing my mind. Watching them you just couldn't help but be impressed by the magnitude of shared efficiently. The distribution of food was orderly. We foreigners were given stainless steel containers of piping hot tasty food and as much rice as you could eat. I'd lost weight in the detention cells and was glad to see the food here wasn't as bad as imagined would be. I'd expected to be served up with cockroaches if the detention cell stories were anything to go by. Expecting to be hungry every day but instead slept that night with a full stomach lying in that mini tomb in the downtown necropolis of Shanghai city in the People's Republic of China.

Chapter Fortythree: Wake Up Call

Day two began like a thunderstorm all you could hear was the noise of the Chinese cons rising to greet another day. Whereas I'd slept alone in my 8ft by 4ft cell, the local prisoners were three to a cell. You can imagine the clatter and organized chaos of a corridor of these cell doors opening to excrete three prisoners per cell all trying to escape the overnight cram and stench of human waste I hadn't been prepared for this the noise it was truly brain damaging. There was a wireless blaring off its waveband, screeching at high volume from one of the speakers' right outside my cell door. I sat up crossed legged on the futon mattress began rubbing the sleep from my eyes. The sound of heavy door locks opening marched steadily towards me Then seeing the first image of what lay ahead and for God only knew how long. The door opened with a clatter and the large dark shadow engulfed the whole cell then click and the lock sprung open that it may not close again without a key. Keeping my focus fixed on a spot in my mind and took a deep breath. The shadow moved on. I arose and got dressed amid the babbling clatter of hell on earth. It's beyond me to describe or fully explain the shock of waking up into pure pandemonium standing and watching as waves of Chinese prisoners passed my cell door. Every passing pair of eyes staring at me, having grown another bushy red beard and I had never felt so alienated.

Grad came to my cell and escorted me to a sink where the wash up area faced directly into another cell block housing death row prisoners. I brushed my teeth staring out of the window and saw a basketball court below. The washing and ablutions over, it was now breakfast time. We were served hot steamed bread and rice gruel with pickled root and chili. After breakfast we sat around talking, it was new to all of us. We asked Grad about remission. He diverted that question by saying that he thought that we would all be deported soon. Cranky went along with that view. The two Germans, Vern and Hans, didn't join the group. Suspicion crept back into me remembering what Bull had told me at the Hell Cells. Hans had apparently told the police were he bought the drugs which resulted in Bull and his girlfriend being arrested. In short Hans had informed the mutual enemy.

The day passed and dozens of officials came to stare at us. It's was fact that on the outside in the streets of China people did stare at you. Westerners are so rare and unusual for them to see in real life in some rural places. Inside this prison we were a real commodity. It was the same smile we got from all the passing officials. Apparently from what Grad had said the Cadres also wished that we go home soon. We were just so far beyond their normal routine. The day was a long one. How many more still to go having counted just over 5,000 at the detention cell first night after sentencing. I had lay in my cell that first night and counted from the years counted the months and counted the weeks. I counted the days counted the stars; then counted ten thousand, of these prison bars. No matter how or what way I was counting it. 15 years sounded better.

Forget counting down all those days one at a time.

The first week's routine was the same after breakfast each morning we had a meeting. Grad suggested that we do some self-study. I was looking for something to do with work that would occupy my body and mind and just couldn't handle the sitting on my arse all day doing nothing. I asked JK as he was now called if he could translate for me. He agreed and we went to the red line painted across the floor before you exit our landing. JK stood and called out "Reporting to you Captain" and waited till he was told to enter myself in tow. JK explained that I couldn't sit doing nothing all day and needed to be occupied and wanted to work. Having explained to JK that Painting and decorating is my trade. This only brought a quizzical look to this guard's expression. As if he could not comprehend such a concept. He then went on to agree that labor reform was beneficial but that those foreigners detained here were not allowed to work. I asked about a study program but to no avail and left the office no further on than when I'd gone in.

Chapter Fortyfour: Chopsticks

It was during breakfast Bull had been collecting the remains of our pickle ration that was fine by all. Every morning we were given one container to share Bull had been storing the leftovers in jars. Red chili's peppers were a common part of the pickle. I wanted to collect some also and reached for the container after all had taken what they wanted. Bull reached for it also there was a pulling struggle then with me head butting him and stuck a chopstick up to his eye he then released the container. Being summoned to the office that morning when our leader came on duty. Lenny from Hong Kong and was now doing the interpretation when JK usually did. The word was out JK and me were trading we were becoming too friendly.

Having explained the situation regarding the pickle incident Lenny translated and my punishment was confinement to my cell for one week it also included no bathing. JK came and told me that he had to write a self-criticism report, asking him what exactly what was that? He explained that he was behaving to bourgeois. I didn't have a clue what he was on about he went on to tell me that some inmates had handed reports in against him. Who I asked? He mumbled some curses in a foreign tongue. JK then told me to also write a self-criticism stating that my action had stepped over the line and over reacted in the most negative way with violence. Looking at him could see he looked different and asked what you have done to your hair it has got darker. JK told me that was part reason why he had to write the self-criticism for dying it. As to me writing a self-criticism report had assured myself was only protecting my right to a share of the pickle such trivialities to fight for you may well wonder as I often did during that seven-day confinement. To sit all day and watch others pass your cell from morning till night although you know they aren't going anywhere nice you would rather be out there with them anyway.

Chapter Fortyfive: Consul Visit

On the sixteenth of June 1992 the British Consul visited the prison with me complaining to them at having to sit all day without a work or study program. But it was the appeal verdict that was occupying my mind and held in my hand. I pointed out that my ignorance and inability of reading Chinese written characters had twice led to me being taken advantage of and that in fact I'd been duped. On explaining my point, asked why the consul's translators had not picked up on it and alerted me to this. JK had pointed out to me that the appeal verdict had been altered, underlining the places he showed to me.

First indicted for and tried for possession of cannabis that case was withdrawn.

A.   I was re-indicted for transporting cannabis oil sentenced to 15 years.
B.   I appealed regarding the substance sentenced for, and which didn't possess.
C.   The Appeal paper read "Verdict upheld possession of cannabis" but the sentence erroneously remained unaltered.

The original verdict stated "transportation of cannabis oil" and sentenced to 15 years under that article. The appeal had reverted back to upholding the first charge of possession of cannabis which holds a maximum of 7 years under that article. Yet the sentence of 15 years still remained contrary to the law here in China.

It had been doing my brain severe damage, all those altered charges. I knew it wasn't 't right but just didn't have the necessary knowledge to translate from the Chinese characters. Yet the consul had and could give me no explanation so told the consul about lodging a petition against the altered verdict and left that visit somewhat irate.

The only consolation was that my son Scott had sent more money from Japan. So he is still there I thought. Good for him and signed for FEC at that time in China; foreign travelers were expected to use this Foreign Exchange Certificates as per same in the diplomatic community thus indirectly helping to create a vibrant black market. You could shop at special outlets with better quality commodities where local currency was not accepted. That's communism for you.

Chapter Fortysix: No Talking

I was summoned to the office after my consul meeting and was told by the Criminal Affairs guard that you cannot talk about your case at the visit. It wasn't JK doing the interpretation but with Lenny's interpretive skills he told me to "accept my guilt" and not discuss petitioning as my case was closed. In astonished disbelief, replied irately, I can talk about whatever with my consul and I'll be lodging a petition and shall need a lawyer. Lenny as much as could be in the short period of time we knew each other told me "Don't speak just listen" "Fuck you just do the interpretation" I said and went into a rabble about how the substance charged with was wrong and that the communist thieves stole my family's $3,000 dollars. The office went silent and was told that I had a bad attitude. I exploded back "No fucking wonders!" and left the office fuming. Grad intercepted me asking why there was shouting in the office and told him what had been said and he looked at me in bewilderment. He then advised me to listen to the Cadres education" I turned and walked away mumbling "Cadres education, what a halfwit." Sensing my frustration JK came by my side eventually finding me calm enough to give me the low down on the way this system operated.

JK explained that the prison system works by reform through labor. That through labor you can pay back your debt to society. This brings revenue for the prison upkeep. The food we eat and the guards' wages. The prison must strive to be self-sufficient and not be a further burden upon state or the people or it fails in its duty. Such labor can also bring remission of sentence and success on job quotas brings added monthly bonus to the prison guards. Also, labor helped the prisoner to see the error of their ways and to repent and regret their crime. They must strive to make amends to earn remission. While he does not admit his guilt, he cannot truly repent and there is no hope for him. Further dissatisfaction and denial of his guilt can result in the penalty being changed.

I could try to get to work on the farm thinking as he spoke, then said out of the blue are the foreigners to be sent home? JK told me he hadn't heard such rumors and, if he did, he wouldn't build our hopes up on it. What had prompted me to ask was the past two days there was a movement within the jail. The commotion was about the massive transfer of prisoners which they do every few years. I was assured by JK that I would soon know all about it, as it's televised on the prison channel. Sure enough, within a few days we had lockdowns. The whole prison was banged up except the kitchen and counted. Then names would be read out over the radio. Doors would be opened and those named had to pack. This started in the morning and by noon, hundreds of prisoners ploughed by carrying big hawker's bundles. They boarded buses waiting in the court yards below and even onto the street. They were waiting to be taking to the train station in down town Shanghai. Trains that would carry them to far flung provinces, as far afield as Shandong and Xingjian autonomous region. They would be used as farmers, or factory workers.

That evening we all sat and watched on television the procession of prisoners boarding the train to their new far-flung destinations. We had to watch; it was mandatory. The camera crews filmed the guards guiding the convicts onto the buses then at the station and onto the trains. It was quite a large movement of men. I was told about 800 in total this time. The Prison TV station showed them on the train while they journeyed. Some sleeping, some reading, all seated.

Chapter Fortyseven: Ideological Remolding

We had June 25th 1992. China English Daily Newspaper

Everyone makes mistakes, and the reasons for making them are varied. In the long run it is not the mistakes in themselves but the attitudes of the people towards their mistakes that are more important. Society should always provide opportunities for people to realize their errors, show repentance, mend their ways and begin the lives anew. It cannot be said that a person who has had a black mark in the past won't be any good in the future to judge people fairly; society should concentrate on their words and deeds at the present.

I had written that into my diary from a newspaper the consul brought as something to work towards. It was Grad who had opened this door into his mind he'd been handing in a monthly report to our leading guard. This was known as thought reform. You were to write down your thoughts about your crime but more significantly, you were to write your thoughts about others. Grad explained to us all that he'd been doing this for months. We were shocked to hear this Cranky was quick to point out that this was a violation of his Human Rights but when Grad told us he'd volunteered, that put an end to the story. It was then that Grad came away with the group leader crap again telling us that he had been put in charge. That he had to put in reports on our behavior as well. This was becoming too much to bear.

Since our arrival here at this prison we had all asked to see Grad's indictment and verdict and he'd refused to show it to anyone. All we wanted to know was what his charge had been and what kind of substance it had entailed. We'd been told he was caught boarding a ship from Shanghai to Japan with 7.2Kg cannabis strapped to his body and sentenced to four years and 50,000 FEC fine. Everybody else, even those with lesser charges had received higher sentences. We wanted to know so that we may use his case as a precedent. Nobody was happy that he wouldn't say and wouldn't let us look at his indictment. So, what was going on with the Grad lad? This guy was worth a watching I thought. The two Germans had less cannabis the Welshman had less myself 700 grams more and got fifteen years. Something was seriously wrong here and Grad's secrecy confirmed that something was terribly wrong.

We had been here around one month now and we were allowed to order food and fruit on a monthly basis. Today was order day and some of us wanted coffee and black tea. Grad was telling us there was no coffee but Cranky persisted, he was from the USA and his cultural requirement was coffee as his preferred drink. I wanted black tea and coffee if possible. Grad suggested to Cranky that he write a report requesting coffee and he would hand it in. Bull suggested that we just go to the office and ask, the easiest thing to do, you would imagine and so we did. Grad Hans and Vern stayed behind as we marched up to the red line before the office. J K at our side. It was Cranky who spoke and when he had finished a smile came across the guard's face then he answered. JK explained to us that our request was granted but we could purchase only one jar per month plus it was strictly forbidden that we couldn't give any to the Chinese inmates. We thanked him and agreed. When we came from the office all smiles could see Grad had lost some of his self-importance when coffee was added to the list. We were handed a sheet of items we could purchase all written in English which JK had translated. This order was for July and it was quite interesting what the order list consisted of. In the month of July my first prison order was as follows. Writing paper 10 pads Envelopes 5 pack Notebooks 4. Toilet paper 10 packs. Soap powder 2 boxes. Scrubbing brush 2, Liquid detergent 2. Toothpaste 2, Instant noodles 24, Sesame oil, 1 Chili oil, 1 Tinned pineapple, 5 Tofu paste, 5 and Rabbit meat cooked from the kitchen. There was also Water melon you could order by the kilo we all ordered 50 kilo per person estimating the average melon to weigh 4 to 5 kg a piece. The cost of this order came to £3 pounds sterling the cost of living was low, but so was the standard of life.

Chapter Fortyeight: Football

I had been asking at every opportunity to have a game of football and was well pleased one evening when the guard called me into the office and asked me to play. It was a warm July evening and the guard had arranged for our brigade to play against one block a team who were well known in this event as I was told by JK. Along with our leading guard whom we named Benny, and another two guys named Lee and Chan, prisoners like me and who couldn't speak a word of English, made the team. I stood outside in the hot evening air felt well on my skin. I had been given a pair of canvas shoes from the guard and they fitted well. As soon as the ball was passed around, they knew they had a player who was good and they showed their appreciation with their expressions. As it worked out the guard and me played well together on the field. Having laid off plenty of balls for him to finish and put in a couple ourselves. It was a basketball size court good enough for four aside, like this night, the four aside was a hard and tiring workout which we won. Back upstairs to wash and to get ready for bed feeling the joy of victory from the other two guys. I heard my name used many times and it all sounded okay. I did feel heavy stares on me when passing some of the westerners but what could be done? If they wanted to play, they could ask like me. The word went around that the foreigners had a footballer and it was arranged for all of us to have a game the following evening. Football was taking off in China it was hot news and although foreign imports hadn't yet been here playing, foreign managers were on the scene, mostly from Eastern Europe.

As it turned out, only Bull had some skills. Not much on footwork but solid in defense. Grad was hopeless and the two Germans hadn't kicked a ball in their lives. Cranky was a basketball man. He'd never played football. I had waited all day for this game; and needed, to run and sweat, and to use my mind as one. We had a mixed game, only between guys in our unit but the same guard and me linked up and hammered the other side. I played right into the guard's ego and would jump up triumphantly whenever he scored a goal that I'd set up for him.

Benny as he was to be known, due to him forever telling us during meetings that he was a 'good man'. Vern who was a blues guitar man commented after the meeting that the Goodman should be called Benny after Benny Goodman the Jazz musician. Isn't it strange how you can relate one thing with another and yet to be so far apart in every aspect and it still sticks? That evening after the game sitting with some of the Chinese guys in the guard's office JK was doing the interpretations; there was a lot of laughing at whatever the guard said? I was praised by them all as having a good football mind. The word Hao was repeated often and learned that Hao meant good. That was two days in a row I'd had a game and felt a lot of tension going out of me. I was also informed that evening my son Lochy was coming to visit me and knew what for. Besides seeing his father, he would take away the suitcase his brother Scott had left behind and finally rid me of it once and for all. As well as the worries attached to it.

The following day Cranky who was celebrating his coming 45th birthday had asked for a special lunch of curry. Chancing his hand in the hope they would go along with it, which they did. It was the following afternoon we had a chicken curry and cream cake for dessert. This was something you couldn't even imagine might happen in this dark dismal jail but being part of the cook's brigade, our unit held a lot of sway our guard controlled the nightshift change-over thus power to have whatever food he wanted whenever he liked.

Chapter Fortynine: Good To See You Son

My youngest son Lochy came to visit on the July 5th in a small room near the prison gates. The visit was great, just to see my son again. He looked fine and healthy. He told me about his trip getting to here and his plan on returning to the U.K. The visit just flew by and the suitcase with the 5kg of hashish concealed at the bottom handed out after the contents being itemized. Besides the clothing that was inside I also handed out to him the video camera that Scott had gotten from my brother Rab in London. I reminded my son that this baggage was Scott's and that Scott had taken mine upon his release. I had to make it as clear as could be, just in case something did go wrong going into the United Kingdom with that drug packed suitcase. It was time to depart; and I suggested to have another visit and told Lochy to contact the British consul to arrange it. We shook hands and hugged before saying goodbye. I was returned to the cell area by the guard and sat for awhile talking with Vern who was picking on a guitar that he had just received from the German Consul. I told him about my son visiting and we shared an hour or so chatting. I had found Vern easy to get along with, he didn't have any aspirations nor did he talk much, he mostly sat alone writing songs some of which we would later perform.

Having a lot on my mind thinking for my son's welfare I had also asked Lochy to take a message to the consul regarding me having another visit with my lawyer. Feeling confident now that my son was here to help me and knew that what I'd asked him to do would get done. My son Lochy at the age off seventeen, after all had come to China to his father's rescue. I sleep well that night with just more than a load of my shoulders, and thought what a tremendous risk my son was taking, both sons had come to my rescue first Scott taking the Hashish to Hong Kong and now Lochy prepared to take the suitcase to the UK.

Chapter Fifty: Telegram

It had been over a week and my son hadn't got back to visit me and I was losing my mind. Then being reassured by JK that it takes more than a week to get anything done in communist China, especially anything related with courts or jails. I needed to hear something positive and JK was older and more experienced being a local Shanghai man he knew the script.

JK was serving a life sentence for having sex with his students. He'd been a school teacher who failed in his responsibility to society. I quizzed him on this subject thinking that it must have been a serious rape to get a life sentence. As it happened, it was his third offence, not for rape but for having sex with some of his students, aged sixteen to eighteen he told me. In China that's not allowed as the teacher has a responsibility to the family of his or her students, as well as to the students. Having already served ten years in a work farm for a past offence and still not reformed JK was now doing a life sentence in a rat hole in down town Shanghai. It was while talking with JK that I was summoned to the office this time without him as the escort translator.

I walked into the office where six PSB cops from the detention cells stood around. The office was overcrowded and my belly hollow and nervous; something serious was going on here. Then a few words were exchanged and then I was handed a telegram thinking maybe some family member had died. I read it and then read it again. "Lochy arrested same as you China." I looked up and Alan whom I knew from my investigation said Mr. Campbell you come down stair with us, we have some questions to ask you. Still in shock "Lochy arrested same as you China" flashed in my skull. I immediately spoke with Alan asking is my son here at the Shanghai detention cells? Yes, Alan replied he is under investigation and I was escorted out of the office and taken to another office on the ground floor. I listened to the accusations put to me that I had knowingly passed out drugs to my son during his visit. If confessing to this my son would be released. I didn't give out drugs to my son. I gave him my other son's suitcase which hadn't any drugs inside it stating clearly that it had been thoroughly searched when we were arrested. I started getting new and rather dodgy ideas into my head. Being in a spot I asked Alan why the police hadn't found those drugs during our initial investigation at the detention cells adding, also here at the prison upon arrival. I was continuing on to say then once again when my son was taking the luggage from here. How come it is only now that you have discovered drugs? I raised my eyebrows questioningly. Watching Alan take in what I was suggesting and he spoke rapidly in Shanghai dialect. It was seconds later the room erupted with high pitched talk and a lot of staring at me as they shuffled uncomfortably around the room. Alan stood over me and he was livid by the suggesting that the drugs may have been planted by them. I repeatedly inquired as to my son's welfare but Alan was answering none of my questions. The next route Alan perused was for me to write a statement saying that the luggage belonged to Scott. But wasn't having any of that either but did tell Alan that I had written a letter from this prison to Scott inquiring as to why he had taken my luggage. I had done this with my first letter home covering another angle for myself if it came on top which it now had.

I was escorted back up to my floor with the message ringing loud and clear in my head we shall return tomorrow. It caused quite a stir in the jail what had just happened. I was immediately escorted back to our landing office. It was like a military planned operation. The khaki green uniforms all looked the same but their jobs certainly differed. It was the leader of the prison administration bureau, the criminal affairs leader, education, the Warden and several more. JK had been called and looked frightened and stood straight backed. The questions were to the point first one being, "Did you know there were drugs in that case? "Certainly not" and then answered a few more questions. JK explained to me that now that I'm in prison, the authorities here are in control of what will happen to me while I'm here but that I might be returning to the detention cells after further inquiries. That was certainly not something to look forward to. Then thought the only possible good that might come from it is that I would see Lochy. There was an uncomfortable silence, and could see that nobody knew what more to ask. I tried to convince them by telling them the clothes in that case were all for a young person and certainly not mine. I knew that they translated and censored my letters and reminded them of that. I knew full well and had planned this beforehand and what was written would confirm what I was telling them now.

I was returned to my cell escorted by two guards and could see that the other Westerners were dying to know what was going on and couldn't tell them, not just yet. My cell had been turned over then I was taken to the store room and asked to remove all my belongings, which I did and they were searched. All my belongings were taken to another cell in the middle of the landing cell number 31. My old cell had been 14 so here was me right in among the locals. I then returned to the office for more inquiries. I tried to persuade the guard to let me write a letter to my son. Having pleaded with his humane side asking if he had a son or not, to which he replied proudly that he did have one son. "My son" I continued, is only seventeen years old and those detention cells are dangerous and dirty. Just send one letter for me please. He told me he would consult his leader then after a few more questions I returned to my new cell.

By the time the evening meal came around I still hadn't had enough time to sit and think this dilemma out. Instead, I had just stared vacantly at the surrounding walls. Then when collecting my meal Grad said "Can I ask you something?" I nodded my head to indicate if he wanted to talk, to come and join me he didn't. I picked at my food without much desire to eat having usually looked forward to this meal the end of the day. A good thing to be rid of for prisoners was time. I was focused on Lochy in the detention cells, caught with 5kg cannabis concealed into a suitcase. My fault again, I'd given him the suitcase from here and had warned him in advance that he must stick to one story if anything went wrong, he was collecting his brother Scott's luggage. I searched my brain what could be done to help him now? I had to stick to my story and that was, it wasn't my bag, it was Scott's. Sitting alone again, lost in troubled thought when Cranky and Bull got around me hungry for news or scandal. I told them about Lochy and they said at once astounded. "You had 5kg here in this jail?" We discussed the possible outcome and they all bargained that Lochy would get at least a ten-year sentence. I lay in bed that night thinking of my son having a hard time at the hell cells and was tempted to rush into making a confession and putting myself on the firing line but decided against that. It wouldn't help as they would be more likely to convict us both and for firing a bullet into my head, I wasn't for letting that happen here. I was now in cell 31 and my next-door neighbors in cell 30 were being moved out and that cell was also to be allocated to me as my storeroom. I stood looking in at my new office come storeroom. It now had an old desk and chair in it. A few Chinese inmates were helping me furnish it. Asking JK what was going on and he told me that now to be among the local inmates some of them would be allowed to help me settle in. The two guys who played football with me were among them. It was a sort of isolation treatment until this investigation regarding the 5kg of cannabis was resolved.

What would my ex-wife be thinking? Her two sons meet up with their dad do not pass go. Go straight to jail. No bail in China. Mary would be more than angry with me. The way she'd brought those boys up, they handled themselves well. Her lads were strong, clean and tidy and had intelligence that could be cultivated towards better things. I didn't sleep to well that night and was restless, tossing and turning, fighting off scoundrels who Lochy was battling with over at the detention.

Chapter Fiftyone: Lao Da

It wasn't long after breakfast the following day when I was called to be interrogated by the Shanghai PSB. Alan done most of the talking again and could now see he had changed his approach. Now it was more like him working out a way of ditching his responsibility and avoiding the flack for why it hadn't been discovered in the first place. He wanted me to take the full responsibility. Alan pressed on relentlessly with this point but I didn't take it up and eventually just refused point blank to answer any more questions until speaking with my lawyer, consul and my son. It was a quick meeting and I was told that the PSB would return. The once overconfident Alan and his crew departed.

It was hot news in the jail and as fast as jail rumors and press stories go, I was 'Lao Da' in Chinese that meant 'The Boss' Gangsters, Mafias, whether they were Italian, Russian, or other, their names were as well known as the Triads in China. As far as some of these Chinese convicts were concerned, I could be approached. They knew by the deed I had just done, right under the noses of every security force in China. I had unwittingly opened a door into the jail black market which I had known would be going on somewhere. It always does. Chinese people place a lot of value on not losing face. Just by doing what I'd done, had caused a lot of lost face to our mutual enemy.

I was welcomed into the fold by a small crew who were known as 'Black Jade' JK had approached me regarding some of my clothing asking me if would trade something with his friend so that he could give it to his son on his birthday. Old Hun was the guy JK wanted me to help. His nickname was 'Black Fish' and he was the Triad leader in our wing. He was a good organizer and serving a life sentence and didn't go by the rules and regulations of the prison reform system. I started trading using JK as the go between. I had received a parcel from my brother Robert in London. The contents had brought a few green-eyed monsters to the surface. My brother had sent me a dozen Lacoste polo shirts, still in their wrappers plus another dozen T shirts with all sorts of patterns and prints on them. I got boxes of underwear, dozens of socks, bottles of after shave plus other body perfumes, all designer brands and costing a lot of money. I had soaps from the body shop and enough razor blades to shave for the whole sentence, even if I had to complete every day of it. I got a Walkman and 100 plus cassette tapes with a wide variety of music. I got dozens of pens; one in particular was a much-desired commodity. It had a three in one Red Blue and Black a novelty with a much-required function. Having felt tip pens in every color you could possibly imagine added into the parcel by an old friend Bobby Glen from Glasgow.

It was time to make some inroads. I needed to have a letter sent out without the normal censorship. I asked JK if he could arrange that which he did. I wrote giving TC all the facts regarding the withdrawal of my case from public prosecution and the change of substance in the appeal verdict. I had placed a code word for him to reply thus verifying its delivery. I had given JK one polo shirt for his services but he didn't take it. Saying he can't wear it here at the prison and

and the only person left in his family was his younger brother. JK said he had totally broken away and never came to visit due to JK having a bad reputation in their neighborhood. I asked him if he wanted anything else. JK said I would like a three-ink pen Mr. Campbell" he said it in such a humble voice in expectation that he had no chance of getting the desired pen. I handed him one pen plus some blades and a new razor stick. That had been something else my brother had done. He'd put three sets of Gillette G2 razor it was the in item then. I felt good that my underground letter was going onto someone who knew how to deal with such matters. My brother who knew how to handle legal issues, as he was currently entangled in the biggest legal battle in Scottish history. The Free the Glasgow two campaigns was turning the Scottish legal system inside out.

Chapter Fiftytwo: Young Lochy

It was early July when my son was arrested and that is a very hot season sweating profusely here but the detention cells are much worse. It was a date easy to remember and it was July12th when the Shanghai PSB visited me again. It was on that day when hearing the full story of Lochy 's arrest. I had told him to fly into Japan to a place called Fukuoka but Lochy decided to take the ship to Kobe instead. Alan told me the details and went onto say that if I didn't sign a confession now my son would be charged. I again declined his offer and could see his frustration at my lack of cooperation. It wasn't like the detention cells when admitting to everything and signed most things. Now having some insight into the traps and lies laid before me now had some guidelines. Fifteen fucking years of guidelines to go by, so the smiles and "Don't worry you will be leniently treated" spiel wasn't working this time. I knew they wanted to shoot me in the head and signing one paper could have granted them their wish. I was a total embarrassment to them and to the whole set up of investigation procedure, they needed a scapegoat and I was their first choice and rightly enough viewing it from their eyes. A father who involves his sons with crime would certainly be executed.

Alan showed it all in his eyes; he was going to be the one to suffer besides myself. He was almost pleading to me with his expressions which said to me, "Please confess, and sign here" I looked at him in defiance; his eyes then spoke louder volumes, "Confess and sign here" then going onto say just "Confess. I watched as he squirmed knowing he was in trouble with his superiors. It had all gone so sweetly until now. Alan was over confident when we first encountered to the point that he was arrogant and now, by a twist of fate, he was left holding a major problem. Why didn't you confess to me in the detention cells" Alan pursued? "Now your son will go to jail" he went on, still working out a way to get me to sign a paper that would get him off the hook and me shot." It wasn't in the suitcase" I replied, and felt a little sorry for him. Then woke up and remembered how nasty he could be. It would be his responsibility for not getting the full confession and finding the drugs during the initial investigation period. I didn't dwell to long on that subject having enough to worry about regarding my own hellish predicament and furthermore my sons.

I never signed any papers and was escorted back to the wing, with another headache coming on, I was getting to much pressure from those PSB, and the thought of my son in that hell hole wasn't helping matters either. Sitting alone in my cell pained in mind and body, even my psychic barrier was penetrated that day and it hurts when your family bloodline and love cuts cold and for real.

Chapter Fiftythree: Dalai Lama

It was an unexpected visit from his Holiness the Dalai Lama. This transpired through us all being told to clean up our store room. Whilst Cranky was clearing out he came across a few post cards printed in Thailand with his Holiness on them. He had that calm smile and worldly face with an aura of wisdom. It was at our end of the month outgoing letter hand in time. Cranky had included one postcard to his family. It wasn't until after the evening meal was finished, we were called to sit and have a meeting. At least three high ranking officials were present. The postcard of his Holiness the Dalai Lama was produced. The bottom line was that our Holy friend was considered anti-communist and was trying to divide China. Cranky was criticized, the rest of us just looked at each other in bewilderment what the fuck had a postcard of the spiritual leader to do with communism. That was a short visit by his Holiness, but he did revisit again as Crank had held firm to his stash, he never tried to send anymore but at least his Holiness was in the building. O Mani Padme Hum.

Chapter Fiftyfour: Jail Games

The 1992 summer Olympic Games in Barcelona were coming up creating an atmosphere for sport and a football competition was to be arranged within the jail. In total there would be eight teams forming two groups. This was great for me as getting out training every morning and evening took my mind away from Lochy and got lost in the competitive aspect of the game During training I called for a pass at every opportunity and ran myself into the ground seeking fatigue for the night's sleep ahead. The games had started and the competition was fierce between eight brigades we had football, basketball, tug of war plus board games and ping pong. It was fun whilst it lasted.

I was talking with Vern one evening after playing football; Hans was having a joke with Grad and I could hear that it was due to Grad being a vegan and not eating certain products. Hans was quick to point out that the leather coat Grad had been grooming down in anticipation of going home would have taken at least two cows to make. "I thought you were against cruelty to animals and a vegan" Hans joked. Grad responded with a rather bitter remark saying that he was "More against Nazi concentration camp products made from human skin" It was a bit below the belt and Hans turned away shaking his head in disgust. I wasn't interested in this tit for tat negativity and was more anxious to hear about Lochy. I asked JK to escort me to the office which he did, then inquired if a visit with my son could be arranged as he was untried, then asked if he could come here while waiting for trial. I was just trying and saying anything that came into my head, anything to get me closer to my son. All I got was permission to write one extra letter home.

As it was, the regulations allowed we all had a one letter per month ration. This incident was deemed to be important enough to warrant one more but could only address it to my son's mother, my ex-wife. It wasn't something to look forward to doing but felt obligated to do so. After writing the letter held onto it, reading and rereading adding something here and there, and then putting it away again. I was harboring plans to pass it over to the consul when they next visited and didn't trust the mail system here, especially when his Holiness the Dalai Lama was refused exit last month or entry for that matter, not even on postcards.

Suffering badly from the heat; it was becoming unbearable, especially at night when the fans were switched off while you slept. It was quite an unusual sight to see that all the Chinese prisoners slept outside their cells during these hot and humid Shanghai summers not a cell door was closed. The whole area was covered in bodies, guys slept on top of tables and every space on the cool stone floor was used up. It would have been torture to make people share a cell in this sort of heat and anyone who didn't abide by the rules often found them three to a cell were your body is never dry. This was the season of high tension, people freaking out and a lot of violent eruptions occurred. The weather seemed to take over your whole life, day and night you were constantly wiping yourself down or fanning yourself or drinking lots of water, warm water but wet enough to quench a parched thirst and prevent dehydration.

I recall one morning whilst mopping the floor outside my cell area. A large rat come out and started licking up the water. It had no fear what so ever, its head was down and it was thirsty. Rats were a common site on our wing there would always be a chase after them at one point of the day or another. I hated them, especially when they came into my cell and could hear and feel them walking around me whilst keeping my head wrapped in a bed sheet, hiding. Or I would jump up and shout, hoping to frighten them away. As it happens, you become accustomed to them and just didn't encourage them by keeping food in my cell.

This jail was really run down and badly in need of a whole new sanitation renovation. Being a traveller, I'd slept in places just as infested with vermin as this jail and even paid for it. One place in particular, called Sukarachi Street in Bombay an old dilapidated opium den housing underage girls in cages. I paid for the pipes to smoke and my opium dreams were not of having sex. I'm old fashioned that way no interest in underage teenage girls. It was a hot summer and yet we managed to play football, most games in the evenings but some due to schedules needing to be kept were held in the heat of the day hot and sweaty drinking constantly to re hydrate it was that hot your feet felt it through the concrete but just to get out and expel energy was a godsend for me.

Chapter Fiftyfive: The Shit Patrol

I had seen the Pakistani cons most days they were housed in the two buildings that could be seen from our block. My meeting up with one of them started when our yard drainage pipes got blocked. It was a job for us foreigners to do usually as it was considered hygiene duty and not labor. We had to carry those shit filled buckets four at a time down three flights of stairs walking sideways due to the narrow passage. The size and weight alone were difficult to manage. We then crossed the yard which led us into another cellblock then through their hall into their yard. It was an awful humiliating job.

Haled was from Rawalpindi he was serving six years for passing off counterfeit money. His associates in crime were also serving ten years and seven years respectively. They were kept in other cell blocks and I hadn't met up with them yet but knew their names to be Aktar and Butt. Haled had told me about them and also about Mir who was in cell block one and doing 10 years for a different charge from them but also fraud. It must have been known at this cell block that I had items for trade. Haled was looking magazines, and told me he was trading in photos of Pakistani women cut out from ones sent by his family. In the prisons in Shanghai, you weren't allowed to have photos of your wife or family and thought that to be an unusual regulation. I had a Thailand Calendar that was sent along with a parcel from my brother in London. The girls were exquisite mature and their lithe bodies and small breasts firm and inviting and skin that made you want to caress it forever.

The following day passing it over to Haled for him to do trade with. I got it returned the next day, and couldn't believe my ears when he told me that the Chinese guys hadn't any use for other Asian girl's photos. He went on to say as they were plentiful in China. I couldn't have agreed more after watching a movie with the actress Gong Li I fell in Love. Haled asked did I have any photos of Europeans girls? Even in fashion magazines he could still trade them. Haled then gave me some magazines from his country. As I slept that night slipped off into the land of dreams with some exotic Pakistani beauty. Allah made women in that land a treasure to look at and I slept that night in Lahore, with Miss Gong Li.

Chapter Fiftysix: Blanked

I noted it in my diary as I counted twelve inmates tagged at their lapels for identification purpose being led out from death row to be transported for execution. I could see them from our landing window which faced that building of fear and inhumanity. It housed those prisoners who would never see their family again never see anyone again. I couldn't come to terms at how little regard was given to taking another's life here. In the Chinese legal system, the death penalty was given for crimes that wouldn't warrant much more than five years in the UK for example dumping waste causing river pollution or car theft. I took my mind away from that scene below and thought about my son.

The British consul had come to visit in August and was eager to hear about Lochy and I expected to be called to the visit first my anxiety being on the wellbeing of my son. The other two Brits were called and visited one at a time. I waited patiently till Grad came back timing the visit calculating the walk to the visiting room and back fifty minutes. It was then Bull was called another fifty minutes he returned I was never called and no explanation and no reason given as to why. I was fucking raging and didn't know who was to blame. I barged into the office crossing the red line without first calling and waiting permission. I demanded to see the consul and was informed that I couldn't see them while my son was under investigation. Then I'm on a hunger protest" then stormed out of the office. That evening I didn't eat and followed up by missing breakfast the next morning. I was called to the office again and this time threatened that, if I didn't eat then would be force fed. I smiled in contempt but still didn't eat.

The following afternoon Benny our guard called a meeting with the foreigners. We sat listening to the range of punishments meted out to inmates who broke the rules. Not eating was a violation of those rules. The group was asked what they thought of my action with JK doing the translations. Grad disagreed with what I was doing and tried to persuade me to have some food. This followed suit around the table, all except Cranky made a comment advising me to eat. Needless to say, I ignored them. It was the third morning and I didn't touch breakfast again was now becoming a headache for them. They didn't yet know how to deal with foreigners. We were still a novel enigma. That morning around 11 o'clock I was summoned to the office again and I finally got JK to compromise that I would eat if being allowed to send a telegram that day. This was agreed after our unit leader made a phone call. I left the office, and drafted a short telegram letter to my family regarding my son's wellbeing and handed it over. I was given a receipt a couple of hours later when signing for 150 Renminbi thus verifying that my telegram had been sent. If being honest had been looking for some out from this no eating stint it wasn't pleasant to go hungry but had to do it without losing face. I knew it wouldn't solve my immediate worries but the telegram idea had given me that out. I ate the evening meal slowly and really enjoyed it. Fasting for a few days at a time was nothing new to me and used to do it at a Yoga retreat in Katmandu. It was not like my brother, 100 day fasts for justice losing around 35Kg in body weight but that's TC. He's always been one seriously determined man.

Chapter Fiftyseven: Cooling Parties

It is called a cooling party because the jail gets so hot in summer that you need some escape from the heat. We would all sit outside in the yard basketball court, come car park and now our concert arena. It was also used just for playing chess games and cards or just trying to catch some breeze. This was our second outing since arrival. This was to be a special occasion however; we the foreigners were to visit all the outdoor prison blocks. and to entertain with a couple of songs. Vern, Bull, Cranky and I had formed a little band called 'The Reformers.' Vern had the guitar and could play quite well. Cranky had got hold of a washboard and me a set of maracas made from empty washing liquid bottles and dried rice inside. Bull was the vocals except when I sang 'Smoky Joes café.' The Loudon Wainright rendition or 'summertime blues was Crank's number. We had done a little rehearsing starting with the Beatles number 'Help' then onto Bob Marley 'Baby Don't worry' and if we had time for another we would do 'By the Rivers of Babylon'

It was quite an experience going up onto a stage to perform. We couldn't see anything in front of us except lights. We were singing the chorus to the Rivers of Babylon and adding "Do you remember Tiananmen?" It was Cranky who got that in first, then Bull, Vern and we all joined in once we caught the drift. At the finish off our band was taken onto the roof of number eight block which was all women. It was mind blowing to see some of these beautiful ladies dressed in prison uniforms. Some of them showed out to us, and bumping deliberately into them just for the touch. It was worth risking any sort of punishment just to be in contact with the opposite sex. The closeness to so many women was painfully aching but in a pleasurable way.

That was a night to remember performing in a downtown Shanghai city jail in the People's Republic of China. Who would believe it? And it is true. We returned to our section of the party, hot sticky and sweating profusely. The Chinese convicts were putting on all sorts of performances, Magic acts, singing, opera and dance groups, all in costume. We also had a group of female prisoner's dance and sing for us. It was exhausting, the excitement becoming a bit too much. A bit too much like being outside but the main ingredient was missing the door key onto the street. I can honestly say it was like a dream state of mind when the ice cream was being handed out. That sweet cold vanilla flavor wrapped in chocolate filling your mouth and cooling your throat. Here I was singing and tapping my feet to music. Feeling a lot of emotion rising in me and wanted to be with my son and slept with him close by me, safely secure inside my head that night.

Chapter Fiftyeight: Back Stairs Mailman

It was September 18th and the jail Games were over another sports program was in full swing for the upcoming National Day celebration. I was picked for our blocks football team. There was some dispute about whether to be allowed to play due to being a security risk. I got right in amongst the debate arguing that as I was only moving within the jail and not outside of it. What was going on having already taken part in other jail activities but it was resolved and I was included. We had the sports training on fulltime now we also had a volleyball, basketball and tugs of war team, all going outside at the same time together. The jail held up to five thousand convicts there were nine separate resident halls, not including the hospital kitchen and concert hall. Bull was in the tug of war team, Cranky the basketball and me football. The other foreigners were on the sidelines as spectators. It was hard fought games and although Chinese are small in build they are made of iron.

Time seemed to move very quickly during sports outings but the nights were as long two days. I'd been waiting a couple of months to hear the reply to my letter sent by the underground mail service but still hadn't received any yet and was beginning to think had been duped. Then one day whilst in the washing up area, a voice called me from the landing above. Looking up the back stairs and saw Lenny, he whispered in a hurried tone, "Take this letter from him and read it, then return it to me in half an hour." Taking the letter from him and excitedly returned to my cell. It was a letter from my brother TC confirming he had got the underground letter, thus proving that the back door mailman had fulfilled his promise. That was great news and felt a touch of hope creep back into me. It was important that the facts of my case be told to the right people who might be able to rectify this error in law. Tommy more commonly known by the press as TC Campbell was the man for that. I knew my brother to be an intelligent articulate man. This was a side of his character that the scandal press had ignored and being my brother could rely upon him. If need be, he could contact legal experts in Scotland and seek direction if he came up against something he couldn't verify for himself. My brother was still serving the life sentence imposed upon him for a crime he hadn't committed.

I read the letter with hungry eyes this was my first communication in over one year from anyone outside China except for the British consul. I had received money and a parcel and that devastating telegram about Lochy but this was a letter and I needed that connection desperately. Returning the letter and thanked Lenny profusely.

The floor above us was the translation unit. Most of the work they were doing was in English or Russian. Lenny was the English expert as Hong Kong schooling was all carried out using the British education system. It was known throughout Asia that if you had traveled overseas for a university degree, especially to the United Kingdom or the USA, that degree held more weight than the same degree taken at universities in other parts of the world.

The Chinese prison system utilises the skills of inmates to earn money for the upkeep of the jail. This was 1992 China was moving into the world of foreign trade and hoping to join the WTO translation work was good business. Lenny had the job of translating our outgoing and incoming mail informing me a job he didn't enjoy doing. As the time passed this link with Lenny became a vital line to keeping my sanity. I was getting information beforehand about my incoming mail and had several more back door mail drops from him. Lenny was born in Hong Kong but he had family living in London. He was serving fifteen years for money missing from the safe where he managed a five-star hotel in Shanghai.

It seemed like a long time ago that I'd read that letter waiting patiently for it to be given to me officially so that I could reply. I waited another month before being called to the office and handed it officially God only knows how far up the party ladder it had gone before clearance. I kept a straight face when receiving it but wanted to scream this letter arrived a month ago. As the months went by it appeared that there was a pattern forming. Incoming mail took so long to be sent out and delivered that we would often write again asking why they hadn't replied to the last one. This overlapping of correspondence caused a lot of problems not only for me but for everyone. It was a deliberate systematic chipping away process to break down our connection with the outside world, including family. The following month writing all the details that my brother had asked for as I didn't trust to send my only copies of the indictments and verdict papers for fear they may go missing in the post. Or more to the point; not be posted at all. The mail was collected once each month and I was feeling better that thing seemed to be moving along well enough now having drafted my petition outline for my brother to proofread and sort out the proper legal terminology. I had the momentary sense of achievement that you could actually touch, such as a letter; to eventually get the facts out filled me with hope.

Chapter Fiftynine: Letter To The Court

Gao Ji Ren Min Fa Yuan.
Hong Qiao Lu 1200
Shanghai 200335.

To whom it concerns.
My name is Lauchlan Campbell, I am a British national currently serving fifteen
a Year sentence at Shanghai Tilanqiao prison.
I am presenting this appeal petition so that it be viewed with the essential nature
of Equity in mind complying with the ethics of the legal profession.
My appeal petition is based upon two points.
My criminal case number is 24 1992.

I was sentenced to fifteen years imprisonment by the Shanghai Intermediate
People's court on 1992/3/23, this resulted from being wrongly indicted by the
Shanghai People's procuratorate for a substance that I did not possess.
I believe there has been a violation of the Chinese Criminal Law article 136
Clause 1.
I am presenting this statement of facts for your viewing and consideration under
the Chinese Procedural Law Part 3 Chapter 5 Article 149.

Sincerely, Lauchlan Campbell.

Chapter Sixty: Tooth Fairy

I had a very pleasant surprise one cold autumn day when I was called to go see the dentist over at the hospital. I was escorted by JK without a guard. As we strolled by other blocks JK pointed out that this block was also a baseball cap factory, that one makes clothing, another block made leather footballs and so on. I'd wanted to work rather than sit all day and mentioned that to JK he soon assured me I wouldn't like it one little bit. Going on to explain that the assignment tasks had to be met and very often the prisoners worked throughout the night to fulfill them. But I still thought that would be better than doing nothing all day.

On arrival at the hospital a few cons greeted JK, looking at me and then asking a barrage of questions. "Is it true that the foreigners can have cigarettes?" or "if they pay 10,000 Yuan that they can cut off one year of their sentence? I thought if that were only true then could go home for around £14,500 including my ticket. JK ignored most questions and we sat outside the dentist's office. I asked JK what this was all about but he told me he didn't know. I hadn't made any dental appointment or request to see a doctor. This was unusual ground to be on especially being in a hospital area. I was paranoid to say the least walking about without a guard. The office door opened and out came a guy holding his jaw. The dentist, came over to us a lady in her thirties smiled and called something to JK who in turn beckoned me to follow him into the room. I was beckoned to sit on the chair used for dental work and still inquiring from JK as to why I am here. It was the name Lochy that perked my ears up, then hearing it used again, intervened asking JK why she is using my name? She isn't, that is your son's name, isn't it? Yes, that's correct why asking excitedly. The lady told JK that my son was well and healthy and she understood how I was feeling, not being able to see neither him. It was when she told JK that she had arranged for Lochy to return for further treatment, this time with me in mind that really broke me up. There were tears in my eyes and I almost cried in front of her. It was arranged that we return to the hospital on Tuesday of the next week.

I wouldn't be able to meet him but would get to see him and was told never to mention this to anyone, as the lady would suffer the consequences. I walked across the yard back to our cellblock my heart pumping blood with renewed faith in mankind. The Chinese legal system was new to me but one thing was clear, you never went against the Communist Party or any authority for that matter. I was humbled by what this lady was prepared to do from her compassionate heart.

Chapter Sixtyone: Close To The Government

I had often lay at night thinking of killing people in my mind putting up a fight against tyrants and dictators. I saw myself doing what was right by eliminating police and government corruption. It was just another fantasy and kept it close to my chest in the fear that maybe was going insane. I was like a light switch going off and on and could easily be wired up to the eyeballs by some of the tactics used against us by the authorities. They wanted us to remain at a distance and because of my already somewhat isolated position, they tried me out. One evening after the October sport events were underway myself along with the Chinese prisoner, who normally took charge of the locals plus JK and our unit leader Benny the Goodman Benny was telling me that from the local convicts had heard that Campbell has leadership qualities and that he wants to work. The Goodman went on about labor is the best method of reform; the rewards are good if you work hand in hand with the government. I was getting a reform spiel till he said we would want you to take note on the other foreigners and report your findings to Jin Feng. I was gob smacked and looked at JK as if he was a traitor and being somewhat naïve when answered. No, I couldn't do that. Policing others is not my job and was really annoyed at the very idea of him asking me to be an informer. Benny the Goodman had a thin smile and a confident straight back. He got up from his chair and stood with his hands behind his back and could see that maybe had upset him in some way but didn't know how or why until after that little meeting.

After leaving the office I went directly over to Cranky and Bull and told them the story about this reporting on them business. It was something you just didn't do and if this Grad had been reporting, then we would have to be more careful, whatever we said in front of him. I left it at that and went off to get ready for bed. JK spoke with me while brushing my teeth explaining that you cannot refuse to cooperate with the government. I asked him what the fuck he was talking about by "Not refuse to cooperate with the government?"

JK went on to tell me that when asked to cooperate by reporting on the others I should have agreed. I retorted and asked him are you a fucking spy as well? I got the surprise of my life when he said yes and then went on to explain that he didn't report anything useful. It was all 'Glue mixing' His choice of words baffled me and had to inquire as to the intended meaning of 'Glue mixing 'He explained that every month he handed in his ideological report to prove he was reforming and to gain the model prisoner award he put in good reports on what he sees around him. This would reduce his sentence he explained. Then went on to tell me he gave some reports on others behavior, which aren't good. He saw mistrust in my expression now but he pushed on to try winning me over to his side again. I would have to re assess my opinion about JK; but then after all, he did get my letter out. I now needed to get my petition out and was preparing it and would need his help. I left the suggestion with JK about getting out a large document with all translation work done by him to be sent onto the Supreme court in Beijing and another to Scotland. I could see his eyes reflect a wicked glint at the prospect of doing business with the Triads. JK liked to be involved it gave him face plus a profit.

I had been permitted to buy a small typewriter from the education department and was practicing from a book on learning to type, A to Z sort of method. Being impatient with the structure and kept falling onto two fingers one thumb and getting on with whatever job needed done. I'd drafted six pages since my chat with JK and passed them onto him for translation. He wanted one thousand Yuan that was a lot of money then, £120 at the bank exchange rate during that period. That was equal to more than three-month wages for a guard. I asked him if he had gone crazy or what but he went on to explain this letter is going to the Beijing court. If anyone was caught passing it out, he would be punished very severely by the party. JK went on to say "You don't have to pay me anything for translation; you're my friend and the money is for this guard." "Does he know it's for me?" "No!" JK lied.

Chapter Sixtytwo: Psychic Pain

I was closing the window opposite my cell one day when hearing a commotion in the yard below. Despite the noise my curiosity had got the better of me and looked down. I saw two Chinese cons pulling a basket into the yard. Hearing the wailing screams of a cat I tried to get my head further out of the barred window to see more. The two cons appeared square in the yard right in under me. Another con came out with a bucket full of boiling water and threw it over the cat. It was a sound that should have broken the glass. The cat screamed continuously, my teeth gritted and my skin shrank and then a minute later another bucket was thrown over it. This went on for what seemed ages until the cat went silent then seeing it being tipped out of the basket onto the ground it looked tiny. One of the cons picked it up and tied it by the hind legs to wire mesh in the yard. Then he skinned it I couldn't believe what I had just seen it was somewhat disturbing. Going up our corridor I got hold of JK and told him about it. JK didn't seem in any way phased by what happened JK told me that it would be eaten and it wasn't uncommon. I started to lose it a little and raised my voice to him angrily. It annoyed me that JK wasn't bothered. I started to spiel about animal rights then went on into a rap full of pent-up frustrations. I didn't know why but when emotionally upset always returned to what I considered an injustice whether put upon me or someone else. I would lose the plot on what started me off to begin with but knew the cat scenario had triggered something in me. Then other things would return to annoy me.

I returned to sit in my cell to calm down but still wasn't happy about incoming and outgoing mail. The snail mail was still the norm at least one month minimum going out. I hadn't had my petition dealt with and wanted to know why the system was all contradictory. It had effects on my psyche it had a crack in it and pain was seeping in when needing to get it out. JK came over as if by reading my mind and explained that my petition would go out to a Chinese address first and be re posted from there. On hearing this good sense of security, and nodding my approval. The way to pay was also arranged by JK and was to have my family send money to the address JK would put in along with the petition letter. I would also pay our triad connection by buying things from the monthly shop or give some clothing or other contraband of which I still had plenty and being only too pleased at utilizing it by finding a way out of here without censorship. A Letter getting to where you want it to be is often vital. I had already drafted my petition and handed it over to authorities here at the prison. I'd sent it by registered mail and received a receipt in confirmation of when it was sent. Three months passed and I still hadn't received any notice of whether it was received or not. I was ripping with paranoia and just didn't believe a word these Chinese authorities told me. I wanted to have it sent for sure and had asked the British consul to send it for me which they did then months later they received a letter from the Chinese justice bureau stating the petition must come from the Petitioner. It would be sent by underground mail to my son Scott. He would pass the petition to be redrafted by my brother then given to a translating company in Glasgow and finally sent to the court in Beijing by a family member. Having also enclosed him the article in Chinese law where it states that family can petition on my behalf. It would get out regardless of the cost. I still struggled on with writing letters to the court and to the British Consul seeking their help on this legal issue. I was informed by the consul office that they could not assist further than they already had. The consul had sent me a copy of a letter which I signed at the detention cells regarding me signing over money from their office into my possession. I had to prove that the confiscated money on my verdict wasn't illegal earnings. The fact was it was sent to the consul office in Shanghai via the Foreign office in London. It was sent by my brother Robert. It was just plain common sense that my brother's money couldn't be confiscated as he wasn't accused nor involved in any part of my travels in China. My head was thumping and I asked JK to get me something for it he returned minutes later and handed me one white pill saying this will help. I swallowed the pill lay my head down and rested no screaming cat. I then awoke hours later to the sound of cons returning from work with one head ache gone and another beginning.

Chapter Sixtythree: Chinese Angel

As was promised I saw Lochy on November 18th 1992 and was dying to shout out to him but kept my cool knowing that I could get someone else into serious trouble. I could only watch him walking along the yard, going into the hospital building. I was watching from the widow above. Then once more half hour later coming out again, I must have only set eyes on him thirty seconds in total but enough to let me see that he looked strong and carried his posture well. The experience of those detention cells would be causing some scarring to his youthful psyche. I returned to my cell block at least knowing my son he looked good from a distance but in reality, had no idea how he was coping in those dungeons of doom. The detention holding cells were really dirty and who knows who he sharing that cell with.

Chapter Sixtyfour: Visiting MP

November moved into December and we had two British MPs visit the jail. I didn't say much other than asked had they seen my son to which they replied simply "No. Any chance of getting me a transfer back to the UK?" they said no "I mentioned my petition but it seemed the legal system in China was a closed shop even to them. I couldn't get a response from my inquiries from anyone nor get these authorities to adhere to anything and wasn't allowed to see my lawyer anymore because the case was closed. It was the writing and re –writing to the court waiting that was grinding me down. Letters took at least one month and longer before they got sent. It was a deliberate stalling tactic for all despot systems the world over. Communications are the key.

The first principle of control in a siege cut the communication and isolate from assistance to control and oppress. All the while their prison law stated that "Any prisoner who appeals or petitions or does not accept the verdict of the court cannot have their sentence reduced" It was a typical 'catch 22' position. I was pursuing a petition against being dealt with under the terms of the wrong article erroneously allowing a sentence over the maximum of 7 years and was now serving 8 years over the lawful maximum allowed by law but to pursue this point meant that I couldn't get remission or reduction from my sentence until with-drawing that petition. Truly thinking I was entitled to at least eight years knocked off my sentence once the High court saw the error of substance change on the appeal verdict so waited with the belief that one day, they would have to acknowledge my petition. After all, it is in their legal system that all inmates have that right to appeal. I still had faith then and patiently waited. The two MPs departed with words similar to well stick in their old boy and left me batting for Britain but they departed with at least some insight that we were at least being fed.

Chapter Sixtyfive: Good News

The next news received was the best I'd heard since my sentence. I was visited again by Alan and the Shanghai PSB. Alan was less cocksure and seemed to have been knocked down a peg somewhere along the line. It was another young guy who did the talking now and asked me with a smile "How are you Mr. Campbell fine until meeting him nodding towards his comrade" expecting more of their intimidation tactics. The humor went over his head. He proceeded to tell me that my "Son can go home" if I would send a telegram to my family telling them to send five thousand pounds into my account at the Consuls office. I agreed immediately to comply with that ransom demand but added the condition that wouldn't sign any money over to them or the court unless first assured by the British consul that my son would be released.

It was a short visit and was given the permission to write home and a letter and also to the consul office in Shanghai. It was on December 24th Christmas eve1992 after spending six months in the Shanghai Sheridan. My son arrived back in the United Kingdom having paid fifty thousand Yuan fine. The equivalent of five thousand pounds sterling and was deported. He spent Christmas day with his family and friends at home Lochy by name Lucky by nature. That was a massive burden from my back and had expected he would get 5 to 10 years and sharing that with him in these surroundings would have been another story and experience. I was just so happy that he was home.

Chapter Sixtysix: The Unspoken Word

 When the other guys heard the news about my son, instead of being happy about the outcome, some moaned and complained about the severity of theirs sentences in comparison with Lochy. I could relate with what they were saying but Lochy was the innocent party in all this, that's was the difference fooling myself never letting them know he knew the contents. He was only taking the chance to help prevent his father being possibly shot for a piece of cannabis. I had also expected Lochy to cop at least a minimum of five years with what he was bust with. As it worked out, he couldn't be held responsible at all as a juvenile and was given the substance by the prison authorities during a visit. He never opened the case and never saw the contents. The cannabis was concealed thanking all the Gods and Buddha twice for taking care over my son and not letting him dwell in this world of prison darkness. That karma was mine. It was quite a happy ending for me to the year 1992. That was one year and four months of incarceration now only awaiting the response to my petition. But beyond that had nothing on my agenda to worry about now that Lochy was home safe with his family and friends and no more dope concealed.

Chapter Sixtyseven: Prisoners Abroad

The cameras rolled as they started calling our name out one by one. When he called 'Campbell' I would step forward and be handed my mail, shake hands, smiles all around. Next! Having received two letters; one was my first correspondence from a group of very decent people forming an organization called Prisoners Abroad. It was a newsletter and their Christmas card spread inside was drawn by other prisoners. It was something we foreigners could relate with here and I felt I could contribute something by writing back. It was quite an eye opener when I read how many British are imprisoned abroad and the conditions some lived under, I hadn't any complaints this day eating Christmas remote parts of the world It was a pleasant afternoon we were at ease with one another, past conflicts put aside. It was just three British guys, two German, and one guy from the USA sitting around a table on Christmas day eating Christmas dinner.

The Christmas festivities were of no consequence to the communist run Chinese Prison system. So, it was quite a surprise then when they did serve the Christmas meal. We had previously got permission and together to hang decorations supplied to us by the guard's gofers. Christmas lights and a tree were also set up. Bull and I designed a blackboard with a Christmas theme in the background using color paper and chalks. A round table was set up outside the guard's door where the space was biggest and could seat enough for eight people with space to move around. There was also a karaoke machine with the entire kit and caboodle to record as well.

The propaganda camera crew turned up to film us being served and so well treated. It was quite an event. Once we were all seated, we were served with plates of roast turkey, roast chicken, grilled fish, roast beef and numerous plates of vegetables adding color to the already wonderful spread. The education guard called for silence for his little speech. He wished us all a happy Christmas and knowing that we were far away from our homes and families, he wished that we could at least enjoy the hospitality of the Chinese People's Republic prison during our festive season. I was quite taken aback by his correctness towards the Christian festivities as had already experienced one guard's anger when asking about Buddha via JK. The guard only followed the principles of Mao's red book where Gods were to be avoided.

You would never have expected that this little scene was inside one of the harshest prisons in Asia and known throughout China to be the cruelest, most murderous by executions, held the most prisoners, serving the longest sentences, and the prison reform program the fiercest. They were getting more than their money's worth out of us in propaganda value and momentarily felt that the way things were going; could cope well enough with prison in China. The Christmas food lasted three days. We ate like Kings and watched television we even had a video in English and watched a film. It is cold in late December so we sat around wrapped in thick coats with woolly scarves and hats. I had just received another parcel from my brother Robert in London. One of the clothing items was a thick woolen car coat styled jacket, really thick and warm. The label inside said 'London Fog' that label would become a familiar sight the following year mass produced in the prison workshops. China didn't adhere to copy right laws. It was now into the New Year. First January 1993 and the same applied with the food again. Served up a full on spreads that would be welcome at any table on the planet. It was very clear from the start that the prison system would respect the traditions of the foreigners in their festivities. The prison department wanted the foreigners to take part in a safety play. The good food had to be repaid in some form or other. It was all good fun for a while doing something different contributing to more propaganda.

1.   DO NOT LITTER.
     Bull and I did the fruit peeling scene. This is someone throws the banana skin onto the floor and that causes an accident
2.   FORBIDDEN KNIFE. Cranky Grad and Hans were huddled together cutting water melon with a jail made knife.
3.   SWITCH OFF.

Vern was simulating putting his hand into a mincing machine in the kitchen while the power was still on thus getting an electric shock. JK told us this safety play we put on would go onto the reform file. saying that several departments within the prison need to stamp the approval before our remission papers can be sent to the court. It wasn't just one third automatic reductions. In China you had to be re sentenced again by a Judge. So that was our first clue to that we might be getting something taken off. It was the prison department preparing papers for the court to prove that we are active in our reform. As it happened, we won a prize for our performance. We were told we would all be given a certificate of merit. JK told us that were the first step to getting your sentence cut. We were all delighted to hear this having to admit my fantasy and hope of release scenes were fading fast. The illusion bubble never ever burst completely though.

Chapter Sixtyeight: Does Time Fly?

I had been taking clippings from the China Daily English Newspaper 1993/1/9 paper Stated.

Xiao Yang Vice President of the Supreme people's procuratorate.
"Feedback on their mistakes can be passed onto the procuratorate at different levels.
Through public opinion and supervision, it can be redressed and reduce mistakes.

I wrote him a letter but never got any reply what was going on with my petition. This was madness and I was just completely ignored.

Chapter Sixtynine: Fireworks

The Chinese New Year was the main annual event although they celebrate many times, during the year. It was quite different from our Christmas celebrations. The Chinese New Year date differs depending on the position of the moon. When it came to setting up decorations and the laying out of food etc.it was nothing short of spectacular. Here was where you find out who are who and the guys who do what needs to be done. Black Fish Triads were obvious in that they smoked cigarettes in places were all would never dare and also only on holiday occasions. They also had swaggering antics and were over loud. Some prisoners less financially off had been collecting all year as a group to be able to put out a spread at this special time of year. It was their way of showing face and respect to their ancestors Gods friends and family. What a weird system this country has where the communist party propagates non-religious reasoning yet the jail was full of ancient tradition and believers.

The Chinese New Year was a very special event and the place was rocking. It's the same the world over when Karaoke is concerned; people all think them brilliant singers and had a great time considering the venue location. Every table in the place had invited me to join them and out of respect for them, ate from every table. The other westerners were invited to the one table, along with JK and the Chinese guard's gofer. I did the rounds and had a few drinks of Mai Tai a strong alcohol spirit that Lao Hun from the Black Jade Triad had supplied plus also acquired myself two packets of 555 cigarettes and a lighter. Having secured a small bottle of Mai Tai which JK told me was put into my storeroom along with a bottle of very cold beer. I called Vern first and he had a hit of spirit then a gulp of beer while I kept the watch out. Then one by one they all did except Cranky, who declined. Then handed out the cigarettes as well and because being amongst the locals, could get the guy in charge of the washroom to open up the back gate and let me use it for a quick smoke.

That area was my new domain, and had to secure that space as a place to access whenever needed especially now that Lenny had mail at times. I'd done a bit of trade with the washroom guy, giving him a bar of strawberry soap from the Body Shop, which he'd passed onto his wife at a visit, to her delight. That washroom area was the most vital area for the main reason of reading my mail without waiting a month or so before the authorities passed it out officially. So did more Body shop soap trade with the wash room man in exchange that we could keep contact with the world. It was great for the change in atmosphere.

The Chinese New Year brought all sorts of colourful television shows. We also played a football and basketball competition amongst our own unit. The prison staff was at a minimum and the parties went on until after midnight. It was getting to be just too much noise for me now. The fun had gone and all you could hear were guys shouting much too loud. Chinese chess pieces being slammed onto the board playing cards flutter like a fallen ceiling fan. The constant clicks of the black and white pieces of tiles used in yet another chess game. Being still new to it and couldn't take it all in. The New Year in Scotland is a celebration that people respect and where the tradition is important so felt instinctively that the Chinese were also fiercely patriotic and it wouldn't be wise to disrespect any of their customs or to annoy anyone during this period. I had spoken with my new friend Lenny about what was my acceptance in the jail? Having told him part about JK and my dealings with him his reply was to be careful. This guy Lenny was risking it big time for me by handing over my mail. As far as he was concerned, he came from Hong Kong and not China. As it usually happens during a long period of inactivity, some guys get bored and fights break out. Whilst was going into my cell the last night of festivities when I heard an explosion turning around saw a red plastic thermos bottle take flight. The bottle had been thumped onto the head of a guy sitting in front of the television. Seeing a few guys grab at the attacker and then punches and boots flew in. The guy was dragged into a cell and then a blanket thrown over his head to quite the victim down if he struggles, he suffocates. The con was wise enough just to curl up and take his kicking.

I felt like getting involved as the odds weren't in the favor of the one being set upon but wasn't ready to take that role on, yet had done it in the past at the detention cell, turning back and walked to where the television was and sat down. Seeing most people weren't paying any heed to the situation so we watched what was happening on the screen and ignored what was going on around us.

Chapter Seventy: Lao San Mao

There is this young character age around 12 called San Mao. It means 'Three hairs' in Chinese. San Mao is an orphan living in abject poverty on the streets of Shanghai. It was a television program I never missed and sat eyes glued to the box whilst sitting on the floor in the front row in our wing, surrounded by the locals. I didn't get to watch the other TV set the one that had been put into the small sitting area for Western viewing only. This was due to another clash about what programs to watch. It was a typical jail scenario where there was always someone wanting to control the channels. Cranky was the culprit this time it was usually whoever got there first picked up the remote. Then Cranky and Bull started a monopoly with it. It was bound to happen sooner or later that two people would want to watch different programs running at the same time myself being one that seldom went to watch TV since it was all in Chinese, it didn't make sense to sit and stare at pictures, unless it was football, wildlife or spectacular scenery although I did occasionally watch it and when discovering San Mao that was my spot.

The television workshop was also on our floor, supplying us with a rotten 12 inch black and white set. When saying TV workshop, it really had multiple purposes. It ran back-to-back with our cells. An exact replica of our living area but now turned into a money-making facility making items such as clothes and bags the problem arose when Bull and Cranky both wanted to watch something else something other than San Mao and reasoned that as I didn't watch many programs and I'd slotted this time. We discussed it but nobody wanted to give way. Bull told me that to sit with the locals and watch and Cranky agreed. I knew they would rather just say "Fuck off" but couldn't but took the hint and took up my new seating. I got the message ok; it was a democracy and they had out voted me, growling at Cranky said he was an asshole, using his USA colloquium then smacked him right hook on the jaw, knocking him over backwards. Bull threw his hands up and said nothing. JK came on the scene while Cranky was shouting, "I'm taking a lawsuit against you Campbell"

That incident went into a written report by Cranky and Bull about how the event happened. That was the requirement, if you lodged any complaint it had to be done in writing. I also wrote my account. The outcome was that apologies to Cranky and the group then totally split from the other foreigners. I wasn't to share any of their Space and complied willingly. Now having a front row viewing on a colored set and although I didn't understand what was being said, the scenes spoke for themselves. They reminded me of when a boy in Glasgow living at George Street. One minute walk from 'George Square' and used to run around with the arse torn out of my trousers. Sometimes having a big pair of welfare tackity boots but mostly none at all a street urchin with raggedy clothes and a snotty nose, begging and thieving for my supper. My mother would be waiting for me and my brothers or sisters to bring up a cigarette or better still, a couple of pennies. San Mao being an orphan was close to the heart and really liked the characters in the Chinese period of that time around the 1930s when Shanghai was known as a port with multiple delights. A Shangri-La. It was while watching San Mao one of the local guys joked around with JK and seeing JK wasn't laughing asked him what the problem was. I saw he was still agitated after the show ended and was surprised when he told me "Lao San Mao" was prison slang and it referred to someone within the prison system who had served their time and can go home but had to stay like an orphan with nowhere to go. I listened to the story and it did make sense some people after serving 20 plus years didn't have any other place to go. Or their families disown them as JK's had. These guys who stay on at the jail don't have to work but do have to help out. Now understanding why JK was hurting. He only had one brother and that brother could set him free by signing a responsibility paper for him but wouldn't. 'Bastard' I remember thinking that my brothers would come and serve part of my sentence for me if they could. It was from that day on that JK was adopted he was my brother and I stood by him.

Chapter Seventyone: I Like Pandas

I was sitting on my own looking out to nowhere on a warm June day when this new guy walked up to me with a spring in his step, stuck out his hand and said, "Hi my name's Dom" He was twenty-eight and had been sentenced to two years for possession of 200 grams of cannabis. I got on with him immediately. He liked football and knew people that I knew in London. Dom was the friend of a lovely lady called Missy who was now living with my brother Roberts friend Camay. It's a small world right enough. Dom also played the guitar. So, Vern and Dom got together and did a lot of practicing. Everyone really got along well with him, maybe because he didn't drip with paranoia as I and the others did. It was typical of him to take whatever came at him, undaunted and with a smile. He would be neither intimidated nor impressed by the guards nor their point nor ideological reprogramming system.

For example, what he wrote as his third monthly ideological report. "I Like Pandas." Full stop. I loved that attitude and it was something special the way he totally cocked his snoot in the faces of the prison regime. He was proof that the rest of us were all in some way tied up with the Chinese prison reform regulations chasing the carrot but still all in self-denial of it. I was certainly counting those merit points and could see my name go up the board quicker than the other foreigners. It was a way out and it was beginning to dawn on me that it was the only way out for me. It was becoming more and more clear that no court decision was going to be reached. I had lodged the petition from every angle and avenue imagined and still had no response coming into to the autumn of 1993.

It was madness all these officials coming from jails outside of Shanghai to see the foreigners and how we were treated. It was like playing the part in a movie. All the Chinese cons would either be at the workshop out of sight, or they would be sitting in an orderly fashion head bowed to the table studying the rules and regulations which they would be quizzed on later. It was now one year plus being in this jail. I done a radio interview, wrote articles for the prison newspaper and played more parts than a Hollywood actor trying to gain favor so as to lead to a reduction in my sentence. It was all to lead to nothing. One day I asked a passing visiting committee, who were a mixture of police, prosecutors and Judges? Why wasn't my petition to the court being dealt with? It was now years since arriving here I was exaggerating and over a year waiting for a reply but wasn't exaggerating and was assured that there was a long waiting list in the Beijing court and my petition would eventually be dealt with. I didn't care what they said as JK had already done the job with the back door mailman.

Chapter Seventytwo: Going Abroad

JK came up with an idea to write a book and make cassette tapes for English study classes. All the foreigners were up for it and wanted to contribute. It was a project to help the Chinese people at any age group. JK said it should be aimed at middle school level, no one complained. JK had written a report to the education department at the prison. Going through the proper channels, first of all to get the permission to do the project and secondly to be financed for purchase of required materials to put the project into action. Weeks passed before someone broached the subject of the English study tapes we were supposed to make. JK hadn't told any of us that he had been refused funding from the prison for his little project. It came to my notice from a smear on his character from that stumped finger guard's gofer who was always prying into everybody else's business and could see from the smirk on his face he was delighted to tell me that JK was taken to the office and criticized for having to close contact with the foreigner's and their ways. I approached JK about this and he confirmed it word for word having already purchased a typewriter and 10 blanks 90-minute tapes and a bunch of batteries gave this all to JK for his use on the project. Vern added 10 more tapes and the use of his recording machine then Cranky added 10 more so we started to record. It was the Total investment of £134 sterling. That was JK in his element. He had a project to work on and didn't realize then that long term prisoners need projects to survive. It was a great big bubble and I jumped right on it and floated into imaginary benefits that we would gain for this worthy project. The book title Going Abroad started out as a trip to the consuls' office. It explained the proper greetings and introduction. It then went on to then teaching how to go about to ask for a visa application. Then helped him through the procedure, booking a ticket, airport tax, arrival and departures. It was the basic A to Z in visa application and airport navigation.

The six of us helped out and having different accents, added quality to the teaching that other professional teaching programs lacked. It really did become JK's baby. As it worked wonders and continued to improve, A few guards from other buildings started to pay interest in learning English. Our tape came into demand all over the jail. Then when the cons wanted to learn English, it became a business. JK and Black Jade handled that. It was even rumored a class was to be set up and we the foreigners could work as teachers. I knew most were willing to do this but prison politics got in the way again. This particular communist administration didn't mix to well with western ways. JK's book 'Going Abroad' went underground. This fucking system didn't want you to achieve anything new.

Chapter Seventythree: Open Window

1994/3/14.
Hello Scott.
This is just a short note to ask you to do a few things for me.
The enclosed letter has to be sent on to the USA the address is on   the one I sent you before and is underlined in green. This is what I want you to do for me.

Send a copy of the drug report to the same address in USA. If you don't have it get it from Tommy and Xerox it. You will probably receive $100 from USA can you make me a special card and conceal the $100 you know how from past messages you sent me.

The code to use is Merry Xmas old man.
Can put £50 into another one I need to pay the mailman here.
You can Xerox copy the mail and keep it on file but make sure you send them.
Send me a message saying Ashton had her eighth birthday when you get this letter.
Take care from Dad.

PS Pass on for me.

Hello Robert Tommy.
This is a stiff I want to say a few things about.
First of all, I have a friend here from Shanghai who just got out.
He can be trusted and will help you in many ways.
If you Pete or Sue plan to come he will guide you around.
Robert this country is booming. I am now working in the fabrics shop making anoraks. It doesn't matter what it is, they make everything in jail. Bobbie Glen and Tommy have been telling me you are trying to help me out. I really appreciate that bro; this place has been cracking me up. They don't send or give us mail. It is a bad regime with no regards to prisoner's rights. I swore at a guard and he set five Chinese cons on me. The scene here is bad 90% grasses so I am a loner. You know there is no remission here 15 years is 15 years. I can get it cut by working hard and I do. But then some big mouth tries to be funny and bang I've decked him. I am trying to get a transfer back to the UK to serve my time if not then to another jail in China less hostile than this place.

I've managed to see a psychiatrist a couple of times but it is not easy the medical set up is nearly nonexistent. It is pure desperation to get attention regarding our mail but they ignore me Can you get Tommy or my MP or Prisoners Abroad to get in touch with the Justice department here asking for a transfer out of this hell hole.
I will list a statement of facts that must be sent onto the British consulate in

Beijing. My petition is being blocked. Thanks, Robert, for all your help and Hello to Tommy and family in Scotland.

Give Vonny Jason Joshua and wee Scottie your Dog a big hello from Lockie. P.S. Thank Big Andy, Marsy and Bobby Glen for sending those parcels.

Chapter Seventyfour: A Rebound

It wasn't until another several months later, nearing the end of 1994 that I was visited by the PSB again along with the prison Warden and every ranking official in the prison system. I was called to the office on our landing. As I passed up the wing, saw eyes dart away from me. It doesn't happen often that you get the full ranks turning up to visit you personally it had happened once in a lifetime with Lochy but surly not twice. The office was jam packed I was crammed in among them. It was such a shock when the PSB guy stuck my petition in my face looking at it and but didn't speak. "Who sent this for you Mr. Campbell?" he inquired. I handed it into this office to be sent" was my reply. There were a few sentences exchanged in Chinese and then the PSB guy said this is not the same one" then a minute later our guard Benny produced the same size and color envelope opened it and retrieved my petition. I was a bit hot under the collar by now being caught with my back door petition and into the bargain, that liar of a guard had just pulled my official petition from his drawer. I said "Hasn't that been sent yet? It had sent it by registered mail and even got the receipt years ago. It then came to dawn on me that these people can give a receipt to your family for a bullet to your brain. What was a registered letter receipt? It was all Government Issue franks. How naive we can become when living in a democracy or at least, the illusion of one.

JK went on to tell me that I had violated a regulation and must confess and inform on the person who sent it for me. Replying said had given it to the British consul during a visit. The PSB was quick to respond and brought to my attention that the British consul had my draft returned along with the message that it should be sent by the petitioner. Having momentarily forgotten that but carried on regardless to say that it had been two copies in total and had asked the consul to copy my petition and send one to my family, which in fact had done. "It must have been sent by my son" I went on denying any knowledge of this petition still loosely held in my hand. A few more words were spoken then JK told me to go to my cell and collect my toothbrush and towel on the way he whispered the frank on the envelope stamps is Chinese. I was arguing the point thinking it was sent from the England I was off to the cooler in winter.

Chapter Seventyfive: Body Parts

I was taken across to another building in the hospital wing and put into a sort of white room. Being escorted by a guard besides JK and asked him what was going on. JK told me that I had gone against the government and was a subversive and would be isolated for a while. He made it clear to me that it had to be sealed lips from my end, by his eye contact and the fear of exposure ripped from him in a way only another prisoner can sense. Going into this confinement without complaint and spent my first night in a hospital like surrounding with a television in the room. Two Chinese cons did the nightshift guard duty. The following day on came the interrogation crew and kept to my story that I had given it to the consul and they had sent it onto my family. Feeling sure that of getting away with that until it was reminded to me that the petition was sent from Shanghai, The postage frank would tell what place it had come from but at least, not the person. For that information if known would cause a lot of pain for someone to suffer a lot more than just loss of remission and just replied I don't know and remained silent. Being threatened with all sorts of punishments from adding to my sentence to not having visits or sending out letters to my family was all nothing new. The two Chinese cons tried to go to the bully while the guards were about showing the party support. All the while JK was interpreting for them and then telling me in English, "Don't bother with them cons they are told to do that by the guards. If you were Chinese, they would beat the shit out of you but because you're connected to Black Fish, they wouldn't dare try" JK told me later that they had asked him if I could trade something with them. JK kept that avenue open as that section of the jail was known to be quite brutal.

It was here at the hospital heard of the death sentence inmates having organs removed after execution. Three days on and my sleeping pattern went haywire. It wasn't until returning found out that I had been away for three days it seemed those days disappeared. But did remember that my petition hadn't been sent and as soon as I got the next consul visit told them the story. I wasn't really surprised when they politely repeated their get out clause "We cannot intervene in your legal matters" and was ready to scream "They aren't sending my fucking legal petition" Instead, just asked him what he personally would do in my situation. If you petition that means you haven't acknowledged or accepted your guilt. According to their law, whilst in that procedure, you are denied remission from your sentence. If the court doesn't or can't acknowledge your petition, then it can never be dealt with and you can never get remission from your sentence. Thus, you are stuck in a catch 22. If it was me Mr. Campbell, I would look at whatever way would get me out of here the quickest then left that consul meeting with other thoughts not only relating with remission.

Being the only foreigner who'd lodged a petition. The others were waiting on the outcome from mine as their outcome when they appealed would likely be the same. This way they could keep both options open for early release Where as I had closed one of mine. The pressure was on me because the others hadn't petitioned, so they were considered to have accepted their guilt, although nobody had put that in writing yet except Grad. On returning to the cell area that night lay in bed thinking what would be the best thing to do in this situation. Weighing it all up, still figured that was in the right by their own law. Sentenced under the wrong article in their law, why should I back down to oppression when that very intimidation and oppression itself shows that they know that I am right? By my reckoning was due a minimum of 8 years cut off, in accordance with the articles of the Chinese procedural law. That's what kept me hanging on in there.

Chapter Seventysix: Psychiatrist

It was after spring 1995 that meeting up with" Big Ivan" again. Now working at the cutting table in the workshop was making car coats for a company named London Fog having even tried some on for size. This was a Russian contractor and had seen the paperwork but kept these things to myself knowing Cranky had become a collector of information. He seemed to be against everything and anything Chinese. Some of the other foreign inmates wanted to be included in some work projects. The number board merit point system had got to them psychologically as it had me. After being been told at a meeting I was to be given the certificate of merit for my contribution in labor. We got the usual Chairman Mao lecture stating that a person can be reformed through labor and that Campbell had worked also in the evenings when required too. As far as myself was really concerned about was off that narrow landing and didn't want to sit all day looking at a wall. It was good for me to be able to work. Some of the jobs such as last Christmas as making toys were a drag.

One in particular was when you clapped your hands the toy played a tune. The fucking work shop was ding ching a fucking ling dong all day. It drove me mad and ended up smacking one guy in the jaw opposite me and kept on working. I had cracked up momentarily. It was a surreal experience just threw a punch onto the jaw of this guy and then continued to work on as if nothing had happened. He hadn't retaliated maybe due to the triads at hand it was just left as it was. It boiled down to the noise and reckoned it did cause disturbance in my mind. In the Chinese language there is a lot of swear words used they are and not always meant to be personal with my short fuse and not knowing what was said often just reacted impulsively. The Shanghai word Na Lou i.e., means foreign penis. It became as common as was your "grandmother's cunt". And also hearing those terms used on a daily basis got under my skin. It was speech of the angry the uneducated and hooligans. China jails were full of those. Yet meeting with intellectuals and artists was also possible.

I had written a report to see the psychiatrist. In only a few days was called from the workshop and was then escorted by Lenny over to another part of the jail. There was the sign above the door entrance in English saying psychological counseling. I entered and was taken to a small room with a window and sat down Lenny was seated beside me. It was a minute later a guard around my age entered the room he smiled and sat behind a desk. Lenny and the guard had exchanged some conversation. The guard stood up and shook my hand and introduced himself in English I am Mister Wang pleased to meet you he said politely replying Mister Campbell and pleased to meet you too. We were seated and he asked what my problem was and explained about the noise giving him several examples of when the sound penetrates my psyche and causes me to get irritated. I was also getting severe pain in the back of my neck upper spine. It really felt like red hot needles shot into my nervous system. So it was a pleasant surprise when he pulled out cigarettes and offered us one Lenny was happy to have a puff of nicotine so we accepted. It was arranged that we would see him every week and have some counseling. Having a feeling this guard wasn't like most of them encountered but we would see. It was arranged to visit every Wednesday from 1am till 3am.

On returning to the cell block Lenny told me to meet him on the back stair. He had got a parcel from his sister in London and wanted to give me some chocolates. He asked for me to pass some onto Grad for him which could do and did. I had started putting out more letters for Cranky and others charging them $50 and a jar of coffee for that service a very reasonable price for getting important letters out and you wouldn't be sending anything underground unless you deemed it important. I didn't keep the coffee for myself that went to Black Fish and his Triad associates. What I did do was in with needs of my own told my son Scott to photo copy the letter ongoing letters. It was something learned at a very young age 1966 in Barlinnie prison Glasgow whilst waiting to be sent to Borstal was told never to pass on a stiff i.e.," underground letter "before first reading it. The reasoning behind this was you might be delivering your own death warrant having Scott to photo copy them and to keep them for me. It is now proof of my good work in jail although restricted in a communist regime still got messages out uncensored. As the years went by Cranky would forget this dangerous risk some took. I wanted to be able to prove things to certain people. Knowing how people can put a spin onto things to know how to say something foolish and deceitful is easy. But when you have the copy of a hand a written letter which I have in Crank's handwriting and are prepared to show it. Then it does turn the picture in my favor. Yet not knowing they existed then at the time still in jail. I was having less and less to do with the other foreigners me being in the workshop all day. My life was taking new turns every other week getting embraced by the locals it had a lot of ups and as many downs. Finding out that I was just a commodity for some a novelty to some, and a means to get something free for others. But by most was accepted.

Cranks Letter

This is a copy of Cranks letters to his family and friends sent via my son Scott from Glasgow in Scotland. Send by me via Black Fish Triad connection. The contents of this letter explain a lot more about Big Ivan. I worked in the factory. It seems Cranky thought this information was of value. It might have been a trading card for him. If this letter had ever been stopped heads would have surely rolled. One being my own. Oh, thoughtless one. This at least gives you Another insight from someone else.

Please read on.

<u>Read carefully do not lose</u>
After you read write me using an asterisk on the envelope and name underlined. Do not refer to this on your letters.

Now learn the truth and once you are contacted by my hombre MURPH help him get factual evidence so I can petition this GOVT for redress against my 15-year sentence and 10000RMB fine. I also need some help to get things together in two lawsuits against people who have lied to the media about my case. One the number two policeman in China told an international press conference 4 days before my trial that I was smuggling to Japan. Not true there is no smuggling or trafficking in my case and if China doesn't lighten my time your CBS friend Sue Mangione and others are to be contacted with the contents of this letter.
Horror story.
Nov 1990, I wrecked I have the scars still an acquaintance restored vintage Norton Commando motorcycle in Malaysia. No insurance so I owed him $8000. No way could I pay up. 6 heavy months of pressure from JJ and his cousin or brother Marc. (2 Frenchmen) Stupidly I agreed to come to China and do some work for them carrying some hash from one city in Chengdu in Sichuan province. I arrived Chengdu 5/11/1991 but instead of being relieved of these drugs and the $8000 debt I was given more drugs and told by one of the Frenchmen who was traveling on a British passport that he would escort me and the drugs to Shanghai. In Shanghai I was met by JJ and co, who rudely told me that my debt would not be cancelled unless I helped them move this gear out of the country. I flat refused.The hashish was re wrapped and put into the ceiling of the room 707 in the Peace Hotel. I left China still heavily in debt and consistently under harassment from these people.
On 5/11/1991 I stayed at the Jin Jiang Hotel in Chengdu Sichuan w/the person w/ the false British passport. I need a photo copy from this hotel at 36 Sec 2 Ren Min Nan Avenue Chengdu 67002 PRC. Fax 028-558-1849 the hotel registration we both signed. My name and US passport Z6469754 and his are on this form. I will need a Chinese lawyer to get these.
I've tried on my own the authorities mess w/my mail so bad they lie to the US consulate as a matter of policy Chinese Communism is evil, vile, ignorant you name it.
I tried to pay this mob back some money but they physically began threatening me and my girlfriend endlessly. I came back to China a couple of times and tried to get into this hotel room and retrieve the hashish for them. I couldn't get the room. Then these people started to harass my girlfriend's sister as well. That was it. The final straw. So, I got the order to get this stuff once and for all.
I got the telephone number of INTERPOL in France. It is in my telephone book and made sure I could get in this room, retrieve the hash store it in a hotel, fly to my sports assignment in Europe, call Interpol so that they could track these low

lives.

Very important my airline ticket- on Lufthansa airlines to Denmark 3-220-31224725790 are at the US consulate in Shanghai. Get 6 photocopies of this by writing. J.Garriga ASAP as well as my Shanghai Mansions hotel bill.

There is one more witness (Chinese)on my March 7th indictment that didn't appear at Court I need a copy of that indictment.

Mr Ma Yu Min lawyer has report on cannabis that shows what Dama Zhi is. Now need $ for to facilitate this. Write John and Gavin c/o Alan Nana P.O. Box 1027 Bangkok. And explain legal predicament. Maybe $1500 will do. Also, people at Nana should send me shoes shorts etc.

I've written those 12 times and only one answer mail is not getting there. Also, a lawyer in the US is needed to give this appeal an air of authority, Darryl Farrington is a possibility. I also need some political help. I'll make a deal for this. More on that later.

So being in this huge prison was quite a change from the 3mx5m to a 3m x 1m cell.The food improved we got to shower and shave finally etc.
We started a cooking little Rock n Reggae band. I wrote some songs and jokes we toured the brigades giving some good shows, we began teaching English via tapes and generally staying busy. We made friends with the Chinese underground a bit. They don't want us to speak with the Chinese so as not to taint them with our impure western thoughts.Then we had drunken officials insulting us and threats being leveled at us about accepting our sentences.
What could have been a good stay turned to rot and malaise?
The lies and unsent mail stocked up. I went on hunger strike.

Then after the US consulate meeting with H. Hand on 6/24/93 I was taken to the young people's experiment Brigade for ideological reforming. There I sat in isolation for more than eight months. Here I had watched the Chinese forced to work 12-to-14-hour days on exports to Japan with only 5 to 10 minutes for lunch. I had to watch over a dozen kicking hitting or electric cattle prod beatings for essentially nothing, delivered on a regular basis from officers Ming, Chen Wen Shang and Zhang. And when these guys were drunk the madness, they dished out was horrid.

After many of the beatings some were hog tied hoods put on their heads and thrown into a cell with no food for 5-7 days. So they didn't have to crap and were it was below freezing there were no blankets for them all the windows open.

There is a box just outside our brigade for complaints to the prosecutor about abuse. Criminal law art 189 China prohibits corporal punishment to prisoners. However, anyone attempting to approach this box had to cross a line and if you crossed that line, you would be beaten and charged with attempt escape Catch 22. Prisoners 19526, 26899, 6404, 3323, 3778, 25272, 26411, was all beaten. Keep this for the archives.

Since arriving here I've watched millions of items being shipped to the US and

England. All made by forced prison labour. A clear violation of Chinas law and a June 1992 memorandum between the US and China. Most of the stuff is caps (golf/baseball) and it isn't going to break the US But these prisoners sometimes work from 6 to 9pm 7 days a week. So, the officers and higher ups can wear nice clothes smoke Marlboros get drunk etc.

Senators Barbara Boxer, Diane Feinstein, both in California and House of representative Ms. Nancy Pelosi and Maine senator George Mitchell and State depts Mr. Winston Lord would give their right arm for this info below but I need pressure from to allow me to have the two slander libel lawsuits I've filed in China to be heard and my petition for a retrial or reduction to be given a high priority. i.e. visits to China and my case mentioned to high Chinese officials. If they agree then they can have these facts:

1. Cocktail napkins to over 100 Caliif, Ariz Nevada and Colorado restaurant business from this prison. Colo Spg,s restaurant Jose Muldoon's. The Los Angeles Times newspaper, Hurrahs Casinos, BPOE EIK,s clubs.(Chapter 1015,Alameda, Calif) are among these. The Chinese company doing the shipping is Jiaxing Odia- Hygiene Products Service Co Ltd 5/135-S. Morning Road. Shanghai

2. Over 8000 grosses of golf and baseball caps to USA. Labels   inside say Speedway One size fits all. Made in China.

3. Garments to Winmax Fashion International, 2637 El Presidio St Carson Calif.

4. Multi colored toy stuffed turtles to company in Dover.

5. Golf caps to Cobles London England under Outbound REG trademark.

6. Souvenir soccer balls to Japanese Pro League (J League) Teams such as Yokohama Merinos. On and on.

Still the U S Clinton have backed down on human rights stance in lieu of business interests in China. Big Mistake.
China is going to continue to be a serious problem but once they get money, aircraft carriers, they will rule the Pacific Asia. Commies are not benevolent rulers. Watch Hong Kong after 7/1/1997.
This letter is going to cost money eventually so write John / and US Consul for photocopies See China Daily 7/26/93. Love Garry.
On April 21 1992 I went to court for sentence 15 big ones. But at court I meet a Scottish man who had his appeal trial. He was before chief Judge Zhou Jue who allowed his hash THC content to be retested. The result lowered his THC content by 50% in most cases. 5 of us done for hash oil Dama Zhi is an incomprehensible low blow. I never got to cross examine witnesses. I have been screwed so much by the system here it is a wonder I am not pregnant. Oh at least I didn't spend 1-3 yrs in the detention waiting for trial like the Chinese. Beatings thumbnails ripped out etc.
Aargh! So, on June 2nd 1992 five of us came here. It is a wrongful conviction

and false accusation in my case.

Con when you receive this, please stick a £100 crisp dollar bill in a card and send it to the return address in the UK. This will ensure an open window for some time to come. I already know that you know about my plight thru the first slit in the window. Please type the following two pages out so you can read them more easily. 5 more pages of legal and civil lawsuit material will follow. Don't write me and refer to any of these correspondences. Just by the drop of a hint the window could close permanently and some serious injuries occur. Until Murph contacts you keep this top secret away from friends until a plan is made to hit the media.

When you receive this write me and mention the ski area by name that's closet to Leadville. Now after you read this page photo copy and send to John and Gavin Nana, PO Box 1027 Bangkok Thailand. Also, to Heart of Darkness 26-51 street Khan Daun Phenom Penh Cambodia. Also, on the £100 bill put an x on Ben Franklin engraving on his right side.

From a fetid Communist Gulag 1994.
This message is to Chom Nick and the BKK boys has been smuggled through an open window. Possibly more to follow.
I and the others the gang of five are trying to get outside help to rectify our cases in China. All of us were convicted of hashish oil give 8 to 15 years sentence when we only had Hashish. Judges Police interpreters etc. lied.
The false charges were hidden in the Chinese version of the indictments.
I need financial help to get all my documents together.
I have not received anything from Dave P. no packages no books someone please contact him at Athens Apts 710 26/2 Soi 11 Petchburi Road BKK.
I know Nate gave money to Devo but nothing here.
I've received money from John and I have written twice but commos screw with our mail monthly both in and out and tell our consulates they are sending our letters to the court this is 95% pure lies.
Now after two years there is a brief opening.
I need a couple of thousand dollars.
Please co-ordinate this. Send to US Consulate Shanghai by wire.
My story I have been beaten exiled to torture brigade for 9 months.
Witnessed export sweat shops etc.
When I am free will pay you back with interest.

Chapter Seventyseven: One Gone

It was a day of happiness to see Grad pack his bag for the final time. We had watched him pack and unpack it on numerous occasions over the years. Among the foreigners we all had joked about Grad's antics, nick naming him Wolf. We often watched him pace the landing vigorously munching on fruit if he had it or biting his nails if he hadn't. He was hungry for freedom. It had been like this since day one really, with the foreigners not knowing what was happening with us. So many rumours went around, always related with us going home. There was one time in particular that really got us worked up. Out of the blue one day, while in the workshop, was told to go to the office. Once arriving there, Grad, Bull and Dom had gathered too. It was to give us all passport application forms which we were told to fill in that day. We were then taken over to another block and had our photos taken. It was definitely for sure now that we were going, either to another jail in the UK or going home. Grad was excited and assured us he knew all about it beforehand telling us that the British consul had told him that we'd all leave together. I was ready to believe that and Bull and Dom didn't object. We reasoned that it did make more sense to send us all back together. It was a day of hope and bright expectations for all. As it turned out, it was only Grad who left. It still took a couple of month or so after we'd all had those photos taken waiting in vain and was pissed off with the British consul about it. At the next consul visit saying to them that they were cruel and inconsiderate asses to give us the passport applications to fill out knowing well that we weren't going to get using them. The consul assured me that they hadn't requested that we fill out any application at all but that only Grad was to do so.

The Chinese have a weird way of doing things, having us all fill out forms but not the Germans or American. They made it seem all the more realistic so that it hurts. It was time for Grad to give out what wasn't needed and was given a set of Chinese study tapes and books. A basic course in Chinese sent to Grad by the London based organization Prisoners Abroad. There followed the usual promises of things that would be done and gifts that would soon be on the way to whoever. Then he was gone. It didn't feel any different that day, but in the days to follow you could sense a large presence was gone. Grad was a decent man and although having a couple of clashes with him over the years, he departed giving me a firm handshake.

The years had flown by with many harrowing encounters and many more dashed hopes but could never give up. Serving 15 years is a long, long time to serve in a foreign prison, in any prison and could imagine after 10 years you will still clutch at straws to gain remission even for a single year off your sentence. That year is a year that is yours and not theirs who have controlled your every waking moment and all through your sleep as you struggle in perpetuity in psychological chains. Well one day my day would come and no matter what they did to me I always knew this and held onto myself, kept myself alive in the light of that.

Chapter Seventyeight: No Justice No Peace

I received a letter from my sister Agnes it brought the news my brother was released he wasn't exonerated but got out of jail on a decision made by a higher court He was to remain out of prison until his next court hearing. I thanked the Gods of justice that night the force works in wondrous ways right enough reckoning if TC was on the street, then he would win his case. Nobody would have let such killers walk about if it was them. I wasn't living in the UK when all this happened but instead was living on a paradise called Boracay Island in the Philippines the owner of Jocks Rock School of scuba.

During my early smuggling days having some extra cash had purchased some land and built my house there it was there that the news of my brother's arrest came via a newspaper clipping sent to me at the island post office in Balabag. It was the story of TC Campbell the ice cream war monster it had been sent by my brother Robert from London no sun on any tropical island could have brightened that day but today was another day and things were looking bright for Tommy at last. I was delighted with that news.

Chapter Seventynine: Prison Law

We had started to study the prison law as a group in the beginning of 1996 that was the only time, we would all get together these days that was except for Xmas and New Year. That was when the authorities made the effort to show face by filming us all sitting eating together. The handing out of letters and Xmas cards was a yearly ritual now. The new guard who came to work with us was called Captain Ma he was filling my ears with once you withdrew your petition you will get a big reduction in your sentence telling me also even a bigger reduction because I went to the workshop every day.

It was going on four years now and no sign of any petition being dealt with, it was time to move on. I had been resending my petition every year even had the Consul send it my family and finally the Black fish the underground mail man but nothing seemed to work. I finally withdrew the last petition which I had submitted which cancelled out all the previous ones as well.

Chapter Eighty: Withdrawal Letter

Dear Sir.

My name is Lauchlan Campbell.

I am a British national currently serving a fifteen-year sentence at Shanghai Tilanxaio prison.

I lodged a petition of appeal dated 1996/3/1 to be sent to the Beijing Supreme People's court.

After much thought and consideration, I have decided not to pursue my claim. The reasons are as follows.

1. In the month of June 1996, I was active in creating anti-drug propaganda posters, cards and statements.

    I did this to assist in the worldwide fight against illegal drugs.

    During the anti-drug campaign on 1996/6/26 the recognized international anti-drug day.

    I was part of a group who were being educated by the Cadres about the evils of the drug trade and other drug related problems.

    The Cadres education explained historical facts from the opium war up until the present day. This education had a profound effect on my mind.

    Knowing that the spreading of death, disease, crime and other social disorder was part of my making.

    A flicker of light reached into my shadowed mind but still I remained in doubt.

2. During the month of July 1996 I was visited and interviewed on television by the Beijing Justice Department.

    During the interview I showed my anti-drug posters and cards.I also made a statement apologizing for my criminal action whilst a visitor in the P.R.C.

    After the interview, I had a discussion with two Cadres from the Prison Administration Bureau Cadre Xu and the interpreter Miss Lu Qi.

    The cadres told me I had made good progress in my reform.

    Cadre Xu explained to me that the first and foremost important aspect of reform was the acknowledgement of one's guilt.

    I told the Cadre that I had written a crime acknowledgment.

    Cadre Xu asked me if I was still lodging a petition of complaint.

    I replied that I was and the reasons why.

    I was very surprised when Cadre Xu education was exactly the same as our leading Cadre Captain Yu.

    Those Cadres education stated that I should not compare my crime with that of other peoples. That while I am in the PRC I must adhere to the laws of that land.

    Another flicker of light was cast into my mind but still I remained in doubt.

3.   One night as I lay in bed my mind was in turmoil.
I kept comparing the sentence I got to what some others got.
I kept repeating to myself the drug that I possessed was category B.
After hours of soul searching the light finally came fully on.
I could see clearly were I had gone wrong.
The facts are clear that under Chinese law I was guilty of an illegal drug offence.
The Banning of Narcotics act clearly states I should be sentenced accordingly. In fact, as my indictment carried the death penalty I was treated leniently.
The combined education of the Cadres finally reached my darkened mind.

4.   Once I was thinking that the court was dealing with a minor crime as if it was a major one.
This thinking in my mind was erroneous and caused me to feel dejected and apathetic thus loading my mind with a heavy burden.
I came to realize this thinking was groundless.
Firstly, when I speak of a minor offence, I find for myself a pretext to excuse my misdeeds which is neither reasonable nor realistic.
The substance I possessed was cannabis.
Carrying drugs is not a minor crime.
Such thinking proved that I hadn't realized the perniciousness of narcotics which I now have. Owing to the solution for this problem, my enthusiasm in reform has greatly raised. At present I am engaged in painting pictures propagating anti-drug awareness. I shall keep painting to deepen my acknowledgement on the perniciousness of my crime so as to perform meritorious services to atone for my crime.

It is true that I am stubborn in my attitude if I believe that I am correct. It is also true that if I am wrong, I will admit to my error.
I confess that I was wrong in the past although the cadres gave me good counseling, I refused to accept it.
It is better to be brought into the light than always to remain in the dark.

I Lauchlan Campbell prison number 13499 will no further pursue any petition of complaint and I accept the verdict of the court.

L. Campbell.

Chapter Eightyone: Sentence Reduction

It might have been coincidence but a couple of month later after I sent that letter it was in the air that the Judges would be visiting the prison soon. That meant several things there would be reductions in sentence, liberations, and most importantly commuted death sentences to life imprisonment. When I say commuted death sentence to life imprisonment just think about it for a moment. You have been waiting two years to know your fate. This is China, they don't keep you 20 years on death row you know within a maximum of two year. In cases where it is public execution you can be executed after court but usually within ten days. I was feeling great getting the word from JK the Judges would arrive in the afternoon. We the foreigners except for Cranky had all submitted our crime acknowledgment report. Talking with Bull in excited tones thinking and saying eighteen-month reduction at least for me. Then saying that he Vern and Hans would get a year off being led to believe this from whom I considered someone in the know i.e. Captain Ma.

It happened late that afternoon we all went down stair except Cranky. Bull Vern Hans and I stood there in the office there was tension in the air and still a faded hope of deportation. The four of us lined up there were three judges sitting behind the guard's desk. The judge read from a paper for five minutes and could hear the Chinese word for reform being often used. The judge had finished and JK interpretive skills were much quicker. You all gotten month reduction each he said. That was it a cold hard slap of prison reform Chinese style. I was fucking gutted and had worked in the factory evenings and all hours. Keeping me in check hiding my disappointment and said to Vern going upstairs you did the right thing pal, on what he replied, you studied music and bypassed the whole work for merits crap continuing on as he was listening. I was annoyed by that deception of our educations guard and could see also that the other guys weren't too happy with ten months either. Bull had voiced on our way down they might just set us all free and keep Cranky. Of course he was joking yet for a second thought they just might. Cranky was really giving them a hard time with politics he knew his stuff and read profusely. The only way to get back at him was to not include him in this reduction or to withhold his outgoing and incoming mail.

The back door mailman wasn't open for Cranky at the moment this was due to a falling out we had over me withdrawing my petition. Cranky hadn't shown me any gratitude for my ways of getting things done having gotten out his letters to his family. He insisted at length with me Campbell you're our only hope to get this Dama Zhi issue sorted out. I argued that the petition had been in for years but still got no reply plus it was all at my family's expense for translations and lawyer further adding couldn't even have a sentence reduction when petitioning. I stuck with my withdrawal and told him if he wanted to petition, he could. The others also could as in accord to the newly promulgated prison law. I noticed none of them took up the flag. As to working anymore I would only go to the workshop when felt like it or to do some trading. Staying more on the wing to read and study Chinese. Fuck this working all hours labour reform for a bullshit rubber stamp right on my forehead saying. "No communist party. No new China"

Not being part of any revolutions had just been indoctrinated into the melting pot of experimental reform. Or is more commonly known as brainwashed. To top off the disappointment with our reduction in sentence we had a meeting the following day what they wanted us to do we did it. The reason was because the system wanted you to conform. We knew if you didn't you would suffer more. We were to praise the authorities in writing for showing us the path to reform. We assured them we would. They assured us that they hoped we can go home soon the video camera was off course rolling. It was taking in our fixed Mandarin smiles we had all acquired them except Cranky he still had the contempt unshaven three-day growth looks Vern Hans and me still harboring hopes that we would all go home Dom was leaving tomorrow he had completed his full two years he didn't get one day remission. That would leave five of us.

Chapter Eightytwo: Another Gone Home

It was the same way we all thought we would go home along with Grad and off course it didn't happen that way. Dom packed his bags and went around handing out bits and pieces giving to me the book The Last Emperor. I had read it and when it came to the part in the book the year 1959 ten years after the founding of the Peoples Republic of China there was Amnesty given. The Chinese government had released political as well as war Criminals this was to commemorate ten years of the new China under Mao Tsu Tung thinking to myself 1999 that would be fifty years after the founding of the PRC. There would surely to be an amnesty then setting my sights for that date still ever the optimist. It was now 1996 so, three years to go not long when you say it fast. I had been in prison now five plus years it goes so quick when looking back but not so quick while serving it. Dom wasn't gone long before two more new guys appeared.

Chapter Eightythree: New Arrivals

I first saw them standing outside the office on our landing and walked towards them could see they were from the Sub continent and introduced myself and they shook my hand. The smaller of the two was built like Mike Tyson he was a lot smaller around 5ft 5ins his name was Mustafa. The other was taller and medium built around 5ft11ins his name was Syed. I sat with them and heard their story. They were both in for fraud and came from Pakistan and were surprised that Syed could speak Chinese. Asking him how he had learned Syed explained that he had married a Chinese girl meeting her while he was studying at a university in Beijing then after their studies finished, he returned home to Pakistan to make her his bride left her there the returned to China to commit fraud.

I asked Mustafa how he gotten here Mustafa explained Syed had brought him along with fake I.D. plus stolen checks. It was Mustafa the one was cashing them. I told them about the Pakistani guys over in the other blocks that we rarely saw these days now the drain had been fixed they didn't seem concerned. I explained they would first have to go through briefings of the Ten Don'ts and they had to get to know the prison regulations before they would get any freedom of movement. It was the system here that you got indoctrinated over a ten-day period then after that it meant they could go down stair in the morning for half hour exercise. I was in control of the shit removal and didn't carry the buckets anymore but just stood over and watched them getting hosed down then added the disinfectant it makes me laugh now when thinking back to that job and was glad to have it then it was good trading ground. We all knew that the guards never came into that area or rarely. Both Mustafa and Syed had no real interest in knowing who the other Pakistani guys were. Mustafa had linked up with Bull who was showing interest in becoming a Moslem.

I was getting feedback from Syed who was proving to be a real arrogant bastard he really hated communists and had gone to university here and suffered racist verbal abuse as well as violent attacks and could see for myself quite clearly those Pakistani guys weren't given the respect that the western inmates got. I saw this especially from the Chinese inmate's and sensed he would be a problem in time to come. Syed was serving five years Mustafa was serving six years we would see. The 1996 Xmas festivities were the usual good food we had plenty of pretense and our Mandarins smiles still full on view the new Moslem inmates had no complaints about the food or music. It was another Xmas with the same procedure getting our eventual mail and eating well and all on film.

Chapter Eightyfour: Prison Transfer

It was on December 29th that I really got my Xmas gift being told by JK we were all moving to a brand-new jail. This was to be the following day. He emphasized for me that it had an outdoor grass football pitch. I was glad of any news regarding a move out of this dump. If you ask anyone who has lived a long time in a dilapidated condition, they will exchange that in the hope of better things to come. Spreading the news around but it wasn't really accepted we had all heard it before. Rumors were abundant when it came to the foreigners.

The following morning December 30th 1996 when we got opened up the same as usual but this time, we were told to pack our things. This wasn't any rumor. It was a good feeling handing out some of my possessions to Lenny upstairs also some clothes and soaps to my football buddies Liang and Ho who were still here. JK was coming with us an old friend who would keep me right. Then to my surprise all the other Pakistanis were already on board a bus and had traded with Haled and knew about Parviz and Butt then there was another guy whom I had seen about but was now hearing he had been released. I looked out of the bus window swallowing the daylight like a man suffocating for air and needing to get free soon harboring a fantasy of escaping from the new jail. The road passed the airport and a few called out turn left. The humour wasn't appreciated when a guard called out for us to be quiet. The bus was now going down a country road in the distance buildings with a high electric fence on top came into view. Knowing I had reached my new residence I thought hard what might lay ahead for me and watched the large gates opening electronically. It was not like the old place were two guards had to pull the gate open seeing a lot of green grass and trees. This jail looked ok but would soon discover that in exchange for the impression of good surroundings. A lot would be expected in return.

Part Two: A Civilised Prison In China
Chapter One: Out Of A Hole

On the morning of December 30th 1996 had now been in Chinese prisons nearly six years and had spent ten months with twelve men to a cell at the detention house some of these men being taken to be executed and that had gutted me. I had the death sentence also on my indictment but got leniency in the eyes of Chinese criminal law and was sentenced to fifteen years. After spending five years at Shanghai Tilan Xiao prison living in a windowless cell 3ft by 8ft living with vermin and the stink of human sweat fear and excrement. I along with another British guy two Germans one American and five Pakistanis were now being escorted onto a prison bus. The weather was cold and the air damp looking at the surrounding cell blocks dull and uninviting and was glad to being seeing the back of this place. The Pakistani guys hadn't all met up whilst in jail and immediately bonded and were excitedly chatting away in Urdu. We the westerners had already shared our hopes and dreams of liberation on numerous occasions over the years. Cranky was from the USA serving fifteen years for cannabis possession he had got bust in December 1991 five month after me. Hans and Vern were from Germany serving 7 years apiece for cannabis possession. Bull the other British guy was serving 8 and half years for possession and supplying the two Germans. As I watched the prison gates open caught a glimpse of the outside world again and wanted to run for that gate to freedom but thought better when seeing the arm guards at the exit on the ready.

The drive towards our new abode was in some way exciting for me feeling such a relief to get out of that hellhole Tilan Xiao having been beat up psychologically as well as physically over the years. I was like a paranoid android reflecting on past confrontations with Cranky and Bull plus the fights with local inmates and not forgetting the guards. I wished this new jail would be less confrontational. My head was bursting and was going stir crazy. Staring out of the prison bus window saw that the road out of the city was bustling and my eyes searched for God only knew what. Seeing bicycles were everywhere some scattered and discarded with buckled wheels, people swept by it felt like a new noise for my ears and was soon off again into the safety net of my mind with a Pink Floyd song ringing in my ears "wishing away moments that make up a dull day". I could hear behind me one of the Pakistani guys saying we were heading to the airport we all wished. It was around a two-hour drive mostly along a new built highway seeing buildings were going up all around. China was under reconstruction it was something we heard nearly every day from the news. Taken from my reverie when the bus eventually took off down a dirt road and saw that we had crossed a canal then the surroundings of a high-wired fence arose from nowhere. Vern called out we are here.

The bus entered through a large electric gate it was manned by two armed guards then drove past a few buildings on the right then turned left and came to a halt. Two young guards whom I recognized met us they had been introduced to us as recruits at the old jail. There was another guard coming out from the building he looked scruffy with a trouser shine that screamed no steam iron-ing used here. Looking around me and saw we were standing in a basketball court. There was a brand-new two-story L shaped building. As we entered the building, we gathered on the ground floor. The new guard introduced himself as Captain Wang the other two were Captains Hua and Wu. There were five cells on each floor a total of fifteen cells. We were all placed on the second floor Bull and I were allocated cell two Vern and Hans's cell three Khalid Mustafa and Cranky cell four. Parviz Butt and Syed into cell five. The first cell on the floor was for the four Chinese inmates it had two bunk beds.

When I first entered our cell couldn't believe the contrast from the old jail. This cell was massive around 14ft x 9 ft in size it had a bedside cabinet and a stool to sit on. The most striking feature was a veranda a fucking veranda with a door opening onto it. Stepping onto this amazing feature and stood by a bricked wall up to waist level. It had cemented fixed bars bending upwards and over my head into the wall above. It was bigger than my cell at the old jail then noticed a large electrical fence about 30 feet away from where I stood but it was still a good feeling to be able to open a window or door and breath clean air it had been five years and more breathing in excrement gases in a windowless cell. This cell had three single beds Bull and I took the ones with our heads facing the cell door wall strategically putting us out of view from the night duty patrol. My relations with Bull had always been strained since the chopstick attack at the old jail but we could get by and we mostly did get along ok. We settled in and then were told to gather in the corridor with our stools we sat in silence as the place filled with uniforms. It was the opening speech to introduce the foreigners to Qing Pu jail it was the head Warden Yu Zhong Min who had spoken these words and JK was doing the interpretation.

The speech unfolded Shanghai Qing Pu prison is a modern civilized prison with a strong emphasis on cultural values. Culture can help you to distinguish between true and false while art can help awaken one's conscience. I had taken a mental note of those words to log into my diary. Once the uniforms had their say and we had been told not to form gangs or pray plus the usual spiel if you reform actively, you will be rewarded with a reduction in your sentence then they departed. Captain Wang then went on to tell us that we had to write monthly re-ports acknowledging our crime. The reform through labor process was repeated it was words we had all heard before at the old jail. The meeting was over and walking around the new jail building had ideas of getting me a single cell in the forefront of my mind. Then it was time to eat we got served our food in stainless steel containers with a number on it. The container had a small inner bowl that held a lump of fish and beneath was steamed vegetable and a good portion at that. The rice was given out by one of the Chinese inmates and again there was no shortage. That night was a freezing cold December but I still got out of bed to look out of the window and see the moon and stars.

Chapter Two: A Young Practitioner

Walking into cell one the following morning to speak with JK knowing we would be given some daily hygiene duties at some point in the day. I wanted JK to put me up as head cleaner and was thinking of ways to get around the jail and doing some trade. JK and another three Chinese guys shared cell one. It was exactly the same as ours only difference being they had the bunk beds. I noticed the other three Chinese guys sitting around and hadn't spoken with them yet my eyes were drawn to the cover of a book which lay on one of the stools. Walking over picked it up and got surprised when seeing the face of Bhagwan Rajneesh Shree. He is also known as Osho. Inquiring whose belongs to this book this a little guy about 5ft 5ins tall and slim in build wide in shoulder smiled and said it belonged to him. I immediately related with this young guy his name Mr. Cho. He was to become known to us all as Stanley.

Being somewhat suspicious though as to how could he get to read such books? It was against the regulations to worship you weren't supposed to pray. Listening to his use of English and could hear he was precise in his pronunciations but short of vocabulary at least his English was better than my Chinese. I struck up my first bit of trade at the new jail and would teach him English in exchange he teaches me Chinese. We shook hands on it Stanley was doing a fourteen-year prison sentence this was for his involvement in car theft relating with the Tiananmen square student uprising when it had spread from Beijing to Shanghai. Stanley was fortunate in one-way that he had a family relation at this jail who was quite a high communist party official. Seeing the ocean in Stan's his eyes. He was in search for new knowledge and was still unquenched. Stan and I connected and told him stories about some of my travels. As that day went on, he would seek me out at every opportunity to listen to more. I enjoyed his company especially when he opened up my mind to the Chinese teachings of Lao Tzu. Spiritual healing is needed in prison and we were parched for it. That was the start to a long deep profound and sometime violent friendship.

Chapter Three: 1997

It is not a traditional festive date on the Chinese calendar but knew from past experienced New Years at the old jail a great meal would be put on. Hogmanay was the date close to proclaim that being a Scotsman needed to follow my traditions. I had written down several notes from that first meeting and would be using their terminology whenever submitting anything in writing and would be asking for Chinese language or cooking classes' art and Calligraphy or Tai Chi Chan using the words of our great leader Warden Yu Zhong Ming statement on the importance of cultural values. As it happened, it had been pre-arranged that we would be getting special food.

The large reception room on the ground floor was allocated to us to decorate it was Bull who took over that job most years although the others did their bit. We all got special food and recreation treatment until January the third. That was a nice start to being civilized. The New Year came and went it was not as festive an atmosphere here as was at the old jail but was glad of that. We had plenty karaoke and everyone smiled. That was something you picked up in Chinese jail known as the Mandarin smile those faces with stretched lips some with gums and teeth exposed all thinking the same. Fuck you.

The food was duck, chicken, fish, beef and pork. There was also an abundance of mixed vegetables and roots. It was good food and plenty of it. No complaints as of yet. The kitchen also had a Moslem chef that was so no pork would be given to the followers of that faith. As usual, we had a barrage of high-ranking officials being filmed with us. They did this during dinner or presenting us with gifts i.e. notebooks the notebook gift was given for a purpose we were informed to write our thoughts down and hand them in monthly on it. We were filmed receiving letters from our family and so on and were glad to return to normal. Stir crazy normal if you know what I mean? You cannot expect to be fully functioning up top after six years in a limited space living among people who spoke sounds alien to your ear and sometimes attacked you.

Chapter Four: The Odd One In

Cranky was having it hard at present. It did not take long before he began to feel the first hint of conflict coming towards him. It was a struggle with the Pakistanis Cranky was saying that he should not have to share a cell with Moslems his cellmates agreed they wanted him out. There reasoning was he used plates and utensils that made contact with pork products. This was not true as Cranky had the vegetarian diet. It really boiled down to that Cranky and Bull had secured the television remote control on the first day of arrival. That was really the heart of it there was friction and wanted nothing to do with it. I never watched television now unless it was football. I had not watched television for years since San Mao went off the air. Now some may ask why Cranky was not allowed to share my cell with Bull. The reason was I had already attacked him at the old jail and had verbally insulted him on several occasions. Hans and Vern did not want him in their cell either Cranky had always been confrontational with the authorities.

The two Germans were like mice in the sense they were quiet people kept to themselves. It was the authorities who wanted to show Cranky how to play ball their way. So Cranky remained where he was only with one difference, he kept his utensils in a separate drawer. After being given the job as the cells and living quarter's hygiene inspector having JK arrange for to get that for me. Whilst walking around the basketball court during the morning exercise period that was from 6:30 to 7:00 each morning.

I talked with Vern asking him to sort out a rote system so that over the month each cell got equal points. This was part of the job the authorities had laid on me. The proverbial carrot was still in use at this modern civilized prison. I was to select a cell each day that was looking tidiest. By the end of the week, one cell would get merit points for winning. Therefore, Vern wrote me out a rote system that we all were equally rewarded throughout the month. Bull was put in charge of the hot water container that was delivered twice a day it was a heavy container it needed two strong people getting the handle one at each side to lift it from the electric buggy that delivered it so the giant Khalid assisted him.

Parviz was given the job of cleaning and emptying the bins in the guard's office and was considered a position of trust. Some of the inmates who didn't have a job felt left out it were quite interesting to watch and listen to guys complain experiencing myself and other inmates becoming jealous through job allocations. Having identified that emotion in myself but had not examined it closely enough yet. What were we in competition for? Some preferred not to work like Hans and Vern they studied most of the day Bull was also studying and had learned to read write and speak Chinese. It was down to a power struggle and the Pakistanis who were now a force. Syed was the worse that idiot informed on me to the authorities telling them my hygiene set up was a fraud. He had done it after a couple of weeks of me setting up Vern's rote system losing that job and he took over from me. Was the prison system playing the Pakistanis against the westerners? Was it because they were more obedient? I sometimes wondered and watched closely. I was given another job now distributing the monthly food orders we could put in and pay from personal cash kept in our property. That put me in with the Chinese again like the old jail workshop and that caused quite a stir, as it was usually only the Chinese inmates did this job. Being constantly on my toes in this jail and could not trust yourself never mind any other one. I was offering all sorts of assistance to Stanley to get around the jail and was being guided by him now a new friend who was pushing me to have a good position at this new unit. We were attending meetings two or more times each day it was obvious to me the authorities here had not a clue on how to occupy our time. It was an experimental unit for the Chinese authorities on how to deal with the ever-growing influx of foreign criminals.

We also had new rules on how to dress it was to be prison garb we all had to wear from now on. Khalid had taken to wearing his Shalwar Kamiz, Syed wore skintight jeans with high-heeled cowboy boots with silver toecaps quite a figure for a jailbird. This person was vain as most of the Pakistani people there were. We were issued two light grey cotton uniforms we also got one darker grey a synthetic nylon type plus a thick dark blue cotton sweatshirt. The uniform had a blue and white stripe across the front and back of the jacket. It also ran down the outside of both trouser legs we were also given two white short-sleeved shirts. That was to be our summer and winter attire they again had stripes on back and front. We were issued with ID cards which was to be pinned to our jacket they had our prison number and photograph on them. This foreign unit was slowly taking shape and some order. It certainly was experimental. The first months passed it was without much incident in Shanghai Qing Pu jail a Modern and civilized prison in China.

Chapter Five: Marching Orders

One day we were told to go outside to practice marching we had watched the Chinese inmates doing this they were housed in a building opposite the same size as ours and only difference they were eight to a cell with four bunk beds. We all fell in and the charade began it was pure pandemonium. Cranky Bull and Vern turned left when it should have been right. Khalid bumped into everyone the guard was getting wound up he was used to complete discipline and order at his command. It wasn't happening here. Campbell, he called my name JK told me to go over to the guard and was told to stand at attention and say Duisan hao i.e. (Good Captain) which I did then was told to march around left right left right halt. The guard beamed his lost face being partly regained by my efficient marching. JK went on to tell everyone that's how you should march. I felt like a one-legged man at an arse kicking party having set myself up for this by being eager to please my new turnkeys. It was now time for me to show my appreciation and cooperation.

JK and Stanley were pushing my case as being trustworthy and they needed someone who could help them run the unit. We all needed something to occupy our time having offered to work as a painter and decorator telling them that it was my trade and our building was unfinished. Having got a job for a few days and painted the windows and was rewarded by being given a football holding the new ball in my hands and smelling the leather not yet having a kick about since arrival that's all I wanted just to be occupied to be involved to be useful.

Chapter Six: A Great Leader Dies

One afternoon in February the death of Deng Xiaoping was announced. It was quite an event a whole history of his life was in the newspapers and shown on television. The open-door policies man who spearheaded China into the economic revolution. We the foreigners were told to write a report with our views on this great man. I still had Tony Benn's book with me a Socialist Anthology sent by my brother Cranky still had my History of China and Aristotle's Ethics books from the old jail. Now having a group of Pakistanis at my cell looking for words of wisdom to praise this great man. I can assure you words from Emil Zola to the Suffragettes were handed in for translation deliberately leaving out any quotes from Chairman Mao's Red book. It was the best ever ideological reports in history written in the memory of Deng Xiaoping by foreigners held against their will in China.

Chapter Seven: A Means To An End

Having got my persistent request granted at the beginning of March the foreign unit played their first game of football against the Chinese. It was against the unit across from us. Bull was a solid defender and took no prisoners to coin a phrase. Stanley was as fast as a whippet he now was outcast from many of the Chinese this was because of his position in the foreign unit. This position they wrongly believed was more relaxed than the rest of the jail. I had adopted him as my Chinese brother letting him know clearly whatever help he needed he could depend on me. It was already known before coming here I had played in every football competition at Shanghai Tilan Xiao jail and was known as a good player by Chinese standards. Football was really taking off in China but they were still amateur in comparison with Europe or South America. Hans and Vern couldn't kick a ball straight unusual for Germans. Cranky was a basketball player the Pakistanis were cricketers. We had a good kick about having a good laugh out on the basketball court. It was just fun to run and kick the ball and showing the Chinese guys how to keep the ball up. It was easy for me to roll it onto my foot then keep it up then switch foot onto my knee then up to my head and down to my foot again. Then watched them trying to keep up the ball three to four times nobody done it without touching the ground except one. The guards Captain Wang and his two assistants Captain Hua and Captain Wu also joined us they were eager to show their skills. Captain Wang was a better player than any of the Chinese cons we played against that day. The other two guards had never kicked a ball in their lives but knew they would have good players in other blocks Stanley had told me about the prison team plus each cellblock had their own team now we would have ours. I knew we couldn't yet compete on the pitch with seven or eight aside but if it was three or four aside on the basketball court bring them on. Having got this ball in return for keeping busy with my Mandarin smile but it was soon to be deflated.

Chapter Eight: Reward and Punishment

I was called into the office one evening and was met by the criminal affairs cadre called Captain Ma. He started his conversation by praising my attitude for my willingness to work. He went on to say that supporting the government benefits my and the reform of others and was to be commended at the end of the month and rewarded. JK explained more what he meant by commended and rewarded and told me the modern civilised prison story again this time via Captain Ma. They wanted us to take part in the upcoming Chinese spring festival sports event. I was to ask the other foreigners to compete in other events. They had Tug of War, sprints, and other games such as basketball, ping-pong chess or the card game Bridge and were to make a list of participants then pass it over to JK naming the events and who wanted to take part. I didn't see any fault with this and was enthusiastic to go and tell the others. It was always a confrontation of sorts when you had to pass on suggestions or orders and fucking hated it and would never accept taking orders from another con. Getting JK to do this for me it was mutually felt we didn't want to be playing the guards role but still better coming from him. It came to pass that a certificate of merit was awarded to me it was like a small diploma in bold Chinese characters with my name written both in Chinese as well as English. This was done during a meeting it was clearly stated that if you cooperate like Campbell, you would get this reward. I wasn't the only one to get this certificate the two Germans got one as well also Butt and Parviz. If you have two or more of them you can have your sentence reduced. That was a message everybody wanted to hear but didn't believe a fucking word of it as the last experience proved we all got ten-month reduction except Cranky. I knew this was for the new guys to get them competitive and it worked a treat. The Chinese authorities also knew my character and manipulated it sometimes. Deep within I did still cling to the illusion that this place might be different they might yet set us free if giving a Mandarin smile for whatever propaganda project needed at that time.

It wasn't only me eager to get free a couple of guys had written reform articles that got published in the jail paper. Bull also had been studying Islam these past few months and was more focused these days on his health and studies he had secured the veranda of our cell for privacy when he prayed. Syed didn't accept Bull as being converted to Islam and was stating that he hadn't been circumcised; Khalid was saying that the pastries from the kitchen that Bull ate had pork oil in them. I wasn't interested to listen to all the negative reasons why Bull wasn't taking their religion seriously and had never heard anything mentioned in Bulls favour from these Pakistani guys. It wasn't like that when they first arrived having noticed when Mustafa and Syed were only too eager to pass on word from the Holy Koran i.e. in their search of sharing Bulls wares and goodies. I knew of jail converts from past experience some used it for a means to an early release some others used it to hide behind putting themselves into the pacifist group but also believe some people really do find their spiritual guide. In Bulls case it was out of respect towards his girlfriend and wife to be from Xingjian and she was from a Moslem family. Bull did have that thirst for knowledge then his encounter with Islam came to a stop at least temporary whilst he was at the prison. I know the guards were rather confused when they heard that Bull prayed to Allah.

It is difficult for some people to understand but in the Chinese communist ideology they don't believe in any God so from being a Christian converting to Islam that had got them thinking. They are sincerely amused that we civilised westerners could follow or believe in such unrealistic happenings written about centuries ago. It wasn't permitted to pray here at the prison although it was being done privately. It was a subject of conversation still ongoing but certainly not resolved of as yet. The problem seemed to lie in the ritual of going to wash your hands and feet five times a day. On the entrance to the washroom written in Chinese as well as English was the sign. "Water is the source of life save it." That and also by the fact that they wanted to pray together. The guards didn't want to accept that Moslems could go and wash then kneel and pray as a group. It was in the regulations that you couldn't congregate in groups or form a gang.

Chapter Nine: Holidays

It was now only a few days to the Chinese New Year our sports training had begun. One week prior having been given a dozen Chinese people from the opposite building to train and pick a team from. We passed the ball with me watching their moves and seeing definitely the making of a team here. We were out on the large grass field the pitch was about half size of a professional pitch but lumpy with clods of grass and ditches. Having picked a tall slim person who had better dribbling skills than I did not that I was great but not bad and the best yet till discovering this person Lanky. Another player was about my height 5ft 8 inches he was slimmer built around 68kg I was 73kg but this person was twenty years younger and fast. He had another plus going for him, he could distribute the ball quite well, he could speak some English, and like Hanley he had family connections at the prison. He was called Shu Ming then picked another person from Xingjian autonomous region in China he was the Moslem cook and known to us as Kasha. The night shift worker in our unit could play quite well but he was always asleep when we needed him little Wang was his name so he would be a substitute. I needed more players and selected two people who could run fast that was seven and with little Wang as sub made nine. The game these people played was totally disorganised. Football had really taken off big time nationwide. It was usually seven people's aside chasing the ball whooping all the way; when someone got it they kicked it anywhere as hard as they could. I had our side at least get some passing down. It appeared that everyone just ran about making lots of noise it certainly felt relieving just being able to shout at the top of my voice and not be reprimanded but needed a team who would not just run about. Stanley myself Bull and Shu Ming could easily pass the ball accurately the goalkeeper was brave enough but no positional skill and the other two they could learn while little Wang slept. We never went to the big pitch to train unless we had a game against another cellblock keeping our training to the basketball court it cut the time wasted running for miss kicked balls. I had to show them passes using different parts of the foot and taught them to chip and catch the ball on their chest or knee. I had them shot the ball at the goal, which was 4ft by 4ft had them shooting bouncing balls then had them heading and a lot of passing and running on for the return ball. It was a good period bonding well with these younger people. We played four asides for hours and we were getting fit and must say here we were the only unit in the prison to be able to train as much. The Chinese in other units had to work. They would get the weekend off to train so their games were set up for then. It was a fair system at the big pitch one goal, off you went, and on came the next team.

One afternoon our unit was taken over, we did not have a football strip but Cranky had gathered eight vests and had painted Rasta colours on them. The first game we played we won it was noticeable right away how fit we were in comparison with the other team. On our third game a person flew up the wing scored and knocked us out. It was my reckoning anyways these people should get the use of the pitch at the weekend as they worked all week. The following week we stayed at our unit basketball court honing our skills. It was considered a big occasion by the Chinese authorities setting up competitive sports as part of prison reform. Bull and I were the two foreign imports representing Qing Pu modern and civilized prison in the upcoming spring festival football competition. Before the games began, we had the flag flying ceremony and singing of the national anthem. Then there were the speeches from several ranks and finally the units all had a flag bearer and a group of supporters with matching outfits marching around the track with inmates shouting all sorts. When the games began, we got off to a good start winning our first match but eventually we got beat in the semifinal. I was pleased enough with that outcome. It was not bad for our mixed team from the international foreign unit. I had to give Bull credit for taking a person down hard that final game this person was seriously fouling our Chinese players. Stanley especially was getting it Bull had done a slide tackle on the bad guy from about twenty yard run with 80kg of power full on the opponent went down. Off went the heel hacker not with a red card but on a blue plastic stretcher it was a victory at least over one bully.

The sports had come to a close and a meeting to give out medals and cups began. We picked up a third-place flag also 30-merit points to be shared by those who competed. Cranky had gotten second place at the basketball throw for the whole prison and for that, our unit was awarded 30 more points and a cup. It might have been this appreciation from the authorities of Crank's sporting skill. That may have turned him from being in their face to being on their side. He was now a man in transition it seemed to me.

Chapter Ten: The First Pakistan Incident 1997

I was doing fine in this new jail and already awarded a certificate of merit. Then one day Parviz somehow got under my skin and so head butted him knocking out his front tooth. There was an uprising from the Pakistanis. I was taken upstairs to the second floor, locked into cell five, and told to write an account of what had happened. After writing, this down then handed it over to JK for translation. My cell was opened after a couple of hours and was escorted to the office by Captain Hua. They're stood Captain Ma from Criminal affairs department along with Captain Wang. JK told me that I had not acknowledged the wrongdoing committed. He said but had only given my reason for what had been done which is unacceptable. Asking JK what the guards expected me to write he explained that it was my responsibility for my action and should write that I accept this shortcoming. Taken away locked up again and a meeting was arranged for the following day. Stanley brought up my food and sat outside my cell door that is the system in China if you were in the punishment cell someone had you in view twenty-four hours.

The nightshift started at 9pm and finished at 6am. I lay on my bed and thought about what lay ahead tomorrow having to acknowledge my lack of self-control. It was always someone else's fault or why would I head butt someone telling myself. The night was uncomfortable and my sleep disturbed by the sound of passing footsteps on the concrete floor.

The following afternoon the door was unlocked and standing in front of everyone reading aloud my self-criticism. I was punished by losing that certificate of merit that had worked so hard to get thinking that award would bring me a reduction in sentence next year and now back to square one. Everyone else at the meeting also had to write a report on what they thought of my behavior. The diary given to us all upon arrival at the New Year was for that purpose it was during this period having many people go against me. It was a united Moslem front because of Parviz they stopped talking with me except for Butt. Captain Wang gave him the job as peacemaker and go-between. I was investigated by the criminal affairs department and told criminal charges might well proceed. Then it had been settled that I could pay for the replacement tooth knocked out which was paid immediately. Things had more or less gone back to normal after a week. However, it was in my own ranks the biggest bombshell landed.

Chapter Eleven: A Rat or a Reformer?

Cranky really got my eyes to open up when I stole a hand written report from the guard's desk getting the opportunity in the office that was not yet connected with a phone line. It was being used more as a watch desk as you could see up the full corridor. In the office with JK discussing my letters issue when the captain was called by Hanley to go upstairs to receive a phone call JK followed him. I saw writing paper on the desk, picked it up, and had a look seeing my name pocketed it. This is a copy word for word this is the original letter that smuggled out and kept all those years.

Attacks by 13499 Lauchlan Campbell
- Shanghai detention cells August 1991 to June 1992 attacked and injured 5 to 7 Chinese prisoners.
- June 13th 1992 smashes 13498 in nose with head and attempts to poke Bulls eyes out with chopsticks witnessed by Cranky Hans Vern and officer 31-01-427
- Oct 15th 1992 attacks 13497 twice in one-day 13497 swollen knee can't walk lay in cell. Also attacked Grad same day and cut his lip. Witnessed by Cranky Bull Hans Vern and Grad. 13497 had to be assisted to the hospital for three months.
- Nov 16th 1992 smashes 13497 in head cuts his cheek witnessed by same people above 13497 has scar on his cheek from this attack.
- Feb 1993 he smashes out window in hospital while in a rage many witnesses.
- Dec 1993 breaks 8th brigade Chinese prisoner's nose in attack. Mr. Ni goes to hospital witnessed by Bull, Grad, told by 31-01044 officers Jin that if he ever attacks anyone else, he will be given a further sentence.
- 1993-1994 Spits on officer Zhu 31-01428 and Chinese inmates 7000 and 555
- Oct 12th 1994 Pulls 13497 down and kicks him in face with right foot 13497 nose broken. Witnessed by Bull and Dom.
- Oct 22nd 1994 attacks Grad breaks open lip witnessed by Vern and Bull.
- Feb 12th 1995 Pushes Chinese prisoner.
- Feb 18th 1995 Threatens to burn down Dom's friend's house in London gets address from translation brigade or stole it.
- Jan 27th 1997 tries to attack 13498 but stopped by Chinese prisoner Mr. Liu.
- Mar 25th 1997 attacks Parvaz Akhtar. Many witnesses.

When I got my stomach finally settled my heart rate jumped my anger was going out of control. Taking a long deep breath was thinking that bastard does not have a clue of the why in what he is writing. My defenses were up I was not this bad. How the fuck would, he knows what was going on in the detention hell cells mumbling to myself. I did have a few fights there not wanting them fuck me. How no one would end up in a fight was beyond me choking with anger thinking the fucking wimp probably sat in corner bullied. Did he forget about the risk that was taken to get his letters out? Disappointed to the extreme finding out that someone was taking note of me and passing it onto the guards. Looking closely at this report and justifying my actions thinking he failed to mention that the Dec 1993 attack was one that everyone was let us say not unhappy to hear about, The Chinese inmate known to us as doctor death was an informer and distributed us with the food rations we could order. It was clear from day one that we foreigners were at the bottom of the priority rung. If we were receiving fruit, it would be the bruised ones, he also underweighted us. We all disliked him and it was a regular topic of complaint between us but only I took action and his shenanigans stopped after that. I was locked up but then that is the price you pay for taking the law into your own hands. The way Cranky had written it you would think I just walked up, assaulted people, and if this were true then should have been kept in a lunatic asylum and thought why would this reporter give over these details was it to cover his own shit-filled passage through life? Having learned that people can dirty your name by loose words and rumors had read articles in the British newspapers about my brother T.C. Campbell the Ice cream monster. What a tag to be put onto you. It sounds like you had been messing around stealing children's pocket money out at the van. My brother was serving life in prison for a heinous crime he didn't commit and had fought heart and soul to clear his name setting up a campaign from within the prison" Free the Glasgow two" My brother's co accused was a friend of the family from childhood Joe Steel. This young man had outsmarted the police and prison authorities by escaping from them on more than one occasion. He did this and then arranging his own arrest thus bringing much needed publicity to their case. These were the kind of prisoners I identified myself with not informers and wimps. Now having proof about Cranky all hand written it was not just talking the written word and had uncovered a grass. I would be watching sly old Cranky from now on. The fuck wit Cranky Noodle right enough being paranoid as it was. Then when you find hand a written detailed account of your actions over the years it did add weight to my already stir crazy and weary head.

Chapter Twelve: Three New Faces

I was standing looking onto the basketball court wishing away the time to get out for a game of football. It was late spring and getting warm and the guards would rather be outside. It was our arranged exercise time in the afternoon from 4 to 5 pm. Looking from the window a large man walked towards our unit wearing an Arab headdress he was in front of a little Chinese guy plus a slightly overweight Asian prisoner they were carrying luggage. I had heard rumor two new people were coming but not three. Abdul Latif wearing the headdress was from Iran. The little guy was American Chinese his name was Bo and the third Mir was this person's name he was Kashmiri Indian. Latif was a big man 6ft 4inchs tall and built; powerfully he looked around forties in age and had a long unkempt beard. Seeing the weariness in his face and saw strength in his walk and confidence in his attire Abdul Latif was a jewel thief, he posed a striking figure in his Arab garb.

Bo was full on American accent although he was born in China he was educated in the USA. His crime industrial waste or other Mir had a Pakistani passport but said he was British and was born in Kenya but now went as a Kashmiri Indian his crime fraud. He would be fun to listen to and he had already served at the old jail over seven years why he didn't come along with us was a mystery that was often discussed. I knew that another cell would have to open to house them an opportunity might arise for me to have a cell move Bull and I didn't really see eye-to-eye at times we had a couple of small incidents mostly mouthing and had been trying to get a cell upstairs and now it might just happen.

A meeting was called after about one hour of the new men's arrival. It was a short induction and only to allocate their cells. Latif was put into cell five along with Butt Syed and Parviz. Bo was housed with the two Germans Mir was put into cell three with Cranky Mustafa and Khalid. As you do when new people arrive, you get to hear their story. Bo was charged with bringing garbage into China something along those lines either recycling dumping or some sea faring act of piracy. Bo claimed he was innocent he seemed to be well enough educated and well connected in the USA. Lativ on the other hand said he was guilty we believed him. He was a jewel thief cut from the cloth of Ali Baba and immediately took to him he was a scammer. Mir now here was a man who could not stop lying. Mir told me that he was a multi- millionaire he had made fortunes selling anything and everything from carpets to nuclear warheads. He had fought against the Russians in Afghanistan trained Moslems in bombing raids in the Philippines and married a Taiwanese Generals daughter. That was just for starters Mir was fascinating to listen to you just had to remind yourself it was just good stories like the ones you would hear from any palm reader on the many streets of India all good sir.

Chapter Thirteen: Ramadan

It was the Moslem fasting period of Ramadan the issue of prayer and food hadn't quite been resolved. Bull had been practicing alone on the veranda it was April 18th the fasting was over. Lativ called a meeting in his cell for a group prayer. The group got busted that caused quite a stir Khalid was enraged shouting in the corridor he will kill for his religion. The following day we had another top brass meeting it was decided the guard running our unit wasn't suitable or able enough. Latif, he had only been at the jail weeks when he decided to go on a protest raising the issues of religious freedom. He was saying he was going to hunger strike if his religious rights were denied. Advising him to use the words fasting for justice words I had read written by my brother in his free the Glasgow Two campaign. Lativ wasn't happy regarding the way his religion was being disrespected. It took him only one week to work out what the Pakistanis didn't want to acknowledge that was they were being treated as lesser citizens than we westerners.

The Chinese inmates looked down upon them also some guards were open with their disrespect recalling one occasion when a young guard from another unit was doing a shift at our block and said the Pakistanis smelled like sheep. Cranky, Bull and Hans openly talked about this body odour issue as well. It is true enough about how the body odour differs from country to country the truth was in all honesty Syed in particular really gave off a bad smell. All the Pakistani inmates used scented lotions. The cultural differences were beginning to cause conflict in more ways than one. It was stated in some regulation you weren't allowed to gather in groups. You couldn't have photos of your family or idols or any ornamentation on your walls. Abdul Latif had a prayer rug and a wall hanging of Mecca. In the practice of Islam visiting Mecca is every Moslem wish and when you do then fellow Moslems, acknowledges you as Hajji. Latif had been to the Medina. It is a mark of respect given from other Moslems if you are Hajji. If the Christians were allowed to celebrate according to the Bible, then him as a Moslem would celebrate according to the Holy Koran. Latif refused to take the wall hanging down and made his mark that day he never ate until they fully understood his religion was more important to him than their prison reform. The Chinese prison authorities never forgot nor forgave him for that. Lativ wasn't taking any shit from the communists. He would say to me in all sincerity" Campbell how can this country not believe in God" from that protest by Lativ all Moslem holidays were put onto the Qing Pu Prison calendar. After all it was me who did enlighten Lativ to the wardens' opening statement when we first arrived. The Modern and Civilised prison speech. I would use that phrase time and time again putting their words back to them and questioning the civilised prisons actions. The Moslems would now get equal treatment regarding religious beliefs the Iranian consulate also supported their countryman's right to pray and brought him the Holy Koran during a visit.

There was beginning to be a split in the Moslem camp it was Abdul Lativ who was now running the show one Shiite as opposed to six Sunni but only one Hajji. It was the start of the Chinese prison Holy Jihad that's what Cranky would say whenever any conflict arose between them and that was often.

Chapter Fourteen: Work Detail

It was the Criminal affairs Captain Ma who visited our unit and held a short meeting making the statement that if any inmate can stay out of trouble for one year, they will be eligible for a reduction of sentence. This was his carrot before saying he had organised an outdoor work detail. It was retold to us how good for our reform labour is. No one objected to that plus the weather was really nice in May and was pleased when we were gathered and told we would go outside to clean up the football ground. This was observation time we would be under scrutiny by the surrounding cameras as well as guards. The Chinese authorities used every angle they wanted to experiment with in their desire to know foreign prisoners' reactions to different situations. The sun was up and as a group we paced around uprooting weeds. It didn't take long to see who formed groups and who was picking the weeds and who was taking in the sun. Knowing the system well enough to see this was an attitude observation so kept my head down most times. In the surrounding area of the football ground was another three large cell blocks plus another under construction there was a smaller building that would become more familiar in the not-too-distant future. There was a massive factory building about the size of an aircraft hangar behind the newly constructed cellblock. As we walked back to our unit after an hour or so weeding it felt well better than it had felt in a long time something about doing useful things.

Chapter Fifteen: Green Eye

It was Syed he never ceased to annoy someone and Bull was his target at this moment in time. It was because Bull and Lativ had struck up a good friendship as far as jail pals go. Bull still had some interested in Islam and learning to speak Turkish Lativ was qualified to assist in both plus both of them enjoyed playing chess together. Syed was spitting out venomous words that Bull wasn't circumcised and that he was a Christian and other verbal insult behind Bulls back. When he did hear rumours, it didn't seem to get under Bulls skin. Then one day Bull had the duty to clean the toilet area it was still a rote system he completed his job and went on with his studies. Stanley came to Bulls cell and told him the guard wanted to see him. It was moments later that pandemonium broke out Syed barged into the office and accused Bull of not cleaning the toilet then kicked him. He was shouting all sorts of obscenities when two guards dragged him upstairs and locked him down. The place had an unsettled atmosphere you could cut the air it was thick with pent up emotion. Syed remained in confinement for two days then there was a meeting called. It was the usual self-criticism read from his hand written report. It was cursing the guard's names that resulted in him being locked down in what they termed temporary confinement, which lasted from June till September 1997 three month so much for the prison law on the maximum lock up time which was 30 days. It was assured to us he wasn't locked up he was in temporary confinement upstairs on the top floor. This was true but he didn't get out eating or exercising at all with us it is a severe price you pay when you curse the system having had the experience and the consequences it is not a good one.

Chapter Sixteen: Medical Checkup

One morning after breakfast we were all gathered and taken to the hospital for a full medical check-up. The hospital had one male doctor and four female nurses all of whom turned out to be compassionate considerate people. I struck up a little conversation with my limited Chinese flirting with the nurses who were still in police uniform my Mandarin smile was full on. The hospital building had just been painted and there was still the lingering paint smell in the air. There was a bus stationed outside with X-ray equipment set up. It looked like we would be checked out good. The blood test we got now gave multiple results and nobody seemed to have any immediate medical problem. I already had had this check-up done one time before at the old jail in 1992 when first starting my prison sentence over five years ago. Looking around me all the foreign prisoners seemed over fed and the Chinese ones underfed. Chinese inmates who worked at the factories would be hanging around the hospital looking for any medical excuse to get them some relief from work. It was also difficult to believe that a prison this size didn't have a dentist nor dental equipment. It was a new prison holding three thousand plus inmates. A full medical and dental facility was needed.

It was about a few weeks after those medical tests that Stanley came to me one day and said he was returning to the old jail with Cranky. Telling me Cranky had an incurable disease. Asking Stanley what it was and told he had Hepatitis C. and would be glad to see the back of him. The rumours soon went around that he was dying It was told to me that his liver needed replacing and he would be sent home for this purpose. Cranky complained to his consul and was also taking out a lawsuit against the Chinese government for him catching the virus whilst in prison. Good for him and would have thought he knew that wasn't even an option but it probably made him feel good expressing his right. I wanted to return home and with my health though sometimes had thought of trading my health for freedom. Coming come close once in desperation over mail with the thought of killing myself but struggled with my demon and continued doing my time. It would be the longest time served yet among foreign inmates in China but I didn't know that then.

Chapter Seventeen: Five Fucking Goods

It was another brainwashing session we were being introduced to our new unit leader Captain Qian he was now replacing the old Captain Wang. We all sat and listened to the reform education as the Chinese prison system termed it. Captain Qian was a small man but walked with his chest out after introducing himself he then proceeded to introducing the" Five Goods" I had been here a half year now and every fucking month they came up with a new system on how to cause conflict about merit points. This was deliberate this was mind games.

The Shanghai Qing Pu civilised jail was experimental they did not have a fucking clue on how to set up a system for us. It would have been easier if we were all treated the same after all we were in China. The foreigners had been told at more than one meeting that we are treated better than Chinese inmates are because we do not have to work and we have a higher budget for food rations. I was losing faith fast. The five fucking goods right enough.

1. Acknowledge your guilt in a monthly report.
2. Follow the Cadres education.
3. Be active in self-study.
4. Take part in the unit upkeep.
5. Report any wrong doings by others.

Chapter Eighteen: Helping Hands

I was spending my days designing anti-drug posters. This was for the upcoming UN Anti-drug Day on June 26th. It would be the second display of drug education we had one at the old jail when we all had drew on blackboards drawing anti-drug slogans with color chalks. It was drummed into us that if you acknowledge and accept our guilt you would be free quicker. I wrote a letter to ask the British consul to contact the Home Office for me regarding drug education that they did, and they sent me drug education with posters as well. Having also contacted an old friend of mine Davy Bryce and asked him to assist me with any ideas on drug rehabilitation. Davy was very helpful and sent me some original drawings done by schoolchildren in Scotland making me so chuffed this would add a special touch to the exhibition. True-life experience coming from a group of ex drug addicts now reformed to becoming a football team called Calton Athletic Recovery Group. Davy sent me newsletters from Cannabis to Chaos it was all good stuff and the most important aspect of CARG was abstention from all drugs no methadone or alcohol. Davy was a hard talker and that is what makes it work. We had a good mutual friend William Burns also with CARG helping me out with good advice. It is not easy to break any addiction but I respected Wullie and Davies views that was simply help is here but first clean up your act and prove to yourself you want to quit. Davy always stated CARG would always embrace those who want to make the effort. Therefore, the rule was if you are on drugs done come. Being on a mission to prove I wanted to acknowledge my guilt and wanted to be like the lads CARG men a winner. My brother TC Campbell sent me a few sketches and a poster about addicts sharing needles. I designed and gave out three anti-drug posters giving them to the British Consul in June1997. These posters were to commemorate the 10th anniversary of the UN Anti-Drug Day of June 26th. One was to hand over to the German consulate the other for the USA consulate. The German Consul was a Miss Fevers. This kind person sent me a photo of it hanging in the consulate office and a card of thanks. I was awarded the five goods for this one action of sending anti- drug posters with a clear message.

The head Prison Warden Yu Zhong Ming came to personally praise me for my good contribution to the society. I took this opportunity there and then to ask him if I could put on an anti- drug exhibition here at the prison. Chinese officials are never quick to agree to anything so his reply was he would think it over. JK later on explained to me when we were alone that he had told the Warden about my already designed posters hanging on the walls at three consul offices in Shanghai. JK told me the Wardens reply was he knew JK made it sound special saying that the three foreign consulates supported the U.N. Anti- drug project and further added that he would help me and it would be a worthy project. We sat and discussed ideas in his cell and decided it should be done in four parts. It was only one week later being called into the office and told to write a plan and submit it to the Warden. We sat and wrote out my plan and going to use acrylic paints making the exhibition into four parts ten posters covering each topic. 40 posters in total JK knew all that was needed so I left it with him to make the list. Davy also enclosed the book Pain of Confinement written by a reformed prisoner from the city of Glasgow called Jimmy Boyle and it was signed. I soaked that book up and underlined parts that related with my feelings and although never meeting the author would say thanks Jimmy being on my reform journey to find myself.

Chapter Nineteen: Spy Box

I was standing by my cell door and saw the warden coming into our building. Cranky approached him to ask why there was not a Wardens box on any of the floors in our building. Cranky went on to say it was stated in the prison law that such a box should be exhibited in case someone wanted to accuse or report. This Wardens box on the wall was just another mind game. It was just another way to extract information from you. It was under the guise "For his eyes only "I am the Warden; you can trust me" So my mind jumped to the conclusion Cranky wanted direct contact with a higher authority and wondering why. I used this box at the old jail whenever wanting to raise some issue. The prison reform in China is based upon that you sort out your own shortcomings and point them out in others. I did not cope to well with that especially criticisms about me. The system was structured that any problems should always be contained to that unit so having a box also gave you opportunity to report a guard. It was rumored the guard at our unit was being moved. It was down to him not being able to control us as they had likely envisioned. The reform competition they created was fierce. They had non-stop brainwashing sessions with us as often two or more times a day. Some of these old communist hard liners noted every detail of error whether you are a guard or inmate they took notes.

Chapter Twenty: Hard Work

If a workshop finished an assignment before the deadline, the guards would receive a monetary bonus or a food parcel. The convicts were rewarded with extra food. The benefits from the merit point system for the Chinese was not for all if you were a recidivist then you would be very fortunate to get any remission of sentence. This new and civilized prison at Shanghai Qing Pu was realistically a step forward in an effort to reform prisoners. I also knew some Chinese inmates were the chosen select, at first that annoyed me. It takes time to accept the realities of another culture or their ideology. Those selected ones usually had a skill that would benefit running the prison and was beginning to realize the Chinese prison system was clever labor reform pay back for what you stole by doing hard work. The inmates operate the workshops like clockwork. They maintain the discipline most times and they were the ones who get their sentence reduced quicker. Another much-wanted reward was to be given a meal with your family during a visit. There was a lot of conflict going on over this meal privilege as only so many could have that special visit once a month and foreigners were not included. It was during these times would drop a note into the newly installed Warden's box and request a meal with our Consul but was never grant one. The Modern and Civilized prison worked it was certainly a great leap forward in comparison to the old jail in the city except for the medical facilities.

Chapter Twentyone: Hong Kong July 1997

It had been well published in the China Daily English newspaper we the foreign inmates especially the British were told to write our opinions on the issue of Hong Kong returning to the motherland the Peoples Republic of China. A serious assessment was wanted and had not realized how upset the Chinese people felt about their land being governed by Britain. Stanley had explained to me how China wanted Taiwan and Macao returned to the mainland. I never paid much attention to any of the political scenarios other than harboring the fantasy of being set free by amnesty on this historical occasion. The Chinese made a lot of fuss about it. It was every day in the newspaper first it was the history of British colonies throughout the globe. Then we had the opium war re-run. Then the tales of Jesuit priests drinking the menstrual blood that of young Chinese country girl virgins. The television was also pumping out the same anti- British propaganda. On the day of the handover by Prince Charles, it was televised and sure nearly the whole country watched this. The whole jail did it was a historical event and the Chinese inmates were as patriotic as any other about their country was. I was painting new anti-drug posters that day when the guard captain Qian walked into my cell. He was a small man in height that did not daunt his stature he was confident. Wang had been dismissed as unqualified to run the foreign unit and sensed this guard had something to prove. I continued painting and he started to ask me why wasn't I watching the TV as the others were but didn't reply and he called JK and asked him to ask me why. Explaining to JK that I was not interested in Chinese political affairs saying my understanding of the Chinese language was not good enough to understand Chinese politics or decorum from a television announcer. I could see that this guard was not happy that one of his collectives was going astray. They always wanted us to do things as a group that we had no interest in such as to study as a group. The incident was left at that and continued to paint until the afternoon.

Respected Cadre.

I refer to the televised program regarding the handing over of Hong Kong back to the Peoples Republic of China. I have been criticised for not watching this ceremony it was a program, which I had no interest in and so continued to work on something deemed more worthy of my time I don't like to always follow the collective as we are known through Chinese prison reform. I don't accept also this criticism at the whim of the captain in charge of me and can understand the patriotic feelings of the Chinese people watching Prince Charles go through the decorum of returning Hong Kong to China. I have no interest in the entire trumpet blowing, flag raising, marching with guns scenario. I was provoked by Captain Qian and retaliated verbally. I have been in Chinese jail now over six years. I have acknowledged my guilt as in accordance with the Chinese prison law. It is my opinion this Captains weapon is misuse of power knowing he can control the reports that put you forward for remission of sentence. That would

be in breach of Warden Yu Zhong Ming statement of being a Modern civilised prison.
L. Campbell.

It wasn't long after handing in that report was called to the office and was told to sit on a stool which stood eight inches from the floor this was the looking down at you and you up at them domination game declining and stood. JK was doing the interpretation for me and it unfolded that I had gone against the government this use of words always got my hackles up. It unfolded that I had shown no respect by not watching the Hong Kong handover ceremony and was told that Britain caused a lot of misery to the Chinese people replying saying am Scottish. That was a mistake. This guard knew his history and went on to explain how it was the Scottish in the fore front on Imperial Palace raid then a bit on the Boxer rebellion and finally another Opium War spiel. Sometimes I just felt dejected listening to this history at that moment my head was in overload and didn't want any more information about the past but had to listen and after he finished speaking JK told me to return to my cell and think we're I had gone wrong then write a report about my findings. I did return to my cell but just continued painting my anti-drug posters. The exhibition was scheduled for next year now but it was something I had developed a passion for.

Chapter Twentytwo: One Goes Home

Parviz was the first foreign inmate to leave us since arriving at this new jail. It was always a pleasure to see someone go we had settled our past confrontation and we got along quite well. Hearing all the requests coming from the Pakistani guys to visit their families and to send goods and money. It was their status at stake it depended on how much they could afford to spend each month at the jail canteen. It was only Butt and Parviz whose family sent those cash. Syed had got out of his temporary confinement and had a gold chain he had asked the prison authorities to sell it for him at the current gold value and was surprised when they did and that money put Syed flush for at least one year. Mustafa and Khalid where broke Mustafa's Chinese wife had put in for a divorce his family at home depended upon him to send them money back and that wouldn't be happening from here. Now that Parviz was going those two guys would miss out on help with monthly rations and they knew nothing would be forthcoming from Syed.

Chapter Twentythree: Consul Visits

That was another talking point one that had been going on for years was the German consulate visited the prison every month they had done so since their three citizens were arrested. There was one German woman who had got 6 years for possession of cannabis resin and only saw her on a couple of occasions as she passed below me going to her unit. She was released after 3 years from 9th brigade at the old jail woman's cellblock. The British and the American consulate visited on average five times per year. The Pakistani consulate hadn't yet visited their men at all in seven years. The regulations stated we could have two visits each month. That was fine if you were a local. It was one-upmanship for the Germans for years. Bull had never liked the fact that Hans especially could have extra food from his consul visits. The German consulate would bring smoked sausages cheeses mustard good fresh baked bread and so on. Bull had never forgiven Hans for informing on him. I didn't need special foods or such but could write and request the consul to purchase things for me. Bull's lady had been detained for quite a long time due to his arrest that had all been down to Hans's loose tongue. It was something I related with a living nightmare for me during that period back in 1992 after holding my son six month he got fined five thousand pounds sterling and deported. That incident with my son was still a sore point with the authorities. It was one of those stories news travels fast inside jail then it moves onto other jails with the prisoner transfers. Now my son Lochy and I were deeply rooted in Shanghai prison folklore the story like any other grew as years went by. The truth of the matter is we got one over them at a cost. I was still paying that cost by doing my time. Bull had been arranging over the years for his lady's visa for the U.K. and was now also getting monthly visits and sometimes two from her. His lady was now free from detention living and working in Shanghai. I respected her for what she did to travel all the way from to Shanghai find a job and be by her man. Bull said perfection she dances. Bull was a more contented man during this period and couldn't envision myself receiving any more visits especially when my son had gotten arrested during his last visit to see me in China. It was expected we would be having a Consul visit today and had ordered paints and brushes the consul visits were an uncomfortable time for me. Mostly totally detached. I did talk a lot though and it was a means of expressing my thoughts and getting feedback from people outside of jail and was thankful that they brought my family letters parcels plus art materials. The vice consul usually did a two-year stint then moved on this was the third consul attaché to visit me since 1991. Jackie Barlow was a gentle caring lady she always brought me a small gift she could see in my eyes the reflection of my confusion I felt her warmth and compassion knowing someone is out there and cares. It was akin to receiving news letters from Prisoners Abroad the Phoenix Trust away in far off Britain people like P.A. touched you where it was most needed that was your compassion after reading some articles in their newsletter your tears ducts got a private watering audition.

Chapter Twentyfour: Mail

The mail problem issue was ongoing it never worked out as it should have according to the prison law. Lativ was in a rage at his incoming mail taking so long to get to him and it was explained to him that it took time to get a translator for Persian. What do you need a translator for Lativ went on do you think my wife is sending me escape plans? I am not in here for killing anyone why do you make me and my family suffer? I can pay for translator from Iranian Embassy he went on. We all knew he was correct in his views but also knew it would only delay the process of receiving his mail. It was payback time for standing up for his religious rights during Ramadan and for refusing to shave off his beard since arrival. The other Moslems were clean-shaven as they were told they couldn't get the five goods awards if they had a beard.

Chapter Twentyfive: Diplomatic immunity

The arrival of a new guy caused a stir he was seemingly caught in possession of 10kg of heroin. This happened whilst taking North Korean diplomats to the airport. This was undoubtedly a death sentence offence. It was something that left a smell. After being in jail so long tried avoiding new guys stories these days but to no avail Mister Ho was his name and although born in China his parents were North Korean by birth. It seemed Mr Ho had the job of driving a taxi. This day with North Korean Diplomats as his passengers he was driving them from their office towards the airport. That was when the taxi was pulled over and searched thus resulting in the finding of 10kg heroin. As the other passengers were diplomats, they were released under whatever government agreements. Mr. Ho on the other hand got a ten-year prison sentence after having heard that many stories over the years of guys claiming their innocence didn't pay much attention to his tale knowing of many stories involving diplomats and their immunity to arrest. Wishing I had one diplomatic passport on hand myself but as of till now it is but only another fantasy for a money-making scam. Mr Ho needed bed space there was a meeting held and it was cell change time again. All the Chinese inmates except JK moved to the floor above. I moved into cell one now with two single beds. It was a good set up for me and had space to work on my anti-drug posters JK was now my new cellmate.

Chapter Twentysix: The November 3rd Incident

The air was full of tension this was due to some political whisperings among the Moslem inmates. Cranky was pacing the corridor the night before after hearing news reports of some American plane had been shot down in Iraq. Bull and Cranky sat listening to the news again for further details when Syed let out a mighty laugh saying something derogative about America. I was standing in the background watching. Cranky nor did Bull respond they were to long in the tooth for that petty provocation. Bull got off his stool to return to his cell when Syed half blocked him Bull swivelled leaving Syed leaning on air. Seeing Bull approach Stanley and tell him about Syed and that he had better to be removed or there is going to be trouble. That afternoon we had a supply of our canteen apples arrive the procedure was one cell went down at a time to collect Cranky was on his way in the corridor when Syed ran out of his cell and swung a mop handle stick at him. A few other inmates were out waiting to pick up their fruit but Mir was the first to react and deflected the blow. It was only seconds before things were in control again the only problem now was getting Syed to shut up and he didn't and started calling obscenities. It doesn't matter what happens in jail in China the guards must have a report about it. That is the duty of the Chinese inmates to gather information that would be J.K. or Stanley. Bull had openly stated to the guard that Syed should be removed and also stated he would put it in writing. The foreigners all had to submit a report giving our views on Syeds attempted assault on Cranky. The Chinese are clever at gathering information looking for some alterative motive in someone's report for this attack. The guard on duty didn't punish Syed; that day there was no actual wound. The guard had told Bull after a full investigation Syed would be dealt with later. Lativ didn't get along well with Cranky either but he did get along with Bull. It was a typical jail tug of war pulling and playing mind games are you with him or me. Being out of the equation that's what mattered to me.

The following morning at exercise time Bull was running around the grounds one way as Hans ran the other way those two hadn't spoken a word since day one. Sitting by the side of the exercise yard with Vern we watched and chatted for a while. Hans approached after about fifteen minutes puffing and sweating profusely. I got up and walked around seeing Bull cooling down with a slow walk. Then just as he was about to sit down Syed and Khalid ran towards him seeing Syed throwing punches and hitting Bulls arm then big Khalid had a go. Bull gave Khalid a cracking uppercut while dodging blows from Syed getting butterflies in my stomach and wanted to join in but held back Bull was sorting the two out himself. It was when Mustafa joined in I flew into the fight as well. Giving Syed a right solid smack in the mouth he then took off and grabbed a stick and attacked Cranky. Going after him and shouting you fucking bam you want to use a weapon. I grabbed him by the hair and pulled him lower and kicked him right in the mouth he never took off again. Bull was dragged off Khalid by the Chinese inmates and was taken upstairs. I was approached by the young Guard Wu when Kashmiri Mir ran over and started punching into the other Pakistani Butt shouting you are a traitor meaning he was on good terms with Bull. I sidestepped the guard and walked over and landed a knockout punch on Mir he went down. I was escorted to my cell that was the first time standing my ground to support Bull but as to Cranky was still holding his report about me against him. We all returned to our cells and were told to write about what happened that included those not involved. It was one incident that the authorities were appalled about. It was akin to a riot in their minds. One by one we had to be interviewed the Criminal Affairs Cadres came. Being asked did I take part in the fight or not. Yes, and couldn't deny it but explained that only went to Bull and Crank's defence. Using a common law point that I read from a book my brother had sent me explaining like this" if a little girl was drowning in a pool and a sign said keep of the grass would you let the girl drown "or break the law by going onto the grass.

My explanation didn't go down to well. The next line of inquiry was who started the trouble that was easy to answer and told them Syed had openly attacked Bull. What about the guards could they have prevented the incident seeing JK moving his eyes trying to tell me to say no? And sometimes would answer questions in Chinese especially when suspicious thinking the interpreter isn't saying what I want. Then answered yes they could have prevented it after the attempted attack on Cranky with the brush pole. It turned out the following day we had another meeting and all the brass turned up. We the foreign prisoners had behaved in an uncivilised manner well some of us had. Those of us involved got demerit points that meant it was back to square one again for me with my five no fucking goods. Bull was expecting to get a reduction in sentence or even released by the end of the year it looked like that wouldn't be happening now. Syed was given temporary confinement again we didn't know for how long. Vern came into my cell later on that evening and said to me Campbell why did you get involved? While you were down in the yard fighting, Cranky was upstairs' looking down but had the idea thinking that the odds were against Bull and that gave me the right to take part to even things out and was doing the right thing as far as I was concerned. Still had a lot to learn.

Chapter Twentyseven: Christmas Surprise 1997

It was cold again and everyone was wrapped up in thick woollen sweaters a heavy coat and a head cap made from sleeves of an old sweater. The morning exercise yard was half empty many guys preferred to stay inside rather that walk outside in that biting wind. It was after breakfast that we were called to the ground floor area assuming another meeting no doubt about reform Bull and I had decorated that area for the upcoming Xmas festivities. We were all seated the Prison Administration Bureau boss came into the room we all stood and said Duisan Hao then sat again. It unfolded that Hans and Vern had got another reduction from there sentence and were told to pack their bags as they had a flight home that night. It was always like that with the Chinese authorities they never gave you any hint of coming events regarding remission regarding anything. I watched Vern and Hans walking over the exercise yard carrying their luggage out from jail for the last time. It is nice to see the back of folk especially when going out of jail. Bull was disappointed he felt he should have gone with them. It wasn't just felt by Bull my complaint comparing my crime to that of the Germans and Bull. Hans and Vern had got bust for smuggling. Bull for supplying and possession. It was one of the main reform lectures never to compare my crime or sentence with others easily said hard to live with. I had given Vern and Hans's one oil painting apiece before they left one was of the prison band The Reformers the other a reform meeting, they were my first efforts at depicting our lives in a Chinese jail. Wishing them well as they departed.

Chapter Twentyeight: Hand Delivered

I got a letter in bold type British Consul General Shanghai and in brackets hand delivery.

Shanghai British Consul General

15th December 1997

Dear Lauchlan.

Many thanks for your Christmas and New Year wishes and for the card you sent. I have shown it to all my UK colleagues and will make sure that Lisa sees it too when she returns to work.

As you know, I am more than happy to support your excellent anti-drugs campaign. I have been very impressed with your work to date on it. I wish I were as creative and artistically inclined as you!

It is a bit early to start to drum up support for the exhibition but I will of course do my best a little nearer the time. Meanwhile, I have pencilled 26 June in my diary.

This letter comes by hand of David Oswald, in the absence in London of Sue. (She returns to Shanghai after the holiday period) I would like to have sent him with a bottle of Black Label for you but I am afraid it would be a no-no. I hope you enjoy the gifts we have chosen instead. Thanks for writing, Lauchlan.

Take care Kind regards,
Warren.

It was a good feeling reading that letter someone out there was responding and I had the confirmation in my hand the good old British Consulate.

Chapter Twentynine: Another Year Begins 1998

The guards had been issued with new uniforms getting rid of the ugly green-ish ones and being replaced by smart navy-blue ones. They also changed the ranking system. It was silver stars and silver bars now one bar equalled three stars. If you were a recruit you started with one star unless you had a university degree then you started with three stars moving up to one bar after completing your recruitment test. Christmas and the New Year passed that left only Cranky Bull and myself from the westerners. It made room for another cell change and at last Cranky got to share a cell with Bull. I had been working most days on the anti-drug posters with JK he was doing all the written Chinese characters for me. We got along well most times but we could be often fragile in mind. JK had been going on for years at the old jail and now telling me about how his brother was going to be his guarantee and get him out. Turning on him one day and spat out your brothers a fucking dog continuing on, if it was my brother who was outside, he would be prepared to come and do half my time. That's what a fucking brother does pissed off at his illusion of freedom he had jail time now twenty plus years for having consented sex with his students who he said were not underage this was his second offence. Seeing that I had hurt him and was sorry for trying to take away his only lifeline of hope instinctively knowing it was all imaginary JK wasn't going anywhere. He had stopped dying his hair and started to look very unkempt. I had been buying him food since the first month of meeting him in 1992 we had done a lot together. He was my elder brother my Chinese guardian in the ways of the system.

Chapter Thirty: The Pest

The year had hardly started the beginning of March when Shu Ming accused me of punching him. He had arrived as third in command under Stanley. Having had repeatedly told him to stop causing trouble in our unit corrupting people with his favours of getting them extra food. He told me that his connections are the highest and he doesn't have to be afraid of any Captains. It was the same old power story and was sick of hearing it. It didn't benefit me anything because he had connections so gave him a Manchurian sneer and punched his shoulder hard. Then was called into the office and asked why had I punched Shu Ming denying it and replied only the shoulder in jest. Leaving the office, the guard handed me a bunch of papers and told me to hand them out. It was the mail issue again and here is a copy of that document.

<u>Temporary Provisions on the Correspondence of the Foreign Criminals</u>

1. The foreign criminals have the right of correspondence with close relatives, within China accredited embassy and consulate staff and with other persons after permission by the prison.
2. The foreign criminals can send out correspondence twice every month. In special case circumstances it can be permitted to send more mail if the officer in charge gives permission
3. After translation of the foreign criminals mail the original letter and translation will be stored electronically.
4. After examination and registration of the mail by the officer in charge it will be delivered to the responsible officer of the criminal affairs department of the prison and after examination it will be sent out.
5. If there are obstructions to the reform or damaging opinions on politics and other affairs of China the mail will not be sent out and the criminal will be subject to education.
6. After translation of incoming mail for the criminal it will be given to the criminal affairs department and examined by the responsible officer. The officer in charge will store the original incoming letter and the translation electronically.
7. After examination of the mail, it immediately will be given to the receiver. If there are opinions of obstruction to the reform or other opinions, which are not to be made known, to the criminal it will be reported and with the approval of the criminal affairs department it will be registered and kept on file.
8. Mail of the criminal with regards to petition or accusation should be completely and directly given to the responsible officer of the criminal affairs department for handling. The officer in charge will make a registration.

Chapter Thirtyone: Cherish Life Refuse Drugs

It was late May before completing my anti-drug poster work. It was to be exhibited from June 10th to June 26th 1998 and had designed forty posters all with a message about the evils and perniciousness of drug use and drug trade. I had made the first poster with the U.N. logo on it plus the British, American, German, Russian, Belgium and Chinese flags on it and named my exhibition U.N. against drugs. The Chinese government were also running a campaign for the upcoming U.N. anti-drug day June the 26th spearheaded by Jiang Zemin the great leader of the people. It was titled Cherish Life Refuse drugs. It was suggested that we use the government slogan and I went along with that. J.K. and I were taken over to the visiting area where the posters were set up for a preview before the exhibition. The prison film crew were there as was the Warden and several other high ranking officials Warden Yu Zhong Ming told J.K. I could be given a Li Gong award. That meant a direct reduction in your sentence. In China the actively reforming criminals are given certificates of merit throughout the year and if you accumulate two you get a recommendation for reduction. I didn't have any at this time after losing them through fighting. This was different to be given a reduction for my contribution to the society as promulgated in the prison law article 58 rewards and punishment. Having had heard of guys getting a reduction for some invention or for reporting culprits of a past unsolved crime this surely was one Chinese puzzle of reform. I had received a letter with newspaper clippings showing my brother's co accused Joe Steel of free the Glasgow two campaigns in a crucifix posture super glued to Buckingham Palace gates. I was inspired to paint this image it was a masterstroke on Joe's behalf what better way to bring light to their case than super gluing yourself to Her Majesty's front door. Well-done Joe I took my hat off to you that day.

It was June 2nd 1998 and had a consul visit that day so handed in two oil paintings to the guard to be handed out to the consul. Having done one of my brother sitting in a lotus position holding a bible with his legs in shackles. The other was Joe Steel glued to the Buckingham Palace gate. Being called into the office before the visit and asked why the painting has shackles as I don't have shackles in here. Then explained to them about my brother, which they already knew about and got the newspaper clipping to show them Joe at the gates thus letting them know it wasn't related with me in China. The guard wasn't having any of it and told me to return the paintings to my cell. Making the mistake by answering him in Chinese and saying stick your communist thinking up your ass was heckled away and stuck in the punishment block for fourteen days.

I missed my consul visit and any reduction of sentence that might have been coming was cancelled and was fucking sick to the teeth and felt cheated. To rub more salt into my already aching psyche missed the opening game of the world cup Scotland vs. Brazil played on June 10th 1998. Here was me lying in a cellblock solitary confinement trying to work out what was wrong with my fucking mind. It was just ongoing trouble due to lack of self-control. It was summer, and sticky heat filled the air being stripped then given a dirty prison uniform to put on was told to stand upright. I did this until my legs were getting tired so sat on the floor. The guard immediately shouted stand up, ignoring him pretending not to understand. Shouting something else and another guard arrived with the electric cattle prod. I stood up immediately. Later that day it was explained to me through Stanley who was now the main translator and interpreter that I must follow their discipline while here. Stanley sat outside my cell for observation purposes.

It was a painful experience sitting one hour then standing one hour fifteen hours a day for fourteen days. I still blamed the guard for provoking me those paintings had nothing to do with Chinese jail and had to write several self-criticisms and apologise in front of the group for cursing the Chinese government. Standing there looking at those tired and weary faces thinking how they manage not to lose it at times with this system. The punishment block does work at least for a while then you forget well some did. After the meeting asked Bull about the consul visit was their mail for me, he informed me there was. I asked if they had gone to the exhibition yet. Bull told me the Consul went to view it after the last visit but the foreigners hadn't been although he went on to say the Chinese inmates and families can view it at their visit. My head was still in stir and went to the office to ask for my letters and when could we see the exhibition, I was ready to go into a rant of hay you fuckwits it was me who created this so demanded to see it. The guard looked at my unshaven mosquito bitten face and informed me that it had been arranged for the following day that the foreign inmates view it. "Campbell," he said "you had better shave some outside visitors will be viewing it also." It just happened like a blink of an eye that my mood swung from killing these people to thanking them for exhibiting my art. I left the office and went and told Bull who wasn't overly enthusiastic to hear such news. Then returned to my cell feeling elated grabbed my bathing bag and took a shower and shave.

As I left the shower the Chinese inmate Shu Ming asked me what was I doing taking a shower at this time ignoring him and walked into my cell. He stood at the door and asked did you get the captains permission? I was ready to say go fuck yourself but bit my tongue and said yes. That was it he left knowing he had to do this sort of snooping around and reporting trivial shit but it still got my back up at times. The following afternoon we had a meeting and Campbell was the hero and the fool of the day. I was praised to the high heavens from the highest authority for my contribution to the society. It was stated that two of my posters had been selected for prison education purposes. It felt good. Then came the criticisms, which I won't explain in detail but all resulted in me being the fool. The warden finished of as usual with an old Chinese idiom it translated something like no use to cry over spilled milk. I was thinking it is ok for you it's not your milk that's spilled. We left the meeting and headed straight to the exhibition. It surprised me at how they had set it up it was very professionally done.

They had made temporary walls so that the four parts could be viewed as planned moving from part one to two three then four it was a story I had painted. It was beautiful every painting was framed flowers and plants were placed around and my message was colourful and clear. That was the most satisfying moment in all my time in jail to date it really was meaningful. Requesting the guard if I could have photos taken with me at the exhibition and also photos taken of all the posters. He informed me to ask a higher authority which I did and got permission to have a video made of it and also photographs all to be given to the British consul for safekeeping. Feeling a bit sceptical about the easiness of my request being granted but it did and got to return to the exhibition alone a week later and did a photo session with the education guard the negatives were given to the consul also with a short video clip of my work.

Chapter Thirtytwo: African White Paper

The arrival of two new prisoners from Liberia in July 1998 was a new addition to the already international jailbird collection. Wavi and Eli were both devout Christians and had committed the crime of deception. Liberia was war torn and their story was they had U.S. Dollars millions of them taken from the U.S. safety box office in their country during the civil war and needed a certain chemical to wash the ink-stained money into a usable currency. They showed the interested person a demonstration that they had expertly worked out beforehand. Another part of their story was they had a contact at the American embassy in Beijing or wherever they did a scam and he could get the chemical but at a price. Sometimes they would catch a greedy investor and con them. It worked a treat at times and the more money you give to them to buy the chemical the more you are promised to get back. It was a good con and nobody got hurt.

The authorities move us again. Now cell five was to be the induction cell. This had never been done before and both guys were the first to have this imposed upon them. I went to their cell every evening and sat with them still not fully quenched in my thirst of meeting new and exotic looking people. Wavi told me his father was a police inspector and his house was attacked. He went on to tell me that he had to take up arms at a young age he was twenty-six now and had escaped Liberia and getting eventually to the Ivory coast where he was kept at a refugee camp waiting to be sent to America to link up with his family. It was there he met up with Eli and decided to make their own way to America so they split the camp went onto Ghana where they got fake documents and passports. They were both street wise men and Eli spoke French and had gone to college whereas Wavi couldn't read nor write. This threw suspicion on his story to me of being a police inspector's son.

Chapter Thirtythree: Khalid Goes Home

It was August the weather was hot and getting humid there was excitement in the Pakistani camp tomorrow one was going home and could take messages to families and pleas of financial help. Khalid had got a three-year sentence for fraud he served every day of it. When Parviz had went home, he kept in touch with Butt sending him the occasional parcel. But couldn't see Khalid doing the same as his three-year was without monthly ration purchases due to his economic status. It had been Butt and Lativ who had been getting him fruits and toiletries from their monthly purchase as there was no limit on how much you could spend on such items. We purchased everything from the prison canteen including our socks, underwear, sport shoes to pens paper and stamps. I was neither sad nor glad to see the back of Khalid he was a sort of simpleton and could be dangerous at times.

Chapter Thirtyfour: My Old Friend Died

I was shattered when getting the news of JK dying. He had been staying in bed most of the month of July with me thinking the old codger was just resting due to the excessive heat. He had been taken to the old jail hospital at Tilan Xiao in August and he died there.

I lay on top of my bed thinking about him saddened that he never got to publish his English teaching book that Grad, Bull, Cranky myself and the two Germans had helped him with at the old jail. Saying a silent farewell and reminisced about all the little scams we had done together. I loved JK and would miss him dearly.

Chapter Thirtyfive: Radios

The year was moving on without much happening other than the usual squabble over food rations or someone else's space being invaded. Hans and Bull were the only two with radios and were allowed to keep them because they arrived with them. Hans had sold his to Lativ who paid in advance buying Han's postage stamps there was always some way to do trade and Lativ was good at it.

Cranky was getting annoyed that the music coming from Latifs cell was disturbing him as he had it on an Arab station this led to another meeting. I raised the issue of why couldn't we all have a radio, which resulted in that we all could buy them, but the conditions where we had to use earphones. There was no complaint and a good radio only cost four-pound sterling. The problem was the Pakistani inmates didn't have a consul visit to help do this sort of shopping for them and we were not allowed to help them buy one via our consul. This caused more debate with Syed in the forefront. It was resolved by one of the guards buying them so all could be equally treated. The weather is very hot in September and we played football most afternoons. Wavi and Eli where good football players Eli was an excellent player and claimed to know George Weah the Liberian international who had won world player of the year. Wavi was faster than any person in the whole jail and I hadn't even seen him run a distance yet but just knew. The Pakistani inmates wanted to play cricket so a set of stumps and a bat were made in the wood shop and we would go over to the football ground for a game of cricket. That event took place a few days later and we had a good laugh. It was obvious those guys loved that game of cricket as much as we others loved football. At the end of September, the foreign unit played seven aside footballs against the Qing Pu prison first team. Our team was Wavi, Eli, Bull, Stanley, Mustafa, Kasha and I and we beat those 5-2. That caused quite an upset in the jail sport culture. The competitive streak among us coming out and we all wanted to win it was akin to beating the system. They hadn't broken us yet.

Chapter Thirtysix: Zip It

The Chinese American Bo had been giving the guards a hard time over the food orders saying that we were being overcharged. I thought it to be very trivial as the food orders were so inexpensive it amounted to about four to six pounds sterling each month. The prison food was sufficient and plenty but the old status and ego plays a big part on canteen day. That's when those with inferiority complexes stand out and also the leeches' surface. Bo had connected up with three new Chinese inmates who had moved into the ground floor cells below us they were all elderly men in their sixties. It was rumoured that they were communist party officials who had swayed from the principles of the party and were being re-educated at the prison. It was during this period we got to view a lot of good movies and then it came to a sudden end. The reason for this transpired when seeing Bo being escorted from our building by two guards from the punishment block and at his back was Shu Ming the not long arrived Chinese inmate who also had family connections at the prison. Shu Ming had assured me his connection was the highest up and he could help me to get released early. I wondered now if his connection could stop what was about to happen to him. We never saw him again but heard reports of him working long shifts in the sweatshop. Bull and Cranky had voiced that it was someone who must have informed on Bo and Shu Ming. I had to laugh at that, thinking how the fuck could we all sits and watch a movie and the authorities wouldn't know about it they did know but choose to ignore it till the time was right and that was now. Bo was kept for six weeks at the cells. He had been passing out mail via the guy's downstairs all of whom had confessed and told the full story. As he didn't return for six weeks that was in breach of the prison law. Then when he did return Cranky Bull and Bo were right into the intrigue of what was going on in the prison. Bo had news of factories sending items to the U.K.

So, fucking what I thought having worked seven days a week in the factory at Tilan Xiao often more than twelve hour shifts it was nothing new. It was to Bo as he was still a new guy you would have thought he discovered America in his enthusiasm to enlighten some of us to what we knew was going on. I was suspicious of those two Cranky was for sure an informer and had also read a report written by Bull about myself related to an electric organ that Vern had left behind. The organ had lay in the storeroom for months unused when one day Mustafa asked me who it belonged to and told him Vern had left it behind, he asked if he could use it I said sure why not. It was a couple of days later being called into the office and asked did I give Mustafa the organ and replied yes. I was told that it wasn't my property to give out but replied that it was my property and that Vern had given it to me before he left lying but knew they didn't know that. As it worked out the organ was returned to the storeroom and nobody could use it thanks to Bulls report That's how it was at this jail you couldn't trust anyone and thank the communist party for instilling the wisdom of silence into me in short keep your thoughts to yourself. I couldn't relate sometimes with the cultural difference it was difficult to bridge.

Chapter Thirtyseven: A Horrible Man

The arrival of another new guard Captain Jiang at the end of September who was now to be in charge of us. That was the third guard change since our arrival here. The foreign unit always had conflict usually trivial and mostly verbal. Besides being in a foreign jail the cultural mix among the foreigners was often clashing. The Moslem inmates were saying we don't do any work on Fridays. I said then who has to do your share of the building cleaning that day and offered to do it for Lativ and he could do mine on a Monday but what of the others. These sorts of issues often came up who gets the hot water first in the morning, which should be first in line for canteen and on it went.

Captain Jiang was a man who wanted order and discipline he was slight in build and short in stature. The guard he replaced had lost any chance of promotion due to the November 3rd incident. Stanley had asked me to help him keep this guard happy so as to make sure he himself wasn't transferred to the workshop for not helping to run our unit smoothly. It didn't take long for this guard to show his colours. Captain Jiang would often walk into your cell and try to catch you lying on the bed. The regulations stated you should sit at your table and study or read. It had become a ritual for Jiang to try and catch Lativ who always lay on the bed.; Most of us did at times throughout the day as we had no jobs to do it was a boring existence for most. I had written to the prison education department asking for a Chinese language teacher to start classes having done this on numerous reports regarding equal treatment. Putting forward that the Chinese inmates had avenues for study.

The next avenue pursued was writing to the British consul with a request to buy me an oil paints easel palette brushes and canvas to which they complied and am eternally grateful for that service. I had finished the anti- drug paintings and was looking to be useful. Needing to be active with my restless spirit. The equipment was brought to me at the next visit and got to setting up my workshop on the veranda in my cell and started my first oil painting. I copied a face from a magazine thinking of myself to be the undiscovered Rembrandt. I didn't find it that difficult to paint that first face in fact it reminded me of my ex-wife Mary and enjoyed that first encounter with oil on canvas it did give me a feeling of achievement. Captain Jiang was plotting to cause some trouble he was against the followers of Islam and Christianity he had caught Wavi and Eli praying and warned them not to go on their knees again. Wavi and Eli complied through fear of losing any chance of their remission.

One day Lativ had said to me Campbell we need to cover the toilets we had three squat toilets in the corridor and there were no doors on them. In my eyes this toilet was a big improvement on the old jail and hadn't thought of being behind a closed door whilst having a shit. I guess having to do my daily toilet functions in a cell with twelve men at the detention cells then with the improvement of being able to shit in a bucket alone in my cell this was a great leap forward. Lativ asked me to get him some material from the workshop as I had a connection there through Stanley. It took a couple of days then Stanley got several metres of dark plastic sheeting and Lativ cut out three door size panels then stitching a piece of string and nailed them over the toilet sitting area. It was the following day that we heard a lot of commotion coming from Latifs cell but didn't go to inquire as to why. It was something you learned in jail to mind your own affairs. It was my experience on more than one occasion that when trying to solve certain issues it usually ended up with me getting involved and into trouble.

Chapter Thirtyeight: Two Visits Surprise

It was time for the year-end meeting we were all gathered into the great Hall of the people and it happened to fall on Xmas day there must have been at least one thousand inmates in attendance. On stage was the usual high brass with their giant microphones. The back of the hall and throughout guards sat strategically. I hated these meetings it was hours of repetitious gabble about reform. But knew Bull was half expecting to get released the same way the two Germans had done last Christmas. I expected nothing and that is exactly what transpired Bull on the other hand was rewarded with a reform activist award that entitled him to a reduction of his sentence but when that would be and how much time would be deducted was always kept a mystery. The Criminal affairs guard had visited us before Christmas and taken our photos with the promise we could have some to send to our families. He had now returned after the New Year and he wanted some of us to give an interview for the prison newspaper and was hinting if we didn't then he wouldn't be forthcoming with the photos. I said to him are you blackmailing us. Then went on to say you should have told us your intention was to use them for propaganda you tried to trick us. What he wanted was our permission to publish them in then reform papers around China. After handing in this report the guard This was a total surprise to me and hadn't heard anything then realized they always withhold information regarding letters or visits so as you cannot prepare a story. So, why give me advance notice now thinking was it because of doing the propaganda papers? I wondered. It was the following morning that question got answered and was called downstairs and told had a visit. The bastards, I hadn't even shaved and didn't want to return to have one and keep my brother waiting and anyway he wouldn't give a dam how appeared as long as I wasn't being abused.

Nervously walking into the visiting room and my brother sat there relaxed as a Sacred cow would be in India he stood up and we both embraced. Rab immediately spoke in colloquial Glaswegian asking me did I want a bit of hash or cash. I replied in clear English you could put money into my property. Then back to Glaswegian and the other stuff sling it or swallow it when you leave here and was paranoid my brother defying the system and asking if I needed cannabis. The visit seemed to go by quick and Rab showed me a gold Buddha he had bought he gave me photos of his two sons Jason and Joshua and his granddaughter whom he adored. My brother had arranged to have two visits so he left with a list of requirements I had asked for to make life easier in jail. He handed over 1000 English pounds to the guard and said put that into his property. He then shook my hand and said see you next week brother. I was delighted it was the best surprise in a near decade and bounced on my toes back to the unit with the two of the guards assisting to carry my parcels Sitting watching TV in the corridor with Bull and he asked   me how the visit went it was good but that was taken totally by surprise. Bull had been getting regular visits from his now wife and he told me he was itching to get out of this place are not we all remarked. I had not gotten along that well with Bull but we seldom had any conflict. I knew indeed we would be there for each other. November 3rd incident other than that sort of scenario Bull could handle him well enough. I recall him saying to me one day on the corridor when we first arrived at the new jail Campbell there is nothing to worry about here, nobody does anything bad enough to cause serious trouble relax he told me we are all going nowhere. It is the donkey carrot trick he assured me and knew he was correct but maybe just maybe I would get a bite. It was eight days later that my brother returned this time with a wee bit whiskey inside him and McDonald's hamburgers and hips for us both. Rab informed me that he had left a parcel with the consul, as he couldn't carry it. I hugged him and he did likewise to me the guard stood up and tried to separate us but Rab said fuck off you bam pot and pushed his hand away. I saw the tension in their eyes they didn't know how to handle a visitor who was playing by his own rules. We sat down and had good laugh Rab was making me sniffle like a crying baby making Benny Hill imitations of the guards and enjoyed that freedom of spirit that comes with laughter. It was time to say goodbye but Rab refused to budge from his seat. I was getting a little nervous but sat all the same there was no way I was getting up first not after my brother came all the way from Britain to see me. It extended to another 20 minutes then my brother stood up and again put his arms around me and said Lockie you look well and you sound alright keep it up brother you will be home in no time. I let the tears run down my eyes as watched my brother being escorted from the visiting room door. What a lovely man and thought how fortunate to have brothers who cared for me. That whole week was still in a sort of euphoria seeing my brother again he had also brought good happenings about the case of TC Campbell in Free the Glasgow 2 campaigns love you brother.

Chapter Thirtynine: Backstabber

It was January 21st 1999 ten full years to the day that Mir was arrested he stood there with a smirk across his face dressed to go home. Due to the flight time, he had sat around in the guard's office until midday. Several of us stood at the window to wave farewell he waved back at us as he entered the police escort van. Mir had told me a few stories over the years and mostly far-fetched. What he did do he had planted the seed about how nasty Captain Jiang was and knew he was spot on in his assessment. I began to pay more attention to this guard's motive. I couldn't handle all the back biting this Captain Jiang was doing he was seriously demented which might have been the outcome of a motorbike crash he had just weeks after his arrival to our unit. He had been off sick for one month and now he looked sluggish constantly.

I had been watching Captain Jiang closely sneaking up on inmates when they stayed in their cell. He was a nutcase jumping in your cell after tiptoeing up to it. If he caught you, he would deduct 0.5 merit points from you and that was a lot to the carrot chasers to keep you on edge 0.5 was a lot to lose. In one month if all was good you got 6 to 8 points which if amounted to 90 at the end of the year would entitle you to a reward? Several inmates come to me telling me all sorts of stories about what Jiang had said about me. It was soon discovered that he had been telling stories not only about me but many others he certainly was of bad character this man.

Chapter Forty: A Big Event

It was Chinese New Year coming up again and there was a sports competition being put on. This was to be the biggest event so far with all cellblocks taking part also two other jails were coming to join the event. We had football, basketball; and the 100m 200m 400m sprints and 1500 meters for the final race outing. The grounds were crowded all brigades had their own colors in sportswear. Still being a bit curious looking around trying. It was a cool spring day and everyone was excited at the upcoming   to identify with anyone from the old jail but never saw anyone and proceeded to mingle a little.

The prison reform was broadcast from a stage with the usual high ranking officials being filmed while giving a speech. The flag rising and national anthem had been completed.

It was time to start and the 100m was the first race on the card. The crowds chanted encouragement to their cellblock and we did likewise. The starting pistol fired the race was off and Wavi went on and won the 100m and 200m races easily. Stanley had a place in the 400m now it was Bull who was running next. As the firing gun went off, he was left standing he looked like a dummy as the Chinese runners sprinted off. We were all shouting move it come on Bull do not let the troops down but he lagged behind still as he came around for the second time. Cranky was on his feet and was shouting encouragement as Bull passed. Then when the bell rang for the final round, we all jumped and cheered Bull on as he overtook one after another and sprinted over the finishing line in first place, I was happy to see Bull silence his critics namely the Pakistani contingent. It was the following day that our football games were to begin and we went on to win that final. It was sheer determination from all the foreign participants to win even ping-pong and cards. Cranky was not shooting ball anymore after being diagnosed with Hep C he just stopped caring for himself and started getting fat.

Chapter Fortyone: Black Magic

It was the first week of April 1999 and felt sick one night lying on my bed sweating profusely. The following morning putting my name down to see the doctor and was given a couple of pills, but did not take them. Being told to rest because I had a little fever. That night the same thing happened awakening totally soaked and started to get paranoid. It was Eli and Wavi who started the ongoing story that Cranky was practicing black magic. One day during the exercise, period Wavi called me upstairs to look down at Cranky walking around the yard. He pointed out to me that Cranky dragged one of his feet. Wavi said that was the sign. I told him the story of Cranky damaging his leg at the old jail and Wavi immediately replied that was his other leg. That sudden reply knocked the wind out of me, as I did not even remember which leg it was he had damaged. Wavi went on to tell me he had also seen a snake in the shower after Bull had come out. This was becoming too much the Africans were in constant huddle with stories of the dead from Egypt to Nigeria and along the Ivory Coast. I had read parts of a book written by a Nigerian person about spirits and ghosts now it seemed all too real.

For me the icing on the cake was when going into my cell, which I now shared with Stanley and found nail cuttings on the floor next to my bed. Immediately rushing to get Wavi and tell him and had read somewhere nail cuttings were a voodoo means of getting to you. Wavi examined the nails looking them over and he said toenails it is for making a strong spell. Who the fuck put them there I spoke out? It was a big person look at their size Wavi said I did look but did not touch them and just screwed up my nose and looked at Wavi. Cranky or Bull I asked? Bull Wavi replied.

Chapter Fortytwo: Tail Cut

There was some stir in the air that Bull would be leaving soon it was a common term used at the jails in China known as a tail cut. A tail cut is when you get a little extra jail time deducted before your Liberation date. It is usually anything from one month to six months and everyday remission counts is the final munch at the proverbial carrot you're not really expecting but can easily convince yourself that you deserve to have it. Having to returned to the hospital again after another bout of the sweats and wasn't given any medication but was to be given a few sachets of powder mix for dehydration purposes in addition, was told to take one after the evening meal.

I recall having supper that evenings then having a hot re hydration drink. The following afternoon it hit me that I had been drugged and had kept a diary when starting taking these night sweats and shivers. Knowing my mind was off balance having been caught up in thinking black magic was causing this. Then realising I hadn't awaked until after ten in the morning. Having hadn't slept till that time in eight years and you were not allowed too anyway. It took a several hours more then began to feel the muscle tightness in my body the medicinal pollution had registered. I had slept then woke up and two more inmates were gone on their way home. Butt from Pakistan and Bull from the UK.

The bastards had drugged me. Was it their way of making it easier on me being the only British national left imprisoned in China? More likely, they thought I would stir something up and had been rather volatile over the year's unpredictable to say the least. Therefore, I put it down to them not wanting me to see where I also wanted to go and that was home. With two more gone, that would mean another cell reshuffle and was staying put or getting a single cell would be my next new demand.

Chapter Fortythree: 30 Grand

With two inmates gone, the next day two more new people arrived. Both came from Africa one from the Ivory Coast the other Cameroon. They had been working as a team-selling white paper. It was the same swindle that landed Wavi and Eli here the only difference was the amount swindled. Happy came from Ivory Coast and the same age as myself then forty-nine. He had a bushy head of pure white hair and white beard to match he was overweight and around 175cm tall. Joe his partner was a big well-built guy around 184cm and was as bling as they come. They both spoke in French as well as English and Eli spoke French so that was the beginning of the QPJ African union with Jean Marie Happy at the head. It turned out that Happy had also been on Hajji and him and Lativ struck up a friendship. They also brought news of other foreigners locked up at the detention cells other Pakistanis Japanese and Koreans. The unit was running without much incident until Jiang went on the hunt again. Jiang did not like Moslems and Lativ was still getting hassle from him. Now there were two Hajjis, they got more respect from the other followers of that faith, and Jiang did and did not like it at all. Jiang had called a meeting just a week over from their arrival. He wanted to expose the African inmate Prince Jean Marie Happy from the Ivory Coast for taking stamps on credit from other inmates. This was true and had given him stamps because he needed them to write to his family letting them know about his welfare whereabouts and to request money to be sent onto him. It was Jiang up to his mind games again this time Happy was his victim. It turned out to be a glorious outcome for Jiang. During the meeting, Happy frustratingly asked to have the storeroom door opened which Jiang called the other guard to comply with sensing something had been stirred up. It was when Happy returned back upstairs with 300 US dollars crisp 100-dollar bills waving in his hand and saying don't you insult Africans we are not beggars as you call us. That started it. The search was on for more money and another 29700 US dollar were uncovered lying in the bottom of Prince Jean Marie Happy bag. The popper to Prince back to popper had unfolded right in front of our eyes. The meeting came to an abrupt end and we were all locked up then the place filled with uniforms. The storeroom was quarantined and each inmate was called one by one and identified their belongings, which they then watched being searched. Maybe a flash of what my sons Scott, Lochy and I had gotten away with gave them thought to look closer at us all plus with 30 thousand dollars already uncovered it gave them a good incentive. Happy had declared the money was in his bag since arrest and had assumed the guards new about it at the detention cells. The money was confiscated and that left Happy in the same boat as before he opened his bag. What a fucking halfwit I thought 30 grand would have set him up for going home speaking with him later and suggested all sort of ways he could have gotten it out but as usual who fucking wants to hear it? He did not and neither do I when people try to tell me what I should have done with the cannabis now eight years down the line.

Chapter Fortyfour: June 1999

The unit had been running smoothly recently that should have been a warning sign. I had just received art books from a dear Scottish friend in London called Ralph Maclaren and was sitting reading them when Mr. Ho came into the cell and asked to have a look as he also painted in oils.

I was sharing a cell now with Mustafa due to conflict he had with Mir before he had left in January. Stanley had told me beforehand that Captain Jiang wanted me to share a cell with Mustafa and told me not to agree and to say it isn't culturally acceptable and to use Cranky as an example how conflict could arise between us. I ignored Stanley's advice and agreed to share a cell with Mustafa Stanley knew much more than he let on he knew about Jiang and often confined in me to be careful or to not get involved with what Jiang was brewing. It was made clear to me that trouble would arise so watch out one thought came to my mind was Mir had told me that Jiang had said to him that he will swat Campbell like a mosquito when the time comes. The time had come.

Chapter Fortyfive: Sticky Heat. July 1999

It transpired that Captain Jiang still riding on his high horse with talk of promotion at finding the money had managed to convince Mustafa that I disrespected his religion. Confronting Mustafa and asked what it was all about? He informed me that I had shown Mr. Ho his shrine when he came to our cell to ask to look at the art books. Induced a mini-Jihad and when people think you have disrespected their religion that spells trouble. There was a meeting held and I was smack in the middle. Jiang had set me up and had fallen straight into his trap. It was too late now as Stanley's words rang in my ears do not change cell, ended up losing the plot as usual, and started to curse the communist party, which resulted in another fourteen-day, confinement cell experience. Whilst being carted away still shouting abuse at Jiang. In addition, true to his words spoken to Mir there was me lying in a mosquito-filled cell naked with a rough and dirty hairy blanket that made your skin creep. Whilst in confinement you have to write self-criticisms and this was my first submission.

Dear Sir.
I am a foreign national in Shanghai I am a prisoner under the Chinese prison reform system and have been educated at the prison to express my thoughts honestly and to write a monthly ideological report in accordance with the prison reform demands. I am a sensitive person and attentive to certain comments made by others and also articles read in the China Daily newspaper.
It has been my experience that the China Daily newspaper does not waste space in printing sensationalism. I write this report requesting that you follow up on my accusations by doing some investigation and want to expose the wrongdoing of one man in particular.
Throughout the years whilst serving my sentence has experienced many racial comments towards foreigners even today still hear them. I recall this caused much conflict between the foreigners and Chinese at Tilan Xiao jail. We were often offended and at times angry.
As time went by began to realise that most of the racial slurs were said parrot fashion due to the inmate's lack of worldly knowledge knowing that every language uses words that are uncouth and are often spoken without malice or intentional disrespect. At the end of the year 1998 while having my daily exercise was shocked when a guard spoke to me using racial slurs against two African inmates. I walked away in disgust at this guard's use of words. After the exercise period was finished was called to the office and asked why I showed contempt by walking away from this guard during exercise. I answered his question through the interpreter Mr. Chon that did not want to listen to the captains' racial views about other people or their countries. I could clearly see that this guard was not pleased with my outspokenness. On another occasion whilst walking with the inmate Mustafa Aqbal when this same guard joined us and interrupted our conversation by making the statement in a racial tone about the Iranian

inmate Latifs manner of dress. Mustafa Aqbal changed the conversation by saying the weather was nice for sport today and asked the guard to arrange some event. Once more on another occasion the same guard approached me and again started using racial slurs against the Cameroonian inmate Nesiwe. I immediately stepped up my pace mumbling idiot and forcing my psyche to get the message through to him. When I returned to my cell Mustafa came to me with quite animated eyes, he told me that his religion teaches that people who talk that way are evil. I agreed with him and began to distance myself from this guard's presence telling this guard not to come to my cell unless he was with an interpreter. I have no respect for this type of bigot. What finally determined me to write this report was the meeting held on 1999/3/24 during that meeting the guard openly humiliated the African inmate Jean Marie Happy. The guard openly exposed this man's private affairs in a mocking disrespectful manner which had no relevance to reform or the meeting.

The guard revealed matters regarding his and Neiwe personal property openly stating that these two Africans had no property which later proved to be a lie the guard had told. The guard even stated during that meeting that the Warden of Qing Pu Jail wasn't qualified to talk to Prince Jean Marie only the Justice Minister was qualified. The whole meeting was humiliating and racially bias. If this type of talk is tolerated one day it will get out of hand.

STOP RACIAL DISCRIMINATION AT QING PU JAIL.

L. Campbell.

Chapter Fortysix: Trouble Brewing

When released from confinement was just a red blob of mosquito bites literally hundreds if not thousands covered my face and body. Feeling very shattered my mental state was suspect revenge was on my mind and started my one-man campaign. I was telling no one that my plans were that was always a mistake some of us made thinking you can tell someone. I had made copies of the above report and sent one to the British Consul also one to the Prison procurator and one into the Wardens box and let's see what transpires It did not take long the following day after handing in the consul letter was called to the office by Captain Ma of the criminal affairs department and asked to not send this letter. I asked why? In addition, went onto explain it is my right to correspond with my consul. Telling Captain Ma that one had also been into the warden's box his face frowned. The foreign inmates knew by experience that the guards in our unit kept the problems away from the ears of the higher authorities. By going over the head of Captain Jiang he was not happy about it. It was Stanley who was doing the interpretations and said to me slyly do not push it and withdraw that letter please. I left the office still undecided but with a promise from Captain Ma that he would look closely at my accusations.

The following day the prison procurator visited me and had a surprise in store for them. Syed also writes a report accusing Jiang of discrimination Syed signed it and finger printed it for me this was the sort of leverage needed and thanked him for his support knowing he only did this because he also knew he wasn't getting any remission moreover; he was just happy to stir it up. The prison procurator listened to my story and then also asked me also to retrieve the letter being sent to the consul. They assured me that it would be resolved within the prison. But I told them about past promises from the Prison Administration Bureau that if I withdrew my petition would be paroled. I made it very clear to them that whilst Jiang was running the unit my life was a misery. It was left at that and never retrieved my letter. The following day in the afternoon Captain Ma called a meeting telling us to rearrange our cells as four new inmates from Japan were arriving the following day The unit now consisted of four Africans two Pakistanis two Americans one Iranian one North Korean and me from the UK. The Chinese inmates were now Stanley in charge another new guy we called Eddie plus two nightshift workers Toto and little Wang I got hold of Captain Ma before he escaped downstairs, had Stanley at the ready to ask my question, and took him by surprise when asking for a single cell on the top floor. To my surprise, he immediately replied yes. This was a first from him. They always said let me think it over and never got back to you and perused my request with can you inform Captain Jiang of your decision? Stanley intervened and said to me it will be done Lockie Jiang wont dare go over Captain Ma decision. I was so excited to be having a single cell again but knew it would stir things up with some others and knew that Stanley would be coming to me over the next couple of days and try to persuade me to retract my letter to the Consul.

Chapter Fortyseven: The People Trade

Mr. Funahashi, sentenced to four years a man of slim build height around 174cm head slightly bowed age around 46, Mr. Kamimura, sentence four years overweight around 178cm age 42 walks with chest out. Mr. Matsuda sentence two years slim and fit age 30 around 173cm appears withdrawn. Then there was young Josikawa age 19, sentence two years he is Mr. Funahashi nephew. They arrived the following day as was told to us at the meeting. They got of the prison van carrying bags and bowing as they walked. They were imprisoned for arranging visas for women from China to get into Japan. The sex trade was as ancient as China itself and a big business in Japan for Chinese beauties. They were sending them under many guises some as students with fake college documents others as tourists with set up bank accounts in addition, return tickets. It is known as the oldest trade in the world and still being applied by one of the most cultured and civilized nations Japan. I had got myself moved into a single cell on the top floor there was five cells to each floor. The cell lay out had improved since the four new guys arrived they opened all of the upstairs. The two-nightshift guys moved to cell one also with Elah and Wavi in cell two and the four Japanese in cell three and me alone in cell four. Cell five was our storeroom. I was   getting a consul visit the following day and had my letter at the ready nothing had been done about Jiang and his shenanigans he was still creeping up to cells and catching guys laying on their bed and only too happy to deduct 0.5 merit points.

Chapter Fortyeight: Finding Art

I was called out for my consul visit and had stashed my letter down my briefs. Walking briskly to the visiting room we first crossed our yard then passed the hospital unit and then into the main building. It surprised when the consul showed great concern about my welfare not that they did not usually but today was different. Then out came a clipping from a UK newspaper with an article about the rough treatment that I had not so long ago undergone. The consul read this article out to me as passing correspondence at visits was forbidden. I was elated for more than one reason it proved to me my underground mail system still worked and had given a letter to someone at a risk of putting myself straight back into the mosquito farm and him to the torture seat. The article stated most of the facts that I had sent out i.e. being left handcuffed on my tiptoes overnight secured to the cell door. In return, read the consul my letter and told them I had sent it weeks ago and further inquired had they received it yet? Knowing the answer already. I could see the consul look at her interpreter and she at once started to take notes. The air could have been cut with broken glass the chatter of the guards it sounded to me like buck passing time and who's going to be responsible for this breach of jail security. I had been painting every day since getting oils brushes and canvas with the assistance of the British consul. As the visit was now over collected art materials, I had requested plus some gifts from consul staff and mail from my family was handed in. I really loved painting it was the best discovery of my life until now and it occupied all of my days. It was so interesting to see shapes appear with a resemblance to what I was copying. It made me laugh to myself when discovering the illusions that could be created by a few strokes of a brush. Seeing the improvement in my artistic skills that encouraged me and had been keeping a log of everything I had painted. Here was my list:

The forty plus UN Anti-drug posters from March 1997 until April.
Paintings in oil from April 1998 until Oct 1999.
1.TC Campbell fast for justice.2 Joe Steele Buckingham Palace.3 Cherrie Anne 4 Orange tree Abstract 5. Soldier's head.6 Small orange tree.7 Tommy Fasting.8 Self Portrait.9 Scott's girls.10 Lotus lust.11 Rabs house.12 African girls. 13 Naked ladies. 14 Flowers. 15 Flying carpet.16 Princess Diana.17 CARG.18 Girl on chair.19 George and the dragon.20 Starry night 21 Football match 22 Rabs portrait. 23 Naked women.24 Flower tree 25 Ladies face 26 Landscape Waterfall. 27 Chineseflag.28 Waterfall. 29 Rembrandt 30 Landscape autumn. 31 Landscape trees and 32. Ang Sung Sui Burmese democracy leader.

Paintings with acrylic Sept and Oct 1998.
1.Joshua holding fish. 2 Jason's daughter.3 Nazi eyeglass. 4 Shotts jail guard. 5 Orange tree 6 Chinese wizard 7 Van Gogh self-portrait. 8 Salvador Dali egg. 9 Marilyn Monroe.

Chapter Fortynine: Renovation

It was a surprise welcoming for us all in 1999 when at a meeting known as the year-end assessment or other known as the agitprop show gave us this information. As usual, we were told that we should write about the achievements we made throughout the year and what were our plans for the coming year. It was Captain Ma of the criminal affairs presiding over the meeting. He was in the presence of another guard who was smaller and older and he wore a white shirt. I immediately thought he was a warden. It turned out he was to be a new addition to our unit and that he spoke English. Captain Shao was a slight built man around 168cm in height he was quietly spoken and well educated. The meeting had another purpose Captain Ma informed us that we would be moving over to the building opposite as they were going to renovate our unit. With a smile on his face portraying the look at how civilized we are then continued by saying and putting toilets in your cells. That caused a bit of fidgeting. Then Latif immediately stated that we would prefer it the way it is with the toilets outside the cell. It was ignored the decision was already made. The other thing to be taken away was the veranda. It was good while it lasted to be able to sit outside at times and paint and just chill out. That space was now being used for the new inside toilet. We were asked to write down any suggestions to improve the unit and the meeting was called to an end. I stopped Captain Shao on the stairs going down and asked him where did he learn English? He replied he had traveled overseas as an engineer on a ship the conversation was interrupted when Captain Ma said something and Captain Shao went off to attend to whatever duty. I immediately took a liking to this guard he was very gentle in a humane sort of way.

Chapter Fifty: www.freejudeshao.com

I was sitting outside on the veranda on the third floor it was a warm autumn day hearing voices coming from the cell below called who are you talking with Stanley? A voice with a distinctive American accent replied Hi there my name is Jude Shao an innocent American imprisoned in China. I ran down the stairs immediately thinking he was a pilot who we had heard about on the news and that had been arrested for spying. As it turned out it was a young well-educated native Chinaman age around 36 who greeted me shaking his hand and asked if he had met Cranky or Bo yet the other two Americans imprisoned here. Not yet, he replied and took that as my cue to say well nice talking with you and catch up with you later. I was about to leave Eddie called another new person from Ghana is moving onto your floor. I went upstairs and met Kofi he was a young tall broad shouldered and proud young man. He had been arrested for traveler check fraud and sentenced to four years. Jude on the other had gotten sixteen years for tax evasion that he claimed was all a set up.

Chapter Fiftyone: Cell Block Move

As it turned out regardless of our written reports not to put toilets in the cells or remove the veranda, they shipped out the Chinese from across the way we were all moved to the opposite building and were kept six to a cell. The cheery on the cake for me was on our first day settling in we had a meeting that was the introduction of another new Captain his name was Chang. Now he would take charge of us. He was around 34 years in age and he looked enthusiastic and most importantly that meant Jiang was gone. I had wondered why he wasn't at this meeting now knew and was so happy to hear that evil Jiang was no longer here in fact I felt victorious then thought again he would be in some other cellblock disrupting people's life's a vicious circle.

Chapter Fiftytwo: Mick the Greek

It was news every day what the year 2000 The New Millennium would bring. There were predictions from disaster to a new messiah coming. I was on my illusion bubble ride again thinking that 1999 would be the 50th anniversary of the founding of the Peoples Republic of China and they might grant me amnesty. I had even submitted a report stating that the King of Thailand granted amnesty to drug offenders. As usual no response. The millennium bug had died a death in the end all sorts of predictions made from every nationality in here but they came to nothing lying on top of my bed one day when this person walked into the cell and introduced himself as Mick. I looked at him and saw he was a westerner Hi I said nonchalantly where did you just come from? Mick replied in an offhanded way Oh I came by special escort. I looked at him again; he was dressed in top designer sport wear. Just then Stanley came into the cell and started speaking Chinese to which Mick replied in Chinese and left saying see you later mate in a not very distinguishable Australian accent and immediately thought that he was a Consul Staff member but then remembered there were no Australians here. It turned out that Mick was a new inmate sentenced to 15 years for a mobile phone deal deception between Hong Kong and Shanghai. When his personal gear arrived, it took six of us to carry into the storeroom. Mick was from Greek parents and he had that look and body like a well-sculpted Greek statue. As it happened, he had some medical problem so was kept at a hospital before coming here and not the detention cells.

Chapter Fiftythree: Herbal Medicine

The arrival of five more new inmates caused quite a lot of gossip. It was three South Koreans Mr. Kim the eldest in his seventies Mr. Lee in his sixties and Mr. Chun in his forties along with two Nepalese guys Bijay age 39 Min 32 they had been arrested for attempting to smuggle cannabis into Japan. The story was that Mr. Kim and Mr. Chun really did think they were smuggling herbal medicines and felt a bitter resentment towards Mr. Lee and Bijay the ringleaders of the scam. Mr. Kim and Mr. Chun had gotten five years each whilst Bijay got nine Min eight and Mr. Lee 6. I sat and listened to Chun speak quite a bit and he was angry you could taste it. I knew he had approached Bijay immediately upon arriving at the jail and confronted him for an explanation. Whatever was said until now there was nothing forthcoming to calm Chun so it brewed on? The renovation work was to be finished before spring festival 2000 and there was a lot of friction in the unit due to the shortage of space. That is when if you are aware try to remain silent. It was one of those things when history comes in the Koreans Chinese and the Japanese do not always mix to well. They have there past conflicts and each as equally patriotic.

It was not easy living especially under these conditions. On top of that, there was an ongoing political issue regarding the Japanese government to apologize for past war crimes, and their use of comfort women. You can imagine how the local inmates felt towards them but they were safe in this unit. I also had a run in with Cranky over the remains of the hot water container. After sports, we sometimes collected it to wash after a game. Now you may think a water bucket it is a trivial issue but you become possessive to odd things in jail. Fights can start over something as simple as not acknowledging good morning to someone who greeted you. I was content to be a loner most times and was mostly left to my own. No longer having that curiosity anymore wanting to know what other people were in for I had exhausted that avenue of illusions thinking that I could put them straight with how the system works. I was the worst example being the one with the littlest remission. It was decoration time as Xmas 99 was upon us so we all made an effort to color the place up. The mix of cultures condensed a foreign unit in that small area was invigorating. We had the usual Karaoke Happy did a tribal dance Kofi sang a Chinese song Cranky sang. The Pakistani people danced and the Japanese sat huddled together looking like being at a Japanese freak show. Bijay Min Stanley and I secured a table at the back. The making merry lasted all week plenty of good food. I did not want to celebrate the New Year but wanted to celebrate the ones already survived and to see this year pass with myself still intact.

Chapter Fiftyfour: The Renovated Foreign Unit. 2000

It was February 2000 that we moved back into our old building. The cells were all bigger with the veranda gone. As you went inside the cell on your right-hand side was a flushing toilet with a half door and on the left side a washbasin and running water. Each cell had four beds and by each beds a stool and a small table plus one small wooden cupboard for keeping a variety of things. Above the beds at the entrance wall were four large linen storage spaces. It was the normal procedure now that the building was finished to have a meeting and have our new cell allocation. I had asked Stanley to try to secure my old cell on the third floor. This meeting turned out to be more than the normal humdrum of Chinese prisons reform. It was told to us that we were having a change of staff and that Captain Jin would be our new Brigade unit leader and was introducing transparency in our reform. The two guards who had been with us here since the beginning Captain Hua and Wu were going also. Now it was time for the new guards being introduced. There was Captain Chang who had already taken over from Jiang and now in charge of us. Captain Shao was the eldest with the white collar who spoke English and was doing translation when needed. Then there was Captain Chung and Captain Liu one a university graduate the other a young man of around twenty-two.

Top floor.
Cell 1 Campbell and Stanley.
Cell 2 Josikawa Funahashi Kamimura Matsuda
Cell 3 Jude Kofi and Mick.
Cell.4 Happy Joe Elah Wavi.
Cell 5 Storerooms.

Second floor.
Cell 1 Toto Little Wang and Eddie three Chinese workers.
Cell 2 Mr Lee Mr Kim and Mr Chun.
Cell 3 Mr Ho Bo and Mr Park.
Cell 4 Cranky Bijay and Min.
Cell 5 Lativ Mustafa and Vicky.

I did not have any complaints with the set up but some others did. It would take time to settle in and get used to the new set up. There was one more floor above, which was the dining room area. A large room had been set out with tables and chairs plus an area for serving and collecting food. On the back wall was a fourteen-foot by eight-foot blackboard with a completely new set of conditions and rules. The merit point system under the title transparency you could see how many points you got each month and why you were given them. There was an open rooftop area where you could hang out bedding and was used to sit out on hot summer evenings to play chess or just relax rather civilized one could say.

Chapter Fiftyfive: Jail Remission Meeting

It is something to witness when you go to a mass reduction of sentence meeting having got my first remission of sentence that was ten months behind closed doors back at the old jail. This was open aired and being televised around a jail network. We all sat watching this meeting; Stanley called me and said you are wanted in the office. Captain Shao turned me around and escorted me out to the meeting. Having butterflies in my stomach thinking what sort of reduction would be coming my It is propagated through reform that if you inform on someone and the case leads to confession or conviction whether that is inside or outside of the jail you will be rewarded with remission. That was the scenario going on now rewarding the informers publicly. Sitting along with about 600, Chinese guys on what I named the criticism stools and did not have to pay any attention to the long speeches made by wardens and other would-be reformers of men. That ceremony we saw on television and could not understand it anyway a few words here and there. I perked my ear up only when they started calling names out but how would it ever be possible to hear Campbell amongst this madness.

As it happened, Captain Shao returned taking me from the crowd and escorted me to the guard's office in brigade five passing enroute the hotbox confinement block. Captain Shao told me to wait at the office door and so waiting stood there my best face on of the day. Five minutes later standing in front of three Judges and Captain Shao was given another ten-month reduction from my sentence a present for the May Day holidays. Returning to the unit with a fake smile not wanting the authorities or anyone else for that matter to see how gutted I was. It was usual procedure if you were having a second reduction that it be more than your first. Having gotten ten months first time everyone estimated would get fourteen-month minimum this time. Cranky had gotten fourteen months on his second reduction although he had missed out at the old jail when we had gotten ten-month cut. Now he already had two reductions amounting to 26-month remission and I had 20-month remission. Cranky must have been doing something right or me something wrong. My new liberation date was December 5 2004 and could now see the gate in my mind's eye but did not feel any closer to it.

Chapter Fiftysix: Exercise Yard

The exercise yard had been the forefront of many a debate argument and fight. The issue now was basketball as opposed to football during the afternoon period. It was true that football was played most days unless Captain Jin organized a basketball game against the opposite unit. This he did quite often as he himself enjoyed the game and in the evenings, he was on duty, games were on he was still a very skillful player at his age being fifty and was fit. It was decided three days each and one day rest for those who wanted to walk around without ducking from balls. The football team we had was unbeaten within the jail. Bijay was an ex British army officer and the Gurkas are well known for their loyalty and fierceness he was a good strong and skillful player. Min the other Nepali was small around 160cm but built like an ox he was also not a bad player. Wavi was very fast nobody at the jail could catch him. Grand Joe as we named him was also good and then Happy who often played in goal had surprised us all with how well he read the game. Matsuda had all the best gear sent from Japan and he was someone who ran for every ball everywhere on the field, then there was Stanley the hardest defender in our unit he let nobody pass him he was good. I was still very reliable at my ball distribution and scoring my share of goals. However, none of us was as good as Elah he was as good as George Weah as far as our unit were concerned and a fellow citizen to boot being Liberian. The days they played basketball sometimes sat and watched it seemed to me every move constituted a foul. It did not have the flow of football then one day Jude explained to me the rules, then saw the game from another light, and began to enjoy watching that sport on television. I believe I can fly with air Jordan was big at the time also Kobe Bryant and my favorite was Iverson and learned new words like a Shaq attack but wouldn't trade football for it though and prefer the echo of old chants of football legends. The likes of Jinxy Johnston or Slim Jim Baxter both of whom were rivals from the same city but different clubs I had heard the Hampden roar on many occasions as a boy going to games.

It was a mixed house in Glasgow our family shared my father a protestant my mother a catholic. I was a blue nose my brother Robert was a Tim and Tommy wisely supported Scotland. Football is a passion once possessed it never dies so in my eyes football should have been the exercise yard game but we were the foreign unit and a democracy definitely ruled amongst most of us It remained that way until autumn then another obstacle arrived the complaint was the football was leaving dirty marks on the bedding or clothing of the Chinese inmates that was hanging out and objected to the guard that this is our exercise ground not the drying area. It had not been the first time this problem arose. The Chinese inmates really did not like our set up as opposed to theirs and they had a right to complain regarding daily exercise. The foreigners could play sports twice a day and they were lucky if they could get a game once a week. I had helped a lot with this problem and started to arrange mixed games or at times play against each other. The problem was easily solved in words that was collect your laundry at afternoon exercise period but off course the Chinese didn't have any fixed exercise period so we arranged for Stanley to collect it all at four o'clock and pass it into the building opposite. It was those sorts of obstacles that you could not foresee we had been playing for years without any mention of dirtying the bedding until now.

Chapter Fiftyseven: The China Daily English Newspaper

The foreign unit was supplied with two English papers every day. It was arranged that the paper would go to cell one on Monday then to cell two first on Tuesday then on along the line to five. Cranky was always circling over articles or even cutting them out before some people had read them. By the time cell, five got the paper it was the following day and often later. Therefore, another rote system was set up. Cell one got the newspaper first for one week then it started at cell two and so on same same but different. Bo had come up with the suggestion that we buy our own papers Jude supported that as he wanted papers from other parts of China. This was submitted in a written report and the outcome was that we could buy our own and that stopped anymore squabble over the newspaper. One day Bo was taken over to the hospital and he never returned. He was transferred to the old jail hospital with a heart problem. The story was he was being returned to the USA for surgery Bo had good connections and he was not really a criminal and wished him the best of luck and a speedy recovery.

Chapter Fiftyeight: Two Go Three Come

Mustafa and Syed returned home before October 1st holiday wishing them good fortune because knew what they would be returning to being a traveler there is not the same as living there. Butt and Parviz had written back that they were apprehended at Karachi airport upon their arrival. It was not a major set-back and only took a few hundred dollars to resolve. Butt had made clear that both should have a friend or family waiting with baksheesh. As they departed three more new guys arrived it seemed like a waiting game to get into this jail as stories were coming that a gang of Malaysians were on their way. The new guys one from Burma age 42 doing life for Heroin possession the other a Chinese American doing two years for deception, and the third a Korean guy named Pang four years for smuggling fake alcohol out of China. Burma was what we called the lifer and Matt was the Chinese American the only cell space left for two people was my own or the one Mustafa and Syed had vacated so Lativ didn't get the luxury of a single cell he got the two new guys and the third Pang was put into cell two with another Koreans.

Chapter Fiftynine: Malaysians

It was now a few days before Christmas when three more new people arrived, they came from Malaysia all on separate charges. Jimmy Huang was in his forties and had gotten eight years for company fraud and said he was innocent. Then there was Mr. Tsai age forty-life sentence for possession of a large amount of ecstasy. Then Mr. Wong he had gotten years for possession of a small amount of ecstasy. Cell five our storeroom was cleared and moved to the ground floor again. The unit was getting quite a mix of nationalities all three were Malaysian Chinese so there was a mix of Cantonese Hokkim and other dialects spoken amongst them and this was throwing the local Shanghai boys into confusion.

One of the major problems for foreigners was you mostly needed an interpreter to inquire about certain matters from the guards. The overseas Chinese did not have this invasion of privacy as they could ask directly everything they needed. As to the Non-Chinese speakers, they either had to put it in writing or with the assistance. It was the same with outgoing mail. They wrote in Chinese so it did not need to lie around waiting in a pile to be translated their mail was out within the week. This caused a bit of friction, as the mail issue had been ongoing since my first week of arriving in jail back in 1991. It appeared the overseas Chinese were getting preferential treatment. Lativ had been getting a hard time as his writing was in Persian and it was taking a minimum of one month before his letters went out. He even got permission to pay a government-approved translator to get his letters out quicker which they did for a few months then it slipped back to the snail mail system. Latif also wrote in English to his children he was very loving in his words. Sometimes asking me to put a cartoon drawing on a card to which I gladly obliged. Mail is a well-known power tool for the authorities and it would not be something our voice of discontent would overthrow. It was Jude who came up with what we thought was an eventual solution Jude suggested during a meeting that the mail be photocopied and sent immediately and checked later. Latif stood up shouting out what do you think we are terrorists. The eventual outcome was nothing changed that you could notice.

Chapter Sixty: A Window To The World 2001

The weather is perfect in China during spring, had been doing a lot of painting recently, and was working on an idea for an exhibition. It was to involve myself, Kofi from Ghana and Min from Nepal and had put forward a report to the education department asking for materials. It was accepted and wrote a list of what was needed. The exhibition was titled an Inside insight behind the great wall of prisons in China and was a very interesting experience with the three of us sitting discussing what we should portray. All knowing that propaganda paintings highlighting the modern civilized prison would have to be present so we broke it into four parts.

Part one: Public security issues five paintings. I did the opening three canvases first were with a giant pair of Jiang Zemins eyeglasses reflecting street crime that the police were cleaning up. The second was a drug scene arrest and the third a burglar being caught coming from a window. Kofi did a confession scene at a police station and Min did a court-sentencing scene.

Part two: The cultural gap four paintings Kofi did a broken bridge with one person at each side with one in police uniform indicating that they could not connect. Min did a meeting with the prisoners and guards putting traditional hats on the heads to make no mistake identifying our cultural differences. I did a variety of religious relics falling from the sky into a Chinese urn putting us all into one category that did not mix well at all. I did one other of two inmates arguing eyes turned up in confusion.

Part three: Communication breakdown Min did a landscape broken telephone lines looked at from behind bars with an upturned mailbox in view. Kofi painted a mobile phone and a laptop computer indicating the technology was available for quicker communication. I did a prisoner sitting biting his nails looking worried at a photo of his child on the table with a bird flying with mail in the beak

Part four: Sport and food five paintings I did large an iron rice bowl with a fish on top and a boiled egg at the side. Kofi did a ping-pong game with oranges as the prize. Min did an abstract combining a weightlifting and basketball game scene with a watermelon as the ball. The other two were done by me a scene of cleaning up the unit with mop and dusters and handing in a monthly report to the guard. The final one was an open gate with three judges handing out release papers and me walking onto a plane with Min and Kofi at my back.

I had done a set of four others called Changes but they were not allowed to be shown. These four were the outcome from advice received in a letter from a lady called Sarah Travelon Sarah had told me to give counseling from Scotland to China was impossible but suggested sitting in front of a blank canvas and paint what's in my mind. I sat for days before breaking into my mind and the outcome was not too nice to look at but it was a step forward to accepting who am I and that was mixed up. It was now finished and the time came to exhibit our work. The three of us knew we would be rewarded in some way or another and it was remission we all desired. It was set out in the visiting area in the main building and would be exhibited there during inmates' family visits and Consuls so that the public could see that foreign criminals reformed actively as well as the Chinese At the end of that month of July 2001 Kofi Min and I were told to write crime acknowledgment reports and that usually meant one thing remission of sentence. Asking the guard about my crime acknowledgement report having already gotten remission six month ago and according to the prison law could not have another reduction of sentence until a minimum of one year passed. The guard assured me that this new crime acknowledgment report would be better that adding the exhibition reward will make it good for you. I walked away dejected knowing this report would lie in some desk drawer or file cabinet and when it came time for me to get a reduction, they would ask me to write a new one adding other supposed achievements.

It was easy to convince myself that it would be better getting a bigger reduction with this new report but felt deep down the longer they can delay my reduction I was bound to fuck up and lose it before getting it. They are masters at trips and traps lies and illusions leading you into a false security then kicking your legs away. That is reform your there to suffer so you do not forget so quickly in future to live an honest life.

Chapter Sixtyone: Drug Testing On Foreign Scum

I had been given the test results of a medical checkup we all had back in November 2000 and was shocked to read was HIV+ and Hepatitis C + In a panic immediately wrote to the Consul knowing that I had been infected by the system talk about being fucked and was so God dammed angry wanted to kill someone but who was to blame seething and immediately thought of Cranky could he have managed to put his infected blood into my food? The answer was yes, he could easily do that, but would he? And didn't doubt it so he was my first suspect then recalled what he had to say when he discovered he was HEP C + Cranky was also enraged and swore to sue the Chinese prison authority for infecting him. It seemed to me this time he was on the right tract. We had both been infected with two deadly viruses. If Cranky was Hep C + away back before our previous medical checkup then I must not have been clean as no mention nor was treatment given to me. I was in some sort of shock and could not shake myself from it. HIV+ and HEP C+ and was going to die. My mind screaming it wanted another checkup this time done by the consul doctor and had spoken with the guard about the urgency of this and asked them to arrange a special visit just to give my blood. That night lying in bed thinking that those dirty evil communist bastards had infected me and knew why.

I had always voiced my opinion at meetings and had written numerous articles on the rights of prisoners not with malice but with genuine inquiry. Qing Pu jail was civilized in many aspects that I respected and thought surely, they hadn't intentionally infected me because of my racial discrimination report against Captain Jiang in July 1999 or for telling them to stick their communist thinking up their ass back in June 2nd 1998.I had also gotten shingles, dragon skin disease as it's known in Chinese a ring of painful blisters running from my left nipple over my shoulder down to under my armpit onto my back another virus. I was truly demented during that period and requested a special visit but instead received this letter sent on by the consul.

Consul Letter.
We have sent you the medical check result of British citizen Lauchlan Campbell in the letter dated 14 August. Unfortunately, we had made a mistake in that letter: in one of his check items the check result HIV (-) has been put as HIV (+) by mistake. We apologize for the mistake we made.
Foreign Affairs department Shanghai Justice Bureau. 24/08/01

Chapter Sixtytwo: HIV-+

I did not let out any sigh of relief but instead reacted rather angrily not at the Consul during this visit but by the way, my life was being handled stating one test said HIV+ the other said HIV – which one is correct and did not honestly know. Having wrote and asked the consul to arrange their nurse to take my blood and give me an independent test result this was granted the nurse had taken it and left that consul meeting at least with a feeling to know how long that I would have to live, and not how soon was going to die, one up for the wonders of positive thinking. I have to give credit here to the consul for their efficiency knowing about the psychological damage such news carries and still being in the dark and not knowing if was infected or not. I had the consul test results in print within two weeks stating HIV- HEP C+. It was good news in one respect to not have HIV. The consul also enclosed 30 pages of HEP C information on how to treat it and what dietary requirements are best for infected patients after reading parts of every page it all came down to your slowly dying. No cures just do not drink alcohol or abuse your body.

It is a wonderful sight to see a letter heading British Consulate-General made it official for me that I wasn't HIV+ that is how the mind works British Consul letter signed Amanda Cooper I could trust that the other with the five-star seal that bounced back what a simple mistake with a Mandarin peel of laughter from someone but not me. Cranky and I seldom spoke we came to tolerate each other and live and let live. Having to ask him one day about his Hep C wanting to know how he knew he had it. The doctor at the hospital had told me Cranky specially asked for that test. Is that true I inquired? No way was how Cranky responded it took my consul months to get that information and only recently, he had received it in writing. The system liked to turn us around in circles putting out misinformation. It was well manipulated in these Chinese jails and it worked being kept in the dark for years on the many games they experimented with. During this period, my family had written to the foreign office asking for my return under medical grounds. I didn't see any chance of that happening as Cranky was still here and there had been talk of him going home for a transplant away back there was always talk. Jail thrives on hope even if that hope is killing you, it still might get you home quicker to die.

Chapter Sixtythree: A Determined Man

Mick was proving to be a real thorn in the side of the authorities he was intelligent and spoke reasonably well in Mandarin. Having sat with him and looked through his photos one day it is not something you do unless you feel at ease with someone Mick and me got along ok. His Chinese girlfriend was a beauty but his ex-wife was gorgeous and his two son's fine young lads. Mick was a body builder but the sort with ribbed outlines in short; he liked the look of himself. The parcels of the highest quality proteins vitamins muscle enlarger and so on arrived on a monthly basis. Mick also had an ongoing medical problem and had even managed to get out to a hospital for tests with the assistance of his consul. I shared a cell with him on the third floor after Stanley and I had a punch up and cell change. Mick would get up in the middle of the night and press the buzzer stumbling and moaning and often vomiting. This really got the guards back up as they got out of bed to take him across to the prison doctor who also had to get out of bed.

This went on for months and then the guards stopped opening our door. That was all Mick needed he was a man who took note of every detail and he logged the dates and times not only when getting treatment but also when he had not been attended to. When his consul visited, he read out his notes and embarrassed the face out of the system. For whatever reason Mick did not give a fuck and rang that night bell until some of the cons were shouting Mick gives a sleep tonight mate. Then that extended to shut the fuck up Mick from the cell next-door. Sympathy is harder to come by than remission in a Chinese jail. The arrival of another Chinese inmate with Australian citizenship was a pleasant addition. Simon was in his early forties and doing life imprisonment for embezzlement and had settled in some tax haven of the coast of Australia. Well now, he was in jail. I got on with him and we started doing workouts together. One day he asked me about Mick and why he made so much trouble and answered you had better ask him that yourself.

Chapter Sixtyfour: Merry Christmas

On Christmas day fed up with the pretentious merriments of the festive season. I was happy though an artist called Thomas Kinkade called receiving a book from my friend Ralph McLaren it Paintings of Radiant light. I looked at the paintings, marveled at his distribution of light, wrote into my diary light in a Godless land, and immediately started to copy his work. I was so enwrapped in this that I was doing two paintings a week. The wall in my workplace looked like a gallery every time one finished an old one got took down and rolled up and added to my now mounting collection. The Kinkade paintings were on big demand in our unit and painted one for half the people there charging a jar of coffee. The guards were in on it also, got Stanley to pass them the book to select their choice, and then copied them. Being on an artistic high learning landscapes and came to realize his paintings were just that bit heavenly and that combining art with spirituality was a wise wonderful and colorful way to work.

Chapter Sixtyfive: Consular Agreement

Jude had been fighting to clear his name non-stop from the first his day of arrival and he was not having any of it regarding his Consul mail and his rights being violated. Jude had secured a copy of a Vienna Convention Consular agreement. Article 36 any communication addressed to the consular by the person arrested, in prison custody the said authorities shall also forward detention immediately the said authorities shall inform the person concerned immediately of his rights under this sub paragraph. This was a revelation and the bandwagon started everyone wanted a consular agreement myself included. It was as if you had this piece of paper your rights could not be denied you. It is written in the Vienna convention that makes it official. Along with some of the newfound international law protectors we soon discovered things went along at the pace suiting the Chinese authorities. I should have foreseen it would not matter what convention Vienna Geneva or Miss World we were all in jail in fucking China and no convention tells the Great wall to stand or fall. I will say Jude Shao deserved another trial his case was shaky to say the least and he had now gathered documents to prove his points but would it ever be heard? Moreover, doubted it and voiced this opinion to Jude one day telling him about my brother and his fight for Justice. I had written to my brother and said take a deal, and get out of jail. It was my brothers reply he would die first but innocent and unbroken by the system. I was trying to persuade Jude to do the same make a deal telling him just get out of here sooner the better. Jude as if my brother was having none of it and wanted his name cleared respecting that strength, which I felt, did not have.

Chapter Sixtysix: Three Go Home

It was early February of the year 2002 and you had all sort of dates times seasons and reasons in your head for release dates. One day out of the blue Wavi Eli and Kofi were called down to the office. The subject was about to buy their air tickets home. Kofi was sorted out the Ghanaian consulate in Beijing secured his flight. As the other two were, from Liberia, this proved to be a problem due to the political instability and their civil war Wavi had family now living in the USA and it was arranged he would fly to Paris and meet someone from the UN office regarding refugees. Eli was allowed to fly into the Ivory Coast where he had a wife and son. I watched as they left the building, thought Kofi was a real fine young man with principles and intelligence to go with it, wished him well on his return to Ghana, and gave him my son's email address. The other two were different Smart Street wise guys like me but from another culture different principles and less experienced. The other two to be released was Josikawa and Matsuda from Japan. During their stay at this prison the Japanese and Koreans were quiet never causing trouble and always obedient they did not have much of a cultural gap to bridge as some of us had. The two Japanese inmates Matsuda and Josikawa had paid a little fine and gotten several months cut from their sentence. It was a very unusual situation in China regarding fines nobody ever paid them. The two Germans had paid there is and Bull had paid his in the hope that the system would reduce their time. It had not worked for them but maybe now the communist regime was seeing foreigners would pay their fine if they were assured a reduction in sentence. That assurance was never forthcoming so most never paid. I did not have any fine to pay all my money was confiscated. I wished them well and laughed when Matsuda said gave his football gear to Stanley, that is Japanese for you always polite.

Chapter Sixtyseven: Six New Faces

The six new arrivals put a stir in the air looking out for football players as the two-star men at our unit had gone. There was an old man from Singapore aged 67 serving 6 years for business fraud, a Chinese Bolivian age 38 serving 4 years for fraud, a Chinese American age 50 got 6 years for firearm possession, one more Korean age 35 got 6 years for smuggling technology into China, and finally Abdul from Pakistan 2 years for fraud. The sixth person was a new guard called Captain Li who we nicknamed the Professor because he had a PHD in physics and taught at university for years. I got on well with a guard he was the same age as me but he carried an air of calm, He was tall and thin with a straight back. He called me into the office one day while resting from my painting a Chinese river scene. The professor had me sit while he told me the wonders of drinking Chinese tea. Taking note of what he said and wrote to the consul and requested they buy me a tea making set, which they did. I grew to love the taste of longjin tea. It is not all negative in jail and you could learn a lot if you were willing.

The arrival of our new foreign unit brigade leader Captain Jin and the staff change made awhile back warranted a refresher meeting. We all gathered on the top floor and were seated in silence. On the wall was a white board that was 18 ft in length and 8 ft in height. It stated transparency in bold English writing along the top. All reform related five other slogans. Captain Jin was very smartly kept having a radiance of health about him and introduced himself in a firm tone. I have waited a long time to fully introduce my plans and myself for this unit. I was thinking here we go again more boiled eggs and carrots for the new person's ears. Captain Jin stated it was now going to be clear for everyone to see when he can be eligible for a reduction of sentence. Going to say there will be more transparency that was the new slogan. The board on the wall would be marked on a weekly basis the number of points you got and why you got them. I love the words the Chinese use in prison reform. The 10 don'ts, the 5 goods the 4 cardinals and now it was more transparency. This was getting civilised.

Chapter Sixtyeight: Here Comes The Son

I was happy and somewhat apprehensive that my son Scott was coming to visit me he had booked his ticket for March 20 and assured me he was coming. My mind was in turmoil thinking they might arrest him for the suitcase Lochy junior was arrested with but he was determined and so waited in fear and excitement that my son was coming to visit his old man. I had written to the Prison administration Bureau requesting to have a meal with Scott and had written to the consul that they to request on my behalf, as it is not often that foreigner got visits. This would only be my third visit in eleven years and wanted the equal opportunity as Chinese inmates had. Mick had also had a visit from his parents and had taken over a flask of hot water two plus one coffee packs with coffee cups and biscuits his request for a meal wasn't granted so he broke new ground by bringing his own supply. Well done Mick liking his style at times. Scott arrived and I was elated to see him enquiring immediately as to how be young Lochy. Having been worried that his stay at the Shanghai shackle house would have severely damaged his psyche at the age of seventeen spending six month in a twelve-man cell is hard on the mind. Scott assured me he was fine and all at home are well and still petitioning on my behalf to be returned on medical grounds. Looking at my son and he seemed tired but put that down to the flight having secretly arranged for Scott to meet an old local inmate whom I had got along well with and was now released. Scott and I spoke in colloquial Glaswegian and he told me he had an apartment and my Chinese friend was showing him around town and was glad to hear that as many promises made in jail are seldom fulfilled this one was. I left the visit room both arms full of gifts brought from the UK and gave Scott a list of what to bring on his next visit as I had arranged for two meetings returned to the unit and left my goodies at the office for inspection and went up and laid in my cell. It was great to see my son he looked well enough but a bit pale but that is Scottish weather and dozed into a contented sleep.

The next few days went by and doing a workout with Simon, he was very interesting but a bit above my head when it came to talking about the futures market and how he uses it. I liked Simon he was very softly spoken and never got involved with jail politics. He said to me that he expected to serve fifteen years unless something changes in the remission system. I explained to him all the hopes I had of an early release from the Hong Kong takeover to the 50th anniversary of founding the Peoples Republic of. China all illusions created by me. Simon was under no illusion but did hope something would change. Starting a life sentence at age 40 is not much of a bright future he said.

Chapter Sixtynine: Another Surprise

Sitting in my cell just after lunch it was March 25 2002 and cold wet and windy outside. I had on my feather down jacket my brother had bought when he visited. I was called to the office going down stair expecting to pick up the remains of the parcels my son had brought and ready to enter the office when the guard said you have a Consul visit and directed me towards the exit. I immediately had a panic attack first thought something has happened to Scott and could only think the worst he had been arrested for the suitcase that I had said he left behind in my first letter. Walking into the visit room could see straight away something was wrong. A striking tall blonde woman who introduced herself as Emma met me. Lisa the translator was with her and we sat down. Lauchlan, she said I am sorry to inform you that Scott has taken ill. I nearly shouted Thank fuck but instead said what is wrong with him? Emma in a soft and comforting tone told me it was nothing to worry about it was stress related and he had taken some sort of epileptic fit. Emma also told me he was returning home and that they had arranged for a flight and someone to return with him to make sure he was ok. I was really shaken up but did feel some relief that he was not laying in jail waiting to visit me on a long-term basis. That was such a bummer I could not face anyone who spoke with me, just hung my head, and said my son was on his way home he had taken ill. It was more than a month later Scott sent me a letter explaining it was stress at coming to visit me and he had been billed by the foreign office for six thousand pounds for the escort and fare back to the UK. I was just glad to know he was all right. Scott had enclosed a few photos of Shanghai tower and my granddaughter Ashton who was a little heart breaker.

Chapter Seventy: Great Wall Of Confusion

It was always the same at one point in the week or other someone would have conflict over mail again. This time I was in the office lodging my own complaint regarding using Chinese inmates to give out orders. It was something that could get under your skin being told by an inmate what to do. This delegation of duty was for the guards but the system here allowed the Chinese cons do all the work. Making it clear to the Criminal affairs Captain that had accepted Stanley, as the only Chinese con whom I would deal with and rarely accepted to use some other would-be Chinglish expert. Having got to know Stanley and trusted him as I did JK before he died. When it came to certain personal matters, you did not want to discuss that with a Chinese con at hand. It was told to me that there is no English-speaking guard to handle such matters and replied with a snide remark well it is time you employed one in this modern and civilized prison. To which the guards laughed. What's so funny I asked Captain Shao who did speak good enough English but gave up helping the foreigners for the reason being if our complaint or wish wasn't granted, he would get the blunt end of our frustration I had cursed him myself once then in private apologized to him. Campbell Captain Shao smiled shall we get a Japanese Korean and other foreign speakers to join the force also he was laughing at my narrow vision but he was also spot on why always English-speaking guards was my complaint why not Japanese or other. It had been an issue risen on many occasions before by Lativ and had now resurfaced again as the Nepalese Consul was visiting and Bijay and Min Bijay were called to the office regarding his visit with his consul, they had asked him to speak in English, as they didn't have a Nepali interpreter. Bijay was always the diplomat and in return, he requested that the visit be extended as using English was not his language and as he will not be having visits often and needed to clear all matters now while he had the opportunity. Bijay was told to write a report for the visit extension he requested. Meeting him upstairs and he said to me these people are unbelievable they just asked me to speak in English at my consul visit and then told me to write a report for to extend it as if they are doing me a favor. Mutual respects these people do not know the meaning of it then he cussed in Nepali you could see the hatred in those well-trained killer's eyes. The Nepalese Gurkhas are proud loyal clansmen but can be subservient when required. The British army had taught them well Bijay was proud of that but he also held bitterness in how the British had given the Gurkha's a bad deal when they disbanded. I was getting along well with the Nepalese especially Bijay he started to work out together with Simon and me using his army stamina building skills. It was hard work and him a relentless taskmaster pull ups and push-ups to begin with then combat running for my first time.

Chapter Seventyone: Computers

There was a meeting in July and the new rule was that we would not be staying in our unit all day but from next week, we would go over to the class-room area and study computer skills. What if I don't want to study computers and want to paint all day I asked? The guards replied then bring your paints across with you. When we did transfer over in was a godsend in more than one way for me. Ceiling fans are desperately needed this room had two and the full-length room windows gave great light for painting and a good breeze. July in Shanghai is so hot and to sit for hours you become sweaty wet from head to toe. It is the rash season and the hospital was next door so overall the move was better for the collective. It did not take too long before curiosity as to how a computer worked got hold on me and ventured next door where it was all set up. Tip toeing into the room with a feeling that I might disturb something and was met by Jude. "Hi Lockie" he greeted me. The Chinese inmates had started using my first name also this had begun since Jude's arrival and appreciated his respect for using the proper name calling system of the west and educating the Chinese cons who stayed at our unit with us. Jude lived in America and was a very intelligent young man. It got irritating for me at times when he would sit and talk about his case, he was correct in his views but I also knew he knew how the Chinese system worked. So why was he opposing it I inquired his reply was direct and to the point. The reason is I am innocent he would say determined-ly. Jude then shows me how to work a computer he was in charge of this set up and linked six computers up. Jude then asked Wong the Malaysian person to let him have the computer while he showed me some things. Wong got up and Jude started by showing me how to open a window then went on to some other computer talk. I stood looking over his shoulder in amazement and never remembered a word he had said. After a few minutes telling him to stop then excusing myself said enough for now and will return tomorrow. Leaving that room none the wiser but more afraid of computers now having heard the goggle words spoken by Jude and to type at the same time this wasn't going to be easy as learning to paint.

Chapter Seventytwo: New Law Maker

The arrival of a Chinese Australian inmate was quite a surprise as usually beforehand you heard news about the arrest or information got through one way or another. I never spoke with him when he first arrived but was hearing second hand what he had been sentenced to five years in jail for. It could only be possible in China Jude told me. It seems that Gordon and his girlfriend had gone down to Australia and got another university degree M B A and they were allowed to take residence partly due to these educational qualifications. He and his girlfriend married and settled in Australia building a life and a family with two sons. Being young intelligent and computer literate, he worked at creating programs for a cheaper communications network. Gordon had a contract from the Chinese company related with such network link ups. It was all officially done and so the venture took off. In the first year, massive profits were going to Gordon's network system and bypassing the usual government set up. In the second year, they threw him in jail. It was an unprecedented case there was no law as to why he was arrested. The Australian consulate did all they could but nothing changed the verdict. It was down to money and Gordon was getting a better slice of the pie by using his intelligence. It is still a communist country although it is was supposed to now be free enterprise but money not going to the state and going on to anthers plate was soon stopped. I do not have any explanation as to why innocents are imprisoned but it is dammed well shameful knowing they suffer like the guilty then furthermore to have knowingly set them up in the first place. I can say a couple of the guards here knew the truth and showed Jude and Gordon mutual respect and sometimes one on one they openly excused their systems error in their particular cases. It could never be shown that any guard sympathized with a criminal. Our status was firmly stamped into our psyches remember you're a criminal. I became friendly with the young man who spoke good English with an Australian accent.

Chapter Seventythree: Released October 2002

Abdul came from Pakistan and had been in jail in China several times all for fraud. It was a way of life he told me one day. In Pakistan he can do nothing no job no money no wife nothing. Going on to tell me his connection in Islamabad gets him a new passport and he returns back again to China. He was happy to do this that he now owned his own house and returns to Pakistan once he had changed between 5000 and 8000 dollars and drops it off to his supplier gets his share then returns with more stolen checks and continued to do so until his arrest. He seemed to be only around for weeks then he was gone spending more than one year waiting in detention so his sentence was nearly over when he arrived. I got on all right with him he was a devout Moslem and was proud to show me the hard skin mark on his forehead from praying to Allah. He said in his Pakistani accent see you soon Campbell, he was on the van, and off to the airport one more gone that is always good to see.

I had been waiting on some reduction of sentence for about two years now getting ten months in April 2000. My liberation date was now 5/12/2004 and was hoping to get at least one more year remission. The unit was changing a lot short term people had gone the arrival of a new person from Mexico. There was also a mother, son from Japan convicted of killing her husband his father, and seemingly, he was soon to on his way here. The Mexican person had been arrested in Beijing and was telling us stories that the jail there was much easier. He told us about the guards letting them use their mobile phones in exchange for money or other items they desired. They could buy cigarettes and other foodstuffs. I assured him that would not be happening here and his reply was if they don't get my smokes, I want my patches assuming he was talking about pipe or rolling tobacco and said listen to me my friend there is no smoking here trust me they even add time onto people's sentence if they get caught smoking cigarettes. Then he explained to me what a nicotine patch is and that was fascinating to hear of such a wonder that if you put it onto your arm, it prevented the cravings for nicotine. God the world had changed in the last decade mobiles phones computers and nicotine patches what next. The October reduction of sentences had passed and never got one and was not pleased in the least. Cranky had gotten another reduction and had only four-month left until his release date. I had been inside jail ten month longer and he was going out two years sooner than I was. It was only a couple of weeks before Xmas and was called downstairs to the office were sat Captain Jin and one Judge Captain smiled at me as if to say didn't, I tell you so and was given a one-year remission of sentence. That was it happy as a pig in shit as the saying goes it was December 22 getting the remission and would be going home on December 5 2003 less than one year from now. Now seeing the gate and smell of freedom, it was a feeling that cannot be explained by me it just knew leaving this place civilised jail or not God it felt good.

Chapter Seventyfour: Resolutions

I had decided as my New Year resolution to do the following starting January 1 2003.
1. Monday Wednesday Friday workout Tuesday Thursday stair run.
2. Finish one painting or more a week.
3. Do no more labor voluntarily or other.
4. Don't hand in monthly ideological remolding reports.
5. Start following Prisoners Abroad guidelines to resettle in the UK.

Chapter Seventyfive: The Father Killer

  Sato San was a very quiet operates around thirty-five he had been put into sharing a cell with two Chinese inmates whose job was to observe him. Stanley was telling me that Sato's father had been abusing his mother for years. Then one day the three of them were driving in Shanghai were his father worked it was during this drive that Sato and his mother stabbed the father to death. Sato rarely spoke living with whatever thoughts a father killer may have and could sort of relate with what he had done some drunken men are barbarians. I could murder some people myself easily when seeing how they treat their women. Yet heaven forbid if the same person saw it was his sister or daughter being abused. Having had gathered all my things of what I deemed important and value to me was my writings and paintings. Having had so much paperwork collected over the years, it filled a large box. Then started to sift through it to see what could be discarded. I picked out price lists from the old jail back in 1992 and the prices had tripled and more. I found the prison law copy and other paperwork, wanted to keep so sat for hours one evening and separated it and tore up loads, and binned about half of it. I was not aware of it then but that was gate fever and did not want any surprises now. My hopes were well battered I was not looking for any more 50th anniversary amnesty or other hopes for compassionate parole. I wanted to be ready and prepared.

Last year diary.
Jan 10th 2003 Book ideas. Why do people clap smile and lie at meetings?
Jan 16th 2003 Asian Games Qatar plan to go and study Islam, do paintings go to Qatar consul London. Art idea countdown series using Lanterns dragons Flag ceremonies Firecrackers fans Kung Fu Shoes the great Wall.

Chapter Seventysix: My Last Spring Festival

This was it for me just counting down celebrations still to come all taking me closer to that gate and freedom. I would eat my favorite moon cakes now and still had May Day to come then founding of the Peoples Republic of China Day. That was when we have to eat eight-treasured rice a mixed fruit and dates dish that tasted like heaven to me. The games and karaoke had played its last tune for me and was now fulltime observer.

Chapter Seventyseven: Going Shopping

As part of the transparency policy, the prison had opened a shop and we were allowed to go once per month to buy rations. It was a revelation to us to walk into a small supermarket inside the jail. It was not big but enough for 10 people to shop at a time so we were taken in groups. It also had a bookshop with mostly old classics like Jane Ayres or Dickens books. Jean Marie Happy bought a collection of Mao's writings but all in Chinese. There were some magazines with Chinese art and got myself a few for study and copying. It was set up that we all got a swipe card and that would register what we had in our accounts. There was a limit on how much you could spend which was 200 Yuan around 25 us dollars each month but there was no limit on how much fruit you could buy of what was available in season. The changes to the unit were coming fast we had a small multi gym installed they knocked down the second-floor guards office to make the space and put it in and there. Moreover, there was talk of getting to use the phone

Last Year's Diary.
May 28th 2003 every local inmate who has come to our unit has gotten parole except the nightshift guy Toto. We were all sentenced under the same laws yet we were exempt from the most beneficial aspect of prison law and that was we never go parole.
May 28th 2003, they utilize people's vulnerability they divide when there is conflict then move in underhanded ways to give support. If you don't know these tactics, you are in their hands and that is not good for you. They tried with me on more than one occasions. I was not wise and rebuffed them openly that got me a bad result when it came to remission and in jail that is the real currency. I spoke with Jude about this as he was showing me a letter his classmates sent to the Whitehouse.

Dear President Bush,
As you prepare for your upcoming visit with Chinese President Hu Jintao in Beijing, we urge you to press for the release of Jude Shao, an American entrepreneur who has been wrongfully imprisoned in Shanghai for over seven years.

Jude, a naturalised U.S. citizen and graduate of Stanford Business School, founded China Business Ventures to export U.S. medical equipment to China. He was arrested in 1998 on manufactured charges of tax evasion, and sentenced in 2000 to sixteen years in Qing Pu Prison. Jude was not allowed to prepare a defense for his trial or to present exculpatory evidence his family has recovered from his U.S. office.

In April 2003, six prominent Chinese legal experts at the Centre for Research in Criminal Legal Science in China's People's University reviewed Jude's case and concluded that Jude deserved a retrial. Certified public accountants in Shanghai have reviewed the new exculpatory evidence in Jude's case and declared it to be valid. Despite this, the Supreme People's Court has denied him a retrial, thereby exhausting all his options in the Chinese legal system.

Seven years in a Chinese prison have taken their toll on Jude. He has developed a heart condition that prison doctors are unable to treat. Jude's family filed a petition for medical parole in June 2004, and the U.S. Embassy in Beijing filed a diplomatic note in support of it. However there has been no response from the Chinese government.

Jude is an American businessman who believes firmly in the principles of his adopted homeland - democracy, ethical business conduct, and the rule of law. He was jailed because he refused to compromise his ideals and rejected the opportunity to pay a thinly disguised bribe. His moral character won him the support of high-ranking members of the State Department, Congress, and your Administration, who have made official inquiries about him with Chinese officials.

The Chinese government continues to deny Jude a response on legal or medical grounds. We ardently request your assistance in pressing for Jude's release during your visit with President Hu Jintao. We know that your interest in Jude will help convince the Chinese government to reverse the injustice that was perpetrated against Jude seven years ago. We thank you humbly for your consideration.

Sincerely Jude's classmates. www.freejudeshao.com

Chapter Seventyeight: Telephone

It really happened they had installed a telephone for us to use but off course, there was rules to follow. The first thing to work out was the time zones as we came from all over the world. It was going to be allowed we could call home once per month and talk 20 minutes. It could only be family members and we had to hand in a list of who we would likely phone. On my list, I put my sons and my sisters. The next object was paying for the call and they had installed a telephone card box. The prison shop had them in store for the following month costing 50 to 100 Yuan each and there was no limit on how many you could buy. Mick being the big spender got Yuan 1000 worth myself got 100 as nobody knew the costs of a call or what service was available. Gordon told me it will not cost more than 100 to call England for 20 minutes and trusted his judgment. Gordon had bought cards also for phoning Australia he got two 50-Yuan cards telling me he would not need more. The day arrived when the phone was to be operational it was agreed that the Malaysian people phone first. The stairway was crowded with people leaning over the rail to listen to someone talk on a phone. When those people were finished, we excitedly asked how it was can they hear you ok and they assured us all it was clear? I was going to phone my sister in Glasgow on Sunday and felt excited listening to Mick telling me about talking with his children, Happy had got in touch with his ex-wife he hadn't had contact from anyone in years. When Grand Joe left, he could not locate anyone for Happy as Joe headed for France not Cameroon or Ivory Coast were Happy came from. Jude spoke with his sister, Bijay with his daughter whom he had not seen yet. It was just a stir of excitement from everyone and a calmed atmosphere emerged immediately. When I did call my sister Sarah, she asked me again and again is that you Lockie have you escaped shaking inside shouting No I am here in Shanghai jail we can use the phone now. It was surreal listening to my sister talking then she put on my niece Karen and to hear her clear Scottish voice was amazing to my ear she was talking Glaswegian my mother tongue it sounded unusual coming so rapidly. I had a good talk and assured my family that all was well and healthy doing gym workouts and taking vitamins that they had sent to me. It was something special not likes a family visit but as close and closer that that phantom mail carrier this was instant no more sending mail from now on.

Last Year's Diary.
June 2nd 2003 what will you do if someone provokes you, insults you or your family. Why would someone do this? If someone provokes or challenges you, it means that person has a problem if you neither respond you nor are helping matters. Think about this. If someone is fucked up then you are also fucked up by responding. If someone is just looking for trouble then he is off his tree stay away.
June 5th 2003, I received a parcel from my sister Helen in Fife Scotland she

sent me a full range of vitamins proteins muscle builder it was like receiving one on Nicks parcels. I was delighted I had a year supply to last me six months of serious working out at the gym with Simon and now Bijay. Lativ was a big man, his shape went from fat to really well-built Bijay, and I would join him on doing squats. It was the unit at its best having the gym, shop, computers and now phone.

June 26th 2003 the UN anti- drug day wrote my first article this year for prison newspaper.

July 4th 2003 Cranky and Min goes home.

July 7th 2003 off course you're going to be pissed off if someone calls you a grass, a rip off, but that's the problem with people who think to highly of themselves their image is getting tarnished. I got myself into enough trouble defending my imaginary self-importance. I just had a look at my fantasies I was WBA champion Olympic Gold medalist World cup winner enough said nothing done.

July 12th 2003 it could have been better but it also could have been worse, what really matters is dealing with how it is.

July 14th 2003 try to meet father John Fitzsimons St John Boscos in Erskine.

July 15th 2003 Happy got several thousand dollars returned to him from the confiscated 30000 us dollars and was telling me he is getting it all back. Good news for Happy he is a nice man, set in his ways, and harms no one.

August 4th 2003 finished painting of Jude called Red tape.

August 6th 2003 motivation it is easy to talk about when you read yoga or spiritual books or whatever you can gain knowledge from but it is of no use unless you practice discipline yourself. The benefits are gained from the idiom you reap what you sow.

August 7th 2003, I weight myself in April 2003 I was 74 kg today I am 78 kg the gym and proteins are working.

Chapter Seventynine: Emma

I had been getting my consul visit every month since Emma arrived and looked forward to everyone. This person was bringing in such a refreshing feminine scent. She was married and her husband was a Rugby player Big Baz. I could not put into words what Emma did for me. The closest getting to explaining it was sisterly she really cared for me in a humanitarian way. She was a tall striking blonde-haired woman with a smile that made their Mandarin smile a Mona Lisa in comparison. Emma guided me through some obstacles that would be coming my way upon release. She was more letting me know that things have changed in the UK since was last there. Emma always gave me the latest English newspapers and told me to try catch up on some current affairs. I asked her about not returning to the UK but going to Thailand instead she was informed that I would be deported directly to the UK Emma had also brought me telephone cards and to my surprise she handed me 600 Yuan worth and had asked for only three. Then Lisa explained for me that different companies offer different deals this one was bought 100 and get 100 free. I was delighted and thanked them both for their consideration. As the visit ended and said, see next month handing her an order for some special food goodies for my next visit. The consul was great in that respect and I did not overdo it with my requests. Mick would and did overdo it at times asking his consul to make deliveries of special foods. Mick was still undiagnosed from a mysterious illness that kept him at the doctor's door every other day since his arrival years back. A determined man for sure. When returning and told some of the people about the telephone card deal, they were asking me to buy for them also as their consuls did not visit. Wong the Malaysian person approached me and asked if I wanted to do some trading and business. I asked what the deal was. He asked me to get 1000 worth of cards which would give me 2000 he would pay me 1500 in fruits and foodstuffs. Nevertheless, told him to let me think it over I did not take up his offer but instead ordered them for Bijay and Min whenever they asked. Nick was doing a bit of wheeling and dealing but it all soon came to a stop. All cards handed in by consuls were to be placed in the office.

The calls were now once every week so that cost a bit more for those with children but the guards allowed me to give out cards knowing I wasn't making any profit. Now is not that is civilized.

Last Year's Diary.

August 20th 2003 Charity begins at home when you are in prison for a long period of time you can realize many old sayings. In introspect you can discover what is really of value to you. Is it money, status, or other? For me it was health and family. It seemed like decades had passed and I hardly gave my family much thought. It must be something deep in the psyche that gives you a sense of security even when they are out of sight you just know they care and are there if needed. I did not want to reach out for help that was not my character.

However, once I was put into a bad situation, which was published, in the British press my family got together and rallied to my support. It brought back a lot of memories and emotions that lay dormant. It is a painful experience to be loved but it is worth it. I could understand why a little bit more the support my brother TC Campbell had in his campaign for justice without his family he would have certainly died innocently imprisoned.

August 28th it is my son's birthday today Happy birthday Lochy.

September 1st 2003. Part fasting for 4 days only eating watermelon once a day in the afternoon half melon

September 2nd 2003, I realised that the more willing to help at something they hated me they thought I was spitting in their face showing them willingness when should have been showing contempt. Some of the cons could not work this out they were caught up in others affairs and prison trivialities when they would have fared better looking at themselves. However, that is not easy.

September 3rd 2003 I was lying in bed thinking what Mr. Lee the Korean person once said to me. He said do not masturbate after 50 years of age save it, he told me it is your bodies' gasoline.

Chapter Eighty: Tai Chi Chan

It was mid-October and one of the new guards started doing Tai Chi in the mornings. He was the nightshift guard and he slept while the cons did the patrolling. Therefore, he was fresh in the morning some of us would stand and observe and Gordon started to stand behind the guard and try following his movements. It started some interest and a morning class began. I tried for a week or so but gave up telling myself had not enough time left to learn. Gordon and Malaysian Jimmy got right into it and they had become quite good. Well at least it looked good. Jimmy Wang and Gordon Hu were the sort of people who could do most things they set their minds to both smart and energetic and nice men overall and not criminals not in my eyes.

Chapter Eightyone: Sars

I could not believe what was going on about this new virus called SARS it was killing people all over China. Here was me just about to go home and had less than two months to go. They had stopped flights coming into China and one's going out to try retaining the spread of this deadly disease. All visits stopped no incoming parcels or mail. The whole jail went on shutdown. The guards were not even allowed to go home they stayed on duty one full week. Then went home for one week with very restricted guidelines as to where they could travel. The whole unit was sprayed every morning and evening with a disinfectant. The jail was in upheaval and paranoia spreads fast. The foreigners i.e. non-Chinese felt that the Asian convicts were more likely to catch it than we international convicts were. It was an Asian virus just as mad cow disease was European. It was amazing to watch how we all changed our attitudes towards each other. One Malaysian person Michael was seriously sick and we were all sure it was SARS the poor person was shipped over to the hospital on isolation row. The SARS scare lasted a whole month and we started to get visits again but through a glass pane separating us from any contact what so ever. It sadly reminded me of going to visit my father in the 1950s at Barlinnie jail in Glasgow when he was shipped down from Peterhead prison for visits. It turned out that Michael the Malaysian had another undiagnosed disease and returned to our unit under much suspicion among us all. Everyone was scared to let him or others breathe on us. It was frightening for me afraid of going to die just before my release I had my suspicions okay already surviving HIV+ HEP C + and Shingles now it was SARS what else would these people do to kill me and started to cover my mouth and nose whenever anyone spoke with me so did a few others then SARS had gone and life went back to normal.

Last year's diary.
November 4th 2003, I got a letter from my brother TC Campbell saying he would meet me at the station in Glasgow and to let him know exactly when I would arrive.
November 5th started to do a painting for Mexican Tony of his son and dog.
November 6th started to give out some of my Thomas Kinkade landscapes which everybody liked even the two new Guards got in on two getting one a piece. They were young people one in his early 20s Captain Liu the other in his late 20s Captain Chun these were the new breed of guards with a university degree and had a very open mind to what you inquired from them. It would only be honest to say I liked them. The other two who had been with us from the start Captain Hua and Captain Wu now they were gone promoted and moved on.
November 7th listening to Mick says he does not give a fuck I replied Mick why would you mention something if you did not give a fuck.
November 8th 2003 1000 years ago, there was rape robbery and murder 100 years ago it was still going on every abuse and crime against humanity still

exists. The times change bringing new laws and reforms. Human nature can never be changed only individuals can.

November 13th 2003 I never got the reform activist award like Cranky and Bull. In addition, realized they could not phantom me they did not trust me, I was un-predictable. The system rewarded the red sheep who instead of ba ba went hao hao, which translated as good good like a sheep but with an ass or donkey's grin.

November 14th 2003 art idea navigation to salvation.

Chapter Eightytwo: The Last Concert

This was going to be the last open-air concert before heading home. It was something that was done several times a year and the foreigners always had put on a show. Vern Bull, Cranky, and the old reformers had usually sung a song and I did too. This was time to make a statement Mick was testing me out asking me what you are going to say. If I was you, he advised me just denounce the whole system? Having thought of saying something regarding parole but that was all had in mind. When it came around to my turn sang a song by Loudon Wainwright the third song called Smoky Joes Cafe. I did my usual funny Max Wall walk around the stage then said my few words on parole for foreigners and handed the microphone to the next person. I sat down and Bijay said well-done Campbell and raised his eyebrows towards Mick as if to say let him speak for himself. These cooling parties have ice cream brought around and soft drinks with plenty of watermelon to eat. The guards would also go up and sing that's when the cons got their laughs by shouting all sorts of compliments but that was their style mandarin smiles all the way never showing emotion their way of abuse was its just to nice to be true. November 28th 2003, I packed up my brushes and paints, which handed most over to Lao Ma the Malaysian person whom I had took to drinking Chinese tea with. He was learning from me and wanted to have something to pass his time we worked well together. I liked him he was a professional criminal and never denied other. November 30th 2003, I do not want to hear talk good or bad about others keep your own council. I do not want to hear about your past success or failures keep your own accounts. I do not want to know neither plan nor do I want to know your present stand. I have my own life to handle. December 1st 2003, I heard the rumor five people from Kazakhstan got bust with 4.5kg of heroin two of them were women.

Chapter Eightythree: Goodbye

The time had come I did not sleep well that last night knowing going home the next day. My brother Robert had brought me new suit and other nice clothes during his visit to see me they lay spread on the bed opposite me pressed and ready to be wore. I thought of my brother now buried having taken his own life with a gunshot and would one day meet him in another life. I had said goodbye to most of the people who got along with me the night before. We had a small farewell party having and Pizza delivered by the consul staff for this very special occasion. Jude Gordon and Bijay had given me email addresses this was new to me but I had also gotten one from my son Scott.
I gave that to Jude to pass around Jude as inquisitive as he is when he finds a new word and asked me what scunner meant. I gave him an example when someone is having a party and one guy or girl is the humor of the hour and the drunker, they get their humor turns too humiliation in short saying making a fool of yourself. The next question was why your son would choose such a distasteful name and did not want to try to go into the psychology of it with Jude and said this. You know how Michael Jackson says it is bad but that means it is good. Jude replied yeah well, I went on my son chooses scunner because it may true, he is a scunner at times but to be up front admitting it then it becomes good. You got that Jude I asked. Sort of, he replied then asked what rfc is. That was easy to explain Rangers Football Club.

Chapter Eightyfour: Procedures

I stood in front of cell mirror shaved and dressed like a very well-preserved man of 53 my weight 78 kg and could still play an hour or more football a day. Walking downstairs and nodded, my head at a few guys on the corridor every step my last one inside this place. My hands were free having my luggage put into the office downstairs the night before for inspection entering the office picked up my small suitcase that the consul had bought for me which was now full only of my diaries and writings over the years. Having also a roll of 108 oil canvasses plus 40 UN Anti- drug posters it was a heavy load. I entered the police escort van, turned my head to look up at the unit for the last time, and could see many faces. Sticking out my hand from the window and waved. I looked ahead as the gates opened and a moment later was on the road to freedom.

On the way to the airport a song in my head by John Lennon, "It's a long way to go a hard road to hoe but in the meantime" In the meantime Greenwich meantime here I come. The SARS check was still being done at the airport departures having my blood pressure taken was allowed into the check in area having overweight baggage but did not give a dam as had no money other than a fifty-pound note Emma brought for me to get me across London if nobody was meeting me or got lost. I shook hands with Captain Chang and Captain Shao then headed for immigration with my piece of white stamped paper and no passport it was easy enough and walked into the departure lounge with my Virgin airlines boarding pass and smelled the human mix of international odors. I looked around me the feeling of being in an airport again something once having enjoyed and did regularly in years gone by but now it was all so strange. I did not even look at any duty-free items on sale but instead saw the illusion calling me towards there and once identified, it vanished again. Final boarding for the flight Virgin Airlines sitting back until the last passengers were boarding then getting on. It was Emma the British consul attaché who had secured my flight Emma had worked for Virgin airlines and got me this ticket rather reasonably priced good young Emma and didn't forget that I had offered my services to work as her gardener in her house in London but was politely told Big Baz was a deft hand with a shovel.

Once seated and fastened my seatbelt then looked at the magazines in front of me. A young Canadian man around 36 sat beside me leaving the centre seat free and not wanting to strike up any sort talk being happy to stay locked in my mind. When the plane was up and the sign to unfasten seatbelts was announced the person next to me introduced himself and told me he worked at selling computer programs all across Asia. Then I told mine that had worked at the British consul cultural section studying art and Chinese and teaching English part time. Don set up my movie screen, film programs list for me, and coming to one called Anger Management pressed play. I do not know what the Lord was doing but it was a clear message he was letting me know something or how could it be possible that the new release Anger Management with Jack

Nicholson would be the movie of choice after twelve plus years away in jail. Watching listening opened mouthed and wet eyed. To compare your own situation with others and feel the portrayed emotion from the film some of the Characters seemed worse off than me, then pity creeps in look where did I just came from. Then a little memory flash an article from a Prisoners Abroad newsletter popped back into my mind of the person complaining that he cannot understand or speak the language, he is far away from home, doesn't like the food, and the final straw he was serving six months in France. I recall thinking six month and far from home you wimp. Then sometime later the penny dropped we all suffer equally six month was his suffering fifteen years was mine. I know the feeling and now it was a mixture of excitement and fear. Some of those scenes in that Anger Management movie related so close to many of my own daily happenings in jail that I cried with pain and laughter through the whole film and kept turning my head to see if disturbing anyone else hearing no complaint so cried more this time with a dinner napkin to soak me up.

Chapter Eightyfive: Solid Ground

Walking along the tarmac and upon entering the immigration area was caught in a throng of non-residents pushing to be stamped in and collect their luggage. The sign was large and clear UK passport holders this way. I had just passed through showing my travel paper and was immediately joined by two civilian dressed men, one of which said "Did you have a good flight Mr. Campbell?" Then went onto say that they were Foreign Office workers assigned to ask me a few questions and followed them into a room. They asked me how my health was and I replied fine. "Do you harbour any revenge thoughts against the Chinese people or government?" "No," I said, "Good to be home?" one said. "You bet!" was my reply. My son was there all the way when it began in Islamabad, he had stood by me through my jail journey taking out the cannabis and who was waiting for me in the arrival lounge my son Scott we hugged and headed for the world outside with a friend of mine Jeff and his wife Kath who Scott had linked up with when knowing my liberation date.

Chapter Eightysix: Red Rab

My brother had ended his own life by gun shot to his head he had done this just several months before my release and hadn't mourned him having just jail blocked it all in. I entered the house in Bethnal Green and Vonny embraced me and said welcome back Lockie standing there was her two sons Jason and Joshua and we also shook hands Jason saying welcome back Lock 100% cockney Jason and I had met up in Thailand before my arrest and he was a man of real good character a hard worker and never been to jail. Joshua, I did not know he was a baby sleeping with me when returning from Asia unannounced we slept along with the old Scottie dog that was loved so much. Now here stood a still growing six-foot teenager handsome with strong McLaren features. That evening we all went to the pub to have a drink and meet more in-laws and trust me the McLaren's are a clan eleven girls three boys some of them living in London forty years and more many now had grandchildren. As soon as the bar door opened several old friends of mine waved me over it was Andy McCarthy and James Marr it was a warm exciting atmosphere music playing people talking over each other. My brother-in-Law Jim McLaren approached me and we shook hands and hugged then Jim slipped an envelope into my pocket your looking great Lockie he said and commented on my nice stripped suit Red Rab had brought me when he had visited me in China. You always looked well yourself Jim returning the compliment and it was true Jim was known for his style and enjoyed shopping in Bond Street in his younger days with our mutual friends from our youth. We joined Andy and Marsy at a table and Andy offered me cocaine which politely declined and wasn't drinking alcohol either what about a wee joint son Marsy offered no thanks gave it up don't smoke now. Marsy went on you know Lockie the last time I saw you was walking down the London Road with two empty beer bottles then the next time was from a photo you sent Red Rab ten years later standing on a mountain path in Tibet with a Donkey full of dope you get yourself about a bit Lockie and that is typical Glasgow humor. We reminisced and laughed at past encounters and shared experiences. The names that were brought up all asking me do you remember him or her Lockie and what had happened to them good and bad. Living in Glasgow in the 1960s was producing not only fighting men but also a new breed of entrepreneurs setting up across the UK Jim was telling me Tommy McGuiness whom I had last seen in 1967 had since opened some of the most exclusive clubs and restaurants in the city and became a property developer and millionaire. Andy mentioned Robert Caruthers from Maryhill who took me under his wing in Manchester both of us wearing suits stolen from Frazer's of Perth in Scotland and Pringle crew neck sweaters dating two sisters Barbara and Pauline another name came up who taught me was a guy called Cool this was in London were Cool was King to coin a phrase. These days were gone now and my mind was on the present and was in no way impressed by the amount of alcohol and drug consumption with some of the bar crowd but it was going on openly.

The McLaren family were united against any type of drug even cannabis having had the experience of some of their children getting addicted There was a lot of reminiscing going on Red Rab was talked about nearly as much as old Ray McLaren the mother of them all a lovely lady who wisely foresaw that living in the east end of Glasgow with eleven good looking daughters would spell trouble so were Mum goes the family follows having a very loving family bond. That night sleeping in my brothers old bed lay looking at the ceiling and thinking Rab slept here for years little flashes of his face would sometime skip into my inner vision and I smiled at him then cried my loss and wept away my mourning knowing Red Rab wouldn't want any of us to suffer he was a cracking wee guy and a wife and family that loved him Before leaving for the train to Scotland Vonny took me into Red Rabs wardrobes and told me to take all I wanted it was the finest range of clothing from cashmere coats suits and sweaters casuals for all seasons top designer labels cramming two suitcases with Knightsbridge quality clothing and would have him by me most days see you in heaven Red Rab.

Chapter Eightyseven: Home

The train journey was pleasant Scott looked through some paintings we had unwrapped. My stomach was rattling with nerves my brother and my son Lochy was going to be at the station to meet us. Lochy had spent six months at that detention cell age seventeen now thinking how must have that affected him it had and still has a place in my mind and not a happy one. Then there was TC Campbell although my youngest brother had always been somebody and had earned that respect length and breadth of Scotland, he was a straight talker fair leader and a hard hitter if you crossed him. But what about now after being wrongfully incarcerated for twenty years my mind danced on with the imaginary reunion dialogues that I would have. The train pulled into the station and we were off bundled with excess luggage my brother called out and waved then seeing him walked past the ticked gate to assist with the bags. We embraced and shook hands looking each other up and down. My brother looked well enough to me especially after what he had endured during his campaign for justice. Lockie, he said I was thinking you would be skinnier but you look as if you just came from a health resort rather than a Chinese jail that broke the ice and we laughed. Just then, Lochy arrived, said he was at the wrong arrival gate, came over, and said "Good to see you again Dad." I was choked and we embraced. It was arranged for me to stay with Scott until getting my own place and we all drove there to Haghill where his flat was located. Scott offered me the bedroom but preferred to sleep on the floor in the lounge room. We did not talk for long and TC had arranged for a gathering at my sister Sarah's house for that evening were other family members would join us. TC and Lochy departed leaving Scott and me to relax. It was just past midday now in my own city in Scotland my homeland.

Chapter Eightyeight: We All Aged

In the order of age there was Helen Sarah Agnes and Patricia my brother George wasn't there they had all aged it wasn't just the twelve plus years in jail we hadn't seen each other I hadn't seen Helen in thirty years Sarah and Patricia over twenty and Agnes I had made a short visit to see her in 1990 not long before this past trip through China. They were graying haired and the lines on Sarah's face reminded me of hill tribe women from some minority group in Burma with graceful and intelligent eyes. The house was full of nephews and nieces and many of them with their children god food was served and plenty of it and the Malt whiskey flowed into the glasses of those wanted them myself again declining to which all my sisters commented that's a wise move son now your dry stay that way. It was a wonderful reunion both my sons wlth me again the party carried on till into the morning before Scott and I took a taxi to his place. Lying on the floor that night thinking what would be next what I can do now but just watched my mind and were it was taking me a reformed criminal and anti-drug campaigner I can paint in oils and acrylics can get by with basic Chinese conversation and so slept that night with big ideas of working with drug addicts and counseling them all I wanted was to be useful. The following morning getting off the floor and folding the quilt then put the kettle on to make myself coffee. Sitting looking out from Scott's window you can see Celtic Park also known as Paradise being a lover of that sport thought what a view to see the park of the first British team ever to win the European Champions cup made me feel a sort of pride when comparing the football scene from where I had just come from this view was paradise and smiled inwardly after sleeping my fist night on Scottish soil. Home at last.

By Lauchlan Campbell.

Stephen Sayers is one of the most feared men in the country, with a reputation that's preceded him in the dozens of prisons he's served time.
The Sayers family have been known on the streets of Tyneside for decades. No one else comes close to their level and it is widely known that they 'run Newcastle'. Rumoured to be behind countless violent multi-million pound armed robberies, unsolved gangland murders, extortion rackets and organised crime in general, Stephen, his brothers and associates are an unstoppable force. They've remained tight-lipped about their exploits… until now.
Stephen earned respect at an early age, blazing his own trail and coming out on top by any means necessary. A true bad lad in every sense, he gives us a first-hand account of growing up as a Sayers and living up to the reputation that the name holds.

Buy now at www.badboysbooks.net

Operation Sayers takes a detailed look at the notorious 'Sayers' brothers rise to the top of the criminal ladder on the backstreets of Newcastle's West End and the authorities attempts to bring them crashing back down to earth by any means necessary.

Buy now at www.badboysbooks.net